Great British
Chefs 2

Great British
Chefs 2

Kit Chapman
Mitchell Beazley

For Louise, with my everlasting love

Acknowledgements

Art Director	Jacqui Small
Designer	Paul Tilby
Executive Editor	Susan Haynes
Editor	Elsa Petersen-Schepelern
Production Controller	Melanie Franz
Photographer	James Merrell
Indexer	Hilary Bird

First published in Great Britain in 1995 by Mitchell Beazley, Octopus Publishing Group Ltd, 2-4 Heron Quays, Docklands, London E14 4JP.
Reprinted 1999
The moral rights of the author have been asserted
Text Copyright © 1995 Kit Chapman
Design and Illustration Copyright © 1995 Octopus Publishing Group Ltd

ISBN 1 85732 548 6

A CIP catalogue record for this book is available from the British Library

Printed and bound in Hong Kong

Notes

Both metric and imperial measurements have been given.
Use one set of measurements only and not a mixture of both.
Standard level spoon measurements are used in all recipes.
1 tablespoon = one 15 ml spoon
1 teaspoon = one 5 ml spoon
Eggs should be size 3 unless otherwise stated.
Milk should be full fat unless otherwise stated.
Pepper should be freshly ground black pepper unless otherwise stated.
Fresh herbs should be used unless otherwise stated. If unavailable use dried herbs as an alternative but halve the quantities stated.
Ovens should be preheated to the specified temperature – if using a fan-assisted oven, follow the manufacturer's instructions for adjusting the time and the temperature.

The lines from John Betjeman's *North Coast Recollections* and *Sunday Afternoon Service at St Enodoc's Church, Cornwall*, from *Betjeman's Cornwall*, reprinted by permission of the publishers, John Murray.
The quotation from Sylvia Lovat Corbridge's book *It's an Old Lancashire Custom*, reprinted by permission of the publishers, the *Lancashire Evening Post*.
The lines from *Figs* from D.H. Lawrence's *Collected Poems*, (Penguin), reprinted by permission of Lawrence Pollinger Ltd and the Estate of Frieda Lawrence Ravagli.
The quotation from *Babette's Feast* from *Anecdotes of Destiny*, by Isak Dinesen (Michael Joseph, 1958) © Isak Dinesen 1958, reprinted by permission of the publishers, Michael Joseph Ltd.
The quotations from *Spices, Salt and Aromatics in the English Kitchen* by Elizabeth David (Penguin Books, 1970) © Elizabeth David, 1970, reprinted by permission of the publishers, Penguin Books Ltd.

Contents

Preface

This book is a sequel to the first volume of *Great British Chefs*, published in 1989 and reprinted in paperback in 1994. Throughout, I occasionally refer to the chefs who were featured in that first volume. They are:

Francis Coulson	Sharrow Bay Hotel, Ullswater, Cumbria. After 50 years of service at Sharrow Bay, Francis died in February 1998.
John Tovey	Miller Howe, Windermere, Cumbria. John Tovey has now retired.
Sonia Stevenson	*formerly at The Horn of Plenty in Gulworthy, Devon* and now writing and teaching
Joyce Molyneux	The Carved Angel, Dartmouth, Devon
David Wilson	The Peat Inn, Fife
Richard Shepherd	Langan's Brasserie, London
Brian Turner	Turner's, London
Richard Smith	*formerly at the Royal Oak in Yattendon, Berkshire* now at The Beetle and Wedge in Moulsford, Oxfordshire
Steven Ross	*formerly at Homewood Park near Bath* now at the Olive Tree in Bath
The McCoy Brothers	McCoy's at the Tontine Inn, Staddlebridge, Yorkshire
Shaun Hill	*formerly at Gidleigh Park, Chagford, Devon* now at The Merchant House in Ludlow, Shropshire
Ian McAndrew	*formerly at 116 Knightsbridge, London* now at The Boathouse, Southampton
David Adlard	Adlard's, Norwich, Norfolk
Alastair Little	Alastair Little, London
Simon Hopkinson	now writer and co-proprietor of Bibendum, London
Chris Oakes	*formerly at Oakes, Stroud, Gloucestershire* now at The Stafford, London
Gary Rhodes	*formerly at The Castle at Taunton, Somerset and The Greenhouse, London* now with Gardner Merchant
John Burton-Race	L'Ortolan, Shinfield, Berkshire

This new book is a chronicle of the lives of another eighteen wonderfully gifted people whose work is enlivening the gastronomic culture of this country. But beware: greatness in this Hall of Fame is not necessarily measured in Michelin laureates. The book is a documentary which aims to illustrate what is best in Britain, irrespective of individual celebrity, fashionable location or plushness of fabric.

Grand country houses rank with remote inns, neighbourhood diners with chic metropolitan eateries. As before, the chefs are all British born and bred, exemplars in their chosen environments and individuals who have made an important contribution to the quality of dining in Britain. I am especially grateful for the valuable advice of Derek Brown, Tom Jaine and Jonathan Meades who scrutinized my short-list. Inevitably, it inspired keen debate. Consensus was next to impossible and, once again, omissions are inevitable – but I stand by my final selection.

My introduction considers the contemporary world of cooking and chefs, restaurants and their customers, and sets it in the broader context of society today. It is a blend of status report and polemic. The garden may be in bloom but it constantly needs weeding. I should also note that the paragraphs arguing for the need to rekindle a greater interest in Britain's culinary heritage have been drawn in part from an historical piece I wrote for the *Guardian*, in September, 1991.

My profound thanks first to the eighteen chefs in these pages. They gave generously of their hospitality and suffered my two-day inquisition with extraordinary patience and good humour. My gratitude must also go to their families, their managers and their staffs for welcoming me so warmly.

On my gastronomic journey around Britain in pursuit of the eighteen, I invariably lodged with friends. For their great kindness and hospitality, special thanks to Mark and Diana Guiver, Andrew and Gisella Milne-Watson, David and Rosalind Daukes, Nigel and Nina Lightfoot, Mike and Anne Allen and Mike and Thérèse Duriez. And in Belfast, I must thank May Noble, Anona Robertson and the Northern Ireland Tourist Board for arranging my visit and accommodating me so splendidly.

Through the many months of research and writing, a number of people have inspired and advised, encouraged and assisted. Among them, I especially want to thank Caradoc King, my agent and dear friend, for his constant support and enthusiasm for my work; my wonderful publisher, Susan Haynes, for her gentle wisdom, her light touch and, above all, the freedom she gave me; and Gill Whatmore, my saintly PA, who – as with the first volume of *Great British Chefs* – processed, stored, chased chefs and their recipes, proof read and brilliantly administered this whole work in its progress between author and publisher. Not least, I also want to thank my two editors, Elsa Petersen-Schepelern and Isobel Holland for their sensitive but meticulous work.

Finally, there is my family – all three generations of them. But, perhaps, my two sons deserve particular mention; Dom (a future cook to watch) for presenting me with the most delicious suppers at the end of an evening's work, and Nick, whose room is below my study, for indulging his dad's manic demands for silence by moderating the volume of his CDs.

But my last word has to be for my wife, Louise. Frequently, she accused this author of being 'hell to live with' – but she continued living with him. I love her and this book would never have been written without her.

Introduction

I am no cook, but I reckon to fry an egg as well as the next man. Why is it, then, that the British pub – ancient symbol of our greatest social institution – finds this simple task so difficult to perform properly, let alone produce an appetizing pie, roast or stew? Whatever the pub and restaurant guides may say about the dramatic rise in the quality of our kitchens (and I do not argue with them), in our provinces at least, any tourist who cares about eating is still unwise not to lay careful plans before embarking on an excursion. In the words of A.N. Wilson, 'If you are hungry in a pub you either light a cigarette, buy a bag of nuts, or go home and cook for yourself.'

In my introduction to the first volume of *Great British Chefs*, I argued that the battle for wholesome eating out at affordable prices must take place in the pub – the cultural parallel of continental Europe's cafés and bistros and the environment best suited to foster Britain's incipient restaurant habit outside the capital. Gastronomically, London is another planet, accelerating in its own glittering orbit and accounting for about thirty per cent of the listings in the 1995 edition of *The Good Food Guide*.

According to the corresponding edition of *The Good Pub Guide*, the West of England boasts the highest density of recommended pubs per head of population. In the section on Somerset and Avon, my own home turf, there are fifty-seven principal entries with a subsidiary group aptly headed 'Lucky Dip'. While I will happily vouch for the excellence of the first division, I have yet to strike lucky in the second. In a vast area stretching from Exmoor in the west to the Cotswolds in the east, fifty-seven confident recommendations (of which just four merit the *Good Pub Guide*'s award for 'outstanding' food) do not seem to warrant any special cause for jubilation. You will encounter as many pub signs and more in that mystic triangle bounded by Glastonbury, Wells and Cheddar – a small corner of my county for which I have a great affection.

The tiny cathedral city of Wells is full of old inns with crooked frames, leaning windows and arched entrances beckoning you down their flagged and cobbled passageways. The exteriors of these places draw you inside and seduce you with their nostalgic charm. They put you in mind of lunch. Oak beams and friendly smiles convince you of the sincerity of their landlords. Blackboards may advertise a hotpot with savoury dumplings, a lamb casserole or a steak and kidney pie – all 'homemade'. The beer will be in perfect condition and a stranger might naturally assume that the food will be simple, honest and good. When it is not, the disappointment is acute. I have been gulled too often by tired, Bisto-infused stews, meatless casseroles and asbestos crusts on pies. Whether it be Wells or anywhere else, it is only curiosity and hope that takes me through these miserable archways. Is it any wonder that the millions of foreign tourists who flock to these places still sneer at our food?

On the face of it, times do not seem to have changed much since Raymond Postgate, founder of *The Good Food Guide*, launched his Society for the Prevention of Cruelty to Food in 1949. The best cooking in Britain is still to be found in people's homes, where for centuries there has been a deep-rooted tradition of good eating – a fact instinctively understood by our modern super-grocers and their huge emporia. There is a bizarre paradox at play here. For while our major retail outlets embrace quality as a cardinal principle and actively promote a culture of beneficent education with the exciting variety of produce available in their stores, large sections of the catering trade – bereft of any universal culture enshrining quality as a central canon of business – are still guilty of exploiting consumer passivity. Sainsbury's policy of quality and value began from the day its first shop opened in 1869. It is an ethos driven principally by an unspoken crusading spirit (which the company prefers to define as 'aspirational') rather than by public demand. Television commercials demonstrating recipes for Thai Grilled Chicken and Farfalle Pasta with Parma Ham, presented by Shirley Bassey and Dame Kiri Te Kanawa, vie with Delia Smith to excite the nation's taste-buds and to educate the growing numbers of keen home cooks.

If this brief commentary on aspects of the catering scene should appear somewhat curmudgeonly, so be it. The reality speaks for itself. Too often, eating out – anyway in our provinces – remains a joyless experience.

Excellence through all levels of the trade is a commodity that is still spread too thinly for Britain to make any rash claims of gastronomic apotheosis. However, the real issue – and the one that is fuelling all the excitement – has less to do with scale and is more a matter of an extraordinary dynamism within the restaurant community which is shaping the contours of an increasingly less barren landscape. The 'new dawn' I predicted only six years ago is breaking even faster than I could have imagined, in spite of the crippling recession of the early Nineties.

Again the West Country provides a graphic illustration of what is happening throughout Britain. In 1991, Paul Henderson, the irrepressible owner of Gidleigh Park in Devon, mustered a small gang of like-minded friends to persuade the region's tourist board to publish a guide to its best eating houses – be they hotels, restaurants or pubs. By their very nature, tourist authorities are cautious bodies who avoid any brazen displays of discrimination for fear of undermining the considerable financial support they receive from their commercial members. Within the ranks of the West Country Tourist Board, this sector is a powerful army of over two thousand businesses. But, in an unprecedented move, the Board agreed to publish an unapologetically elitist guide which they saw as a vibrant instrument for trumpeting the region's gastronomic excellence. Now published annually, the criteria for admission to *The Trencherman's West Country* are deliberately exacting – indeed far more so than any of the national guides. No heed is paid to price category, degree of luxury or style of eaterie. What counts is the quality of the food on each table.

The first edition of this slim booklet featured twenty-five outlets. Four years on, the list has risen to thirty-five, ranging from swanky retreats like Gidleigh Park to ancient inns like the Drewe Arms at Broadhembury and the George and Dragon in Rowde. The numbers may not seem impressive, but the growth is remarkable – the more so if this record is contrasted with the scene in the West of England just two decades ago. In today's line-up, Joyce Molyneux of Dartmouth's Carved Angel is the only proprietor who would have qualified for inclusion if an attempt had been made to compile a similar publication in 1975 – and to have done so would have been absurd.

This case history not only demonstrates the accelerating dynamic of recent progress, it illustrates the rich diversity which is rapidly becoming a uniquely British hallmark in the higher reaches of the restaurant trade – especially in London, where trends in culinary catholicity are being led by many of our most lionized chefs. This fascinating development is not altogether surprising and, besides, eclecticism has been in our nature for centuries. But restaurants are also social barometers and the movement

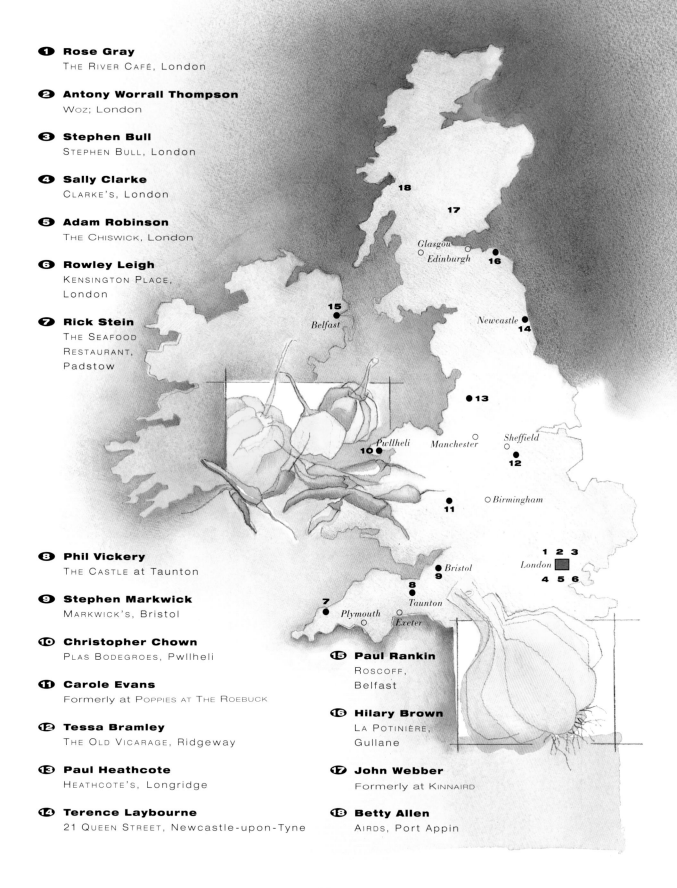

1 **Rose Gray**
THE RIVER CAFÉ, London

2 **Antony Worrall Thompson**
WOZ; London

3 **Stephen Bull**
STEPHEN BULL, London

4 **Sally Clarke**
CLARKE'S, London

5 **Adam Robinson**
THE CHISWICK, London

6 **Rowley Leigh**
KENSINGTON PLACE,
London

7 **Rick Stein**
THE SEAFOOD
RESTAURANT,
Padstow

8 **Phil Vickery**
THE CASTLE at Taunton

9 **Stephen Markwick**
MARKWICK'S, Bristol

10 **Christopher Chown**
PLAS BODEGROES, Pwllheli

11 **Carole Evans**
Formerly at POPPIES AT THE ROEBUCK

12 **Tessa Bramley**
THE OLD VICARAGE, Ridgeway

13 **Paul Heathcote**
HEATHCOTE'S, Longridge

14 **Terence Laybourne**
21 QUEEN STREET, Newcastle-upon-Tyne

15 **Paul Rankin**
ROSCOFF,
Belfast

16 **Hilary Brown**
LA POTINIÈRE,
Gullane

17 **John Webber**
Formerly at KINNAIRD

18 **Betty Allen**
AIRDS, Port Appin

11

which has been gathering headway for the past fifteen or twenty years is a reflection of the changing nature of our society.

The old values of deference, class and hierarchy are shifting – even crumbling – and our institutions are feeling the strain of a rising swell of populism which is now permeating every aspect of our culture and lifestyle. The best chefs in this country do not conform to any social stereotype – they range from the sons of miners to the descendants of courtiers, diplomats and scholars. A generation ago, to be a chef was to count for little on the higher rungs of the social ladder. Today, to be a chef is no barrier to acceptance by the bastions of the old order. Anton Mosimann is a member of the Garrick Club. Oxbridge boasts its own company of distinguished cooks: Little, Leigh, Bull, Stein. And the rising status of women in the professional kitchen is another obvious echo of the changing keys in society. Kitchens, like trench warfare, have traditionally been seen as environments so inimical that only men could possibly endure the blood, the sweat and the tears.

As the homogeneous structures within society loosen up and become more diffuse, so has the character of our restaurants and the food we eat. Like medicine, like religion, we are beginning to experiment with alternatives. Most poignantly, we have at last begun to puncture the gastronomic hegemony of France which has gripped this country for two hundred years. What Britain is now seeing is the passing of an era which began with Antonin Carême in Regency England and continued through a succession of creative masters – Louis-Eustache Ude, Alexis Soyer, Auguste Escoffier and X.M. Boulestin, among others – to the Roux brothers of today. These great chefs occupied the culinary high ground and dictated the style of fashionable dining throughout the nineteenth and twentieth centuries. Raymond Blanc is almost certainly the last in this distinguished line of Frenchmen, as the mantle of influence now passes to a new generation of British stars – among them Marco Pierre White, who is already assured of his place in history as the first Briton to win three Michelin stars and, at thirty-three, the youngest cook ever to fall upon gastronomy's Holy Grail.

Regrettably, White declined my invitation to be included in this book (although he had a sudden change of heart when I telephoned to congratulate him on his third star – by which time it was too late). Thanks to the prurient zeal of our gossip columns, Marco's fame, of course, owes more to an image of intemperance, lubricity and priapism than to his artistic genius – but then Mozart was not noted for the moderation of his behaviour. The fact remains that White's gift to the nation is far greater than the significance of his personal achievements. In a review of Salman Rushdie's *East, West*,

Fay Weldon's observations about 'the wild temperament of the artist' might equally apply to White when she wrote that 'it provides the element of subversion necessary to keep things going at all'. London already bristles with White's ex-pupils, some of whom have won stars in their own right.

It is British chefs like Marco Pierre White (himself a scion of Albert Roux, Raymond Blanc and Nico Ladenis) and John Burton-Race (a student of Blanc) who now carry the torch for the French gastronomic tradition. But whereas their restaurants – like Le Manoir aux Quat'Saisons, Le Gavroche, and Chez Nico at Ninety Park Lane – have historically represented the definitive benchmark of what is 'best', this has become a value judgement which is being increasingly challenged. Given the shift towards a more diffuse and democratized society, these great restaurants – frequently and boringly described as 'shrines' or 'temples' – stand for the Francophile values of the old culinary Establishment; the values of tradition, continuity, paternalism.

But the driving dynamic of Britain's emergent counterculture is, like the spirit of the age, defined more by a sense of diversity and individualism. It is an immensely exciting movement, generating a new wave of mould-breaking restaurants which are inherently British in conception and which are beginning to share an equality of status with their grander French *confrères*.

The first signs of this distinct change of gear came in the mid-Eighties with the arrival of highly individualistic talents like Sally Clarke and Alastair Little. With *nouvelle cuisine* in its death throes, their ideas pumped fresh life into metropolitan dining. But 1987 was, perhaps, British gastronomy's *annus mirabilis* – a watershed year which ushered in a new era of fashionable restaurants the like of which London had not seen since the famous taverns of the eighteenth century. These magnificent eating houses, frequented by the capital's beau monde, moved Samuel Johnson to observe, 'There is nothing which has yet been contrived by man, by which so much happiness is produced as by a good tavern or inn.'

Two centuries later, Johnson's sentiments found a new and radical expression. 1987, the year of Margaret Thatcher's election hat trick, coincided with a quartet of seminal restaurant openings which, in themselves, espoused the very diversity and individualism at the heart of Thatcherite philosophy. Marco Pierre White opened Harvey's in Wandsworth. Simon Hopkinson – with Sir Terence Conran and Paul Hamlyn – opened Bibendum. Rowley Leigh – with Nick Smallwood and Simon Slater – opened Kensington Place. And Rose Gray and Ruthie Rogers – with Sir Richard Rogers – opened the River Café in Thames Wharf.

From this moment, the whole complexion of modish eating in London began to metamorphose rapidly into a multi-coloured, multi-textured, variegated mosaic of places that assimilated different cultures, styles, spaces and price points under a common banner of quality and good value. It is a phenomenon that has grown exponentially into the Nineties, led by entrepreneurial spirits like Sir Terence Conran, Roy Ackerman, Antony Worrall Thompson, Stephen Bull and many others. Cooks trained by the modern pioneers are spilling into new restaurants, brasseries, cafés and pubs all over town. Small colonies of excellent eateries have settled into unlikely neighbourhoods such as Smithfield in East London and Hammersmith in the West.

Crooning approval, the pundits have been lapping up this new gastronomic populism. 'A whiff of bringing civilization to the masses,' pronounced Tom Jaine. 'A realistic alternative to burger culture,' snorted John Whitley. But the issue which critics, guide books and, indeed, the trade are squabbling over is what in Britain today constitutes gastronomic superiority. What is 'best'? Is it possible to draw up any cogent hierarchy of excellence? Writing in the *Daily Telegraph*, John Whitley summarized the argument thus: 'The dominant power in our restaurant culture is still France, sustained by a tribe whose faith in their own antediluvian traditions makes them blind to what's going on around them; they simply can't believe there can be another way of doing things.'

Like the pillars of society itself, Whitley's tribe – those guardians of the received wisdom – is exemplified by the conservatism of its institutions. For all their value and influence, the authority of powers like the *Michelin Guide* and the *Académie Culinaire de France* (the trade's leading professional body) is now being challenged, as the self-confidence of the new British counterculture gathers strength and credibility. In the rank and file of the *Académie*, there is a growing mood – led by militants like Antony Worrall Thompson – that the senior French establishment is behaving like elderly parents who can't let go of their grown-up children. The Brits want their independence.

Although it has shown signs of movement in recent years, there is still a certain predictability about Michelin. The *Guide* remains a prisoner of its long-standing grading system, which makes it look strangely anachronistic in the context of today's more unbuttoned, less starchy and varietal restaurant environment. 'Superb food' is not enough to win three stars. Restaurants in this category are also defined by 'elegant surroundings'. 'One will pay accordingly!' warns the *Guide*. This dislocation between old values and new trends has exposed Michelin to a barrage of criticism. Fay Maschler, London's leading critic, has attacked the *Guide* for having 'little or no understanding of ethnic food or anything that's not French or fancy'. Her censure serves more as a comment on Michelin's unbending traditions than on the quality of its inspectors who, in my experience as a restaurateur, are the most educated and thorough in the business.

Michelin aside, all the principal guide books indulge in points systems which deliver absolute judgements on restaurants and, ultimately, all are flawed – the more so in this new age of idiomatic diversity. League tables just lose their relevance. These subjective scales are, I suppose, designed to enlighten the consumer but too often they result in bewilderment and unfulfilled expectations. Wisely, most newspaper critics steer clear of this minefield. One who does not is Jonathan Meades of *The Times* – an influential arbiter and one of the few who is communicating what is actually happening in this country for the practical benefit of his readers. Meades is the only national restaurant watcher to attempt to make sense of the beauty contest by applying a critical gauge objectively. On a scale of zero to ten, he judges like with like. Superiority – 'best' – is measured in the context of genre. For example, in recent years, his award of a 9 (an honour conferred more sparingly than Michelin stars) has gone to Marco Pierre White (*haute cuisine*), Bistrot Bruno in Soho (bistro), Kensington Place (brasserie), the River Café (Italian), the Castle at Taunton (English) and a handful of others. As exemplars of their kind, these restaurants and their chefs illustrate the kaleidoscope of a British scene which is now unfurling as proudly as a peacock's tail.

The vigour and colour of Britain's gastronomic revival contrast sharply with the evident pallor of France and Italy. Extraordinarily, Europe's two great culinary cultures are showing signs of decay. They may even be withering on their respective vines. Richard and Anne Binns, two Francophiles who have devoted a lifetime to recording their experiences in an authoritative series of guides, claim in Binns's most recent book, *Allez*

France! (Chiltern House, 1994), that standards are at their lowest level in the forty years they have been visiting France. This is a view now widely shared by people who know and care about these things, including those peripatetic chefs in this book, who have scoured the country for much of their inspiration. We all have our dossiers of awfulness in spite of France's conviction that she still has a divine right to govern the palates of Western civilization. Nevertheless, the fact that the nation's youth prefers sitting down to a Big Mac rather than a bowl of cassoulet has spurred the government into setting up a sinister body called the *Conseil National des Arts Culinaires* whose apparent aim is to treat French traditional food products as 'public monuments'.

If the idea is to stop the rot, this initiative misses the point. I have always understood *les arts culinaires* to be a living, breathing, evolving organism – not a monolith. But, of course, this is France's problem: she has become constipated in her own orthodoxy and, as is the way with empires, arrogance and complacency are the conditions which will lead to the demise of her culinary pre-eminence, as countries like Britain, the United States and Australia begin to take over. At present, the edifice of France's international image of supremacy is being propped up by a couple of dozen high-profile, publicity-minded chefs. Beneath the surface, the core is rotting in the *gloire* of its own self-importance.

The situation is much the same in Italy, where guide books lead you to places which are soulless and pretentious – most peddling menus coloured by the tired brush of *déjà vu* – a triumph of form over content. They are a yawn, they lack integrity and, in the starred category, bear no comparison to the quality of their British equivalents. Far better to seek out some remote Tuscan hillside where a family who has never heard

> **" France has become constipated in her own orthodoxy and, as is the way with empires, arrogance and complacency . . . will lead to the demise of her culinary pre-eminence, as countries like Britain, the United States and Australia begin to take over "**

of Michelin will welcome you with a simple but delicious display of antipasti, thick peasant soups, rabbit, wild boar, porcini, pecorino. In cities like Siena and Florence, restaurants have surrendered their standards to the tourist shilling. You will eat better Italian food in London.

But it is the French who lead the PR circus sustaining the triumphalist mythology that rings out across the world. They are absolutely brilliant at it. Powerful associations like *Relais & Châteaux* and *Traditions & Qualité* are justly respected but they are the polished veneer concealing the worm. Another major network, *Jeunes Restaurateurs d'Europe* (these chaps are generously sponsored by the Champagne and spirit industry), wallows gloriously in a vat of self-congratulation – its glossy literature reading like a burlesque recital of the Apostles' Creed:

> 'With a wish to become a full-fledged member of the continent of flavours, colours and aromas, the realm of inventive cuisine, we unite talent and drive and strive to make our name renowned throughout the world . . . [We have] a commitment to beget, along with our associates and counterparts, a great family bound as one, resolute, ever ready to incessantly renew our art, such that our cuisine may serve as an example for generations to come and delight the women and men of our times.'

Mercifully, this sect has failed to establish its church in Britain, although its members run to several hundred on the Continent.

The great thrill about eating with the best British chefs today lies in their infectious spirit of liberation. This is where we differ so markedly from France and Italy. We are unfettered by any orthodoxy. It has made us braver, more curious, more experimental – and somehow we have tuned into the sensuality of perfect, raw ingredients and the opportunities they offer in the kitchen. I marvel at the honesty and beauty of the work of cooks such as Sally Clarke and Rose Gray – indeed all these new pioneers. They seem to have developed an instinctive, almost Florentine Renaissance sensitivity in the balance they have struck between nature and human creativity. Their translations from the raw to the cooked are not abused. Simplicity and integrity prevail.

This great British revival even has its sweet moments of irony. We have started to export our new-found skills back to the sources of their original inspiration. Alastair Little has established a summer school for cooks in Umbria and Antony Worrall Thompson is a popular guest chef just about everywhere in the world. But, while Europe's proud culinary traditions seem to be trapped in their glorious pasts, our own dynamic liberalist movement – tilting headlong into globalism – is ignoring an opportunity to revive and reinterpret Britain's rich and noble gastronomic heritage. It is as if a British tradition never existed, or if it did, its value has been rejected. We may have inquiring, fertile minds; we may be eclectic by nature, but we are showing an astonishing indifference to the modern potential of our own culinary past.

Paul Rankin reckons that traditional British cooking 'will be completely dead within thirty years'. David Adlard believes it is a tradition 'best buried'. Rowley Leigh dismisses it as an 'historical theme park'. Leigh's opinion is also echoed by columnist and restaurant critic A.A. Gill. In a long essay for the *Sunday Times* (3rd April, 1994), Gill acknowledges that once 'British food was as unique and diverse as any in Europe' but eventually he concludes that 'our national cuisine has become a quaint oddity . . . dead history'. Rightly arguing that our food is as much a part of our culture as 'our landscape or our poetry or our music', he then delivers his *coup de grâce* by claiming that 'now, to cook British food is as bizarre as being conversational in Anglo-Saxon'. For all its wry cynicism this is patently ridiculous. Our food culture – like our landscape, music, poetry and language – has the potential for renewal. It is capable of evolution, of contemporary expression. In a civilized society, it demands to be fostered and encouraged because like any other aspect of culture, food is a defining symbol of that society. There is plenty of evidence in this book that traditionally-rooted British cooking is no dead language. Phil Vickery, Tessa Bramley and Carole Evans are outstanding practitioners. And, uniquely, Paul Heathcote has persuaded Michelin to award him two stars on the strength of his British ticket.

Much of the hang-up with our own culture is, as I have already described, the legacy of life under the French gastronomic yoke which relegated British food to the dreary shadows of Mrs Beeton's philosophy of household management. The exigencies of war and austerity aggravated the situation and gave our food an appalling press.

Also, the current British obsession with the cultures of France and Italy is often laid firmly at the door of Elizabeth David. This is manifestly unfair. Our love affair with the Mediterranean stretches back hundreds of years – a fact highlighted by Lisa Chaney, the food historian who reviewed Elizabeth David's *Harvest of the Cold Months* (Michael Joseph, 1994) for the *Spectator*: 'By the last century it was a rare artist or writer who did not make the pilgrimage South. Grand Tourism was eclipsed by Thomas Cook's mass tourism but "... the grand object of travelling" was still, in the words of Dr Johnson, "to see the shores of the Mediterranean".' While Chaney concedes that

David's earlier books on the food of France and Italy tended to alienate the British from their own culinary tradition, she emphasizes that later works – on spices and bread – sought to persuade readers that English cooking was, at its best, at least as good. In Elizabeth David's own words, 'we need to go back to the recipes of a century ago (and further) when an authentic and still strong English cooking tradition flourished'.

In history, Robert May was arguably our greatest chef. His book, *The Accomplisht Cook*, was first published in 1660. It is a classic text with over a thousand recipes and a facsimile copy was published by Prospect Books in 1994. But the eighteenth century was the age which put this country on a gastronomic high. Like our modern generation, many talented cooks of the time enjoyed a certain celebrity. They were keenly sought after – and they even wrote their own books. Patrick Lamb, 'near fifty years Master Cook to their late Majesties King Charles II, King James II, King William and Queen Mary, and to Her Present Majesty Queen Anne', had his book, *Royal Cookery*, published in about 1710. And Lamb's protégé, Robert Smith, cook to King William, published *Court Cookery* ten or so years later. In the second edition of his book, published in 1725, Smith attacks his former mentor 'whose Receipts in Royal Cookery were never made or practic'd by him; and others are extreme defective and imperfect . . . '. Like some chefs today, the eighteenth century produced its own bickering chorus of prima donnas.

The culinary literature of the time is remarkably extensive and many of the chefs who wrote books presided over some of London's fashionable taverns. The most notable was probably John Farley, famous principal cook of the London Tavern in the City – a magnificent establishment with Ionic and Corinthian columned banqueting halls which opened in 1768. Such was England's culinary reputation – and Farley's in particular – that when the first public restaurant opened in Paris in 1782, it was named La Grande Taverne de Londres. It was to become a standard bearer for English food in the French capital and imitated by other restaurants which became known as *les tavernes anglaises*.

These anecdotal jottings illustrate the significance of England's gastronomic heritage. The scope of our native repertoire is huge, and it is sophisticated if the effort is made to examine the evidence. Our cooking traditions reflect our climate and geography, and our history as seafarers and mercantile adventurers. We love pies and puddings – perfect for a cold climate. The Crusades, the British East India Company and the slave trade have all had a profound influence on the national palate. We enjoy matching fruit with meat. We love using spices and nuts, rum and port. Francis Coulson's legendary teas at Sharrow Bay – his spicy fruity bread, Grasmere gingerbread and Cumberland rum nicky – are a rich testimonial to the history of Cumbria when Whitehaven was the most important port after London.

In *Spices, Salt and Aromatics in the English Kitchen*, Elizabeth David praises Cumberland sauce . . . 'certainly one of our most delicious sauces . . . best of all sauces for cold meat'. We are expert at slow cooking methods. And we are expert at preserving – smoking, salting, pickling, drying, candying, potting. Potted tongue, writes Elizabeth David, is 'the best and most subtle of all English potted meat inventions'. Her recipe is an adaptation of John Farley's in *The London Art of Cookery*. And to illustrate our genius for sustaining our great sea-dogs on their long voyages, Dorothy Hartley – in her great classic *Food in England* – offers a sixteenth-century recipe for potted duck which firmly upstages that which we have come to admire as *confit de canard*.

For all the talk of an English revival, chefs like Gary Rhodes, Paul Heathcote, Phil Vickery, Tessa Bramley, Carole Evans and veteran campaigners like Francis Coulson roam their kitchens like prophets in a wilderness. Uniquely, most of our best chefs have ignored the creative potential of our own culinary tradition – an act of dereliction unthinkable to a Frenchman, an Italian, Chinese or Japanese chef. Like magpies, we prefer to steal from their great cultures – seduced by the colour and sensuality of the Mediterranean, or the beguiling flavours of the Orient. The Great British Pudding seems to be the only aspect of our repertoire to have crept in at the margins of our menus.

It is not that I object to this thrust towards gastro-globalism. Nothing should impede honest creativity, diversity and excitement. I have already applauded The Movement and, besides, we have become a multi-cultural society. But equally, we must not neglect the value of regional or national difference, just as we should not ignore the pleasures of seasonality. I do not much care for the advent of the twelve-month season. Strawberries at Christmas, for me, diminishes the delight and anticipation of that domestic fruit in its proper time. This is, if you like, no more than a perfectly natural expression of my personal belief in nationhood and cultural integrity. I am a European but I do not subscribe to the Jacques Santer Euro-federast school of gastronomy.

Social trends also have a bearing on this debate. Historically, the British diet has been strongly carnivorous. The move towards healthier eating, our obsession with sexual desirability, environmental issues and attitudes to animal welfare have resulted in a

" Uniquely, most of our best chefs have ignored the creative potential of our own culinary tradition - an act of dereliction unthinkable to a Frenchman, an Italian, Chinese or Japanese chef "

decline in meat consumption. This makes the attractiveness of eastern cuisines – with their emphasis on fish, rice and vegetables – understandable. Equally, the cuisines of southern Europe are less reliant on meat. But diet and gastronomic tradition should not be confused. As an island race we are also a nation of fishermen and for a millennium we have been keen gardeners. From our earliest monastic foundations through the Victorian and Edwardian eras, the conjunction of the kitchen garden and the English country house has had a direct impact on our culinary heritage. Indeed, this is an aspect of food production in which we can claim world leadership.

Over the past decade, one of the most encouraging developments in this country has been the emergence of a new wave of small producers and growers who care passionately about natural quality, local variety and taste. Nature and regional individuality are reasserting themselves on fruit farms, in vegetable growing, in the revival of rare breeds and in cheese making. At last, the symbiotic relationship between cook and supplier is being re-established. But while many of our chefs have been quick to harvest this new bounty in home-grown produce, they refuse to harness it to their country's rich culinary repertoire. Often, their antipathy is rationalized by claiming that English food is limited, or unsuited to the restaurant kitchen. Both notions are false. As I have been at pains to argue, in a civilized society, a cuisine forms part of a nation's culture. It deserves to be cherished – not abandoned or disparaged.

This overview of prevailing attitudes to our gastronomic heritage may prove to be unduly pessimistic – time will tell. The recession of the early Nineties forced chefs and restaurateurs to rethink their menus and price structures. Suddenly, cheaper and previously unfashionable ingredients became fashionable. Now, in post-recession Britain, we are beginning to see glimpses of a new trend – distinctly more English in its orientation – which seems to be gaining credibility. Stephen Bull has been a leading protagonist at Fulham Road. His ancestor John and the carnivores are biting back. Recent restaurant openings in London have shown a greater interest in slow cooking methods, in knuckles and shins, in heads and cheeks, in trotters, tails and tongues, in

black pudding and all manner of offal. This mood is not just a new flirtation with carnality. Mash and colcannon (Irish bubble and squeak) are popular. That gustatory outcast and non-vegetable, the pea, is now enjoying a modest rehabilitation. And fish 'n' chips on bone china are becoming the new chic item about town.

All this chutzpah can be seen as a signal of our growing maturity and self-confidence as restaurateurs. The Eighties' urge for eponymous branding – the emotional cry: 'Look at Me! I'm a Serious Cook. And, to prove it, my name's over the door!' – has now given way to a less self-conscious approach. The cult of personality, the focus on The Cook has widened to embrace the notion of restaurants as a branch of the fashion industry. Chefs are turning into style gurus and their restaurants are becoming a part of the ornamentation of our social fabric. Design is playing an increasingly important role in shaping the social character of London's eateries. Even the studied absence of 'design' at neighbourhood diners like The Brackenbury is in itself a fashion statement.

Eating out and its setting, food and environment, have become linked and absorbed by the cultural diversity of our new populist age. The trendiest restaurants are to food what the club scene is to dance, what the catwalk is to dress. Intimacy and romantic illusion are out: high decibels and narcissistic display are in. Kensington Place set the tone for light, colour and the clever use of large vibrant spaces. Sir Terence Conran built his Gastrodome on Butler's Wharf. And, at Quaglino's, his staircase may be the oldest trick in the book, but it works. For a night, you too can parade and pout like Elle or Naomi, Linda or Cindy. Of course, there are always the young pretenders, quick to raise the stakes – people like Oliver Peyton who – with his Atlantic Bar and Grill – has been dubbed the 'major domo of groovy London, a Peter Langan in designer clobber'. It is an apt tagline – a reminder that Langan's Brasserie was the original model twenty years ago and a useful metaphor to define the social texture and colour of the London scene today.

This preoccupation with design as an essential accessory to modern eating out has also begun to affect the thinking of a few restaurateurs in the provinces where settings remain deeply conservative and predictable – where whisper rather than whoopee shrouds the atmosphere. In this book, Paul Rankin, Rick Stein and Terry Laybourne are examples of chef-proprietors who have made the break by injecting real vitality into the designs of their restaurants. In North Wales, Chris Chown's Georgian villa also illustrates brilliantly how modern ideas can be grafted harmoniously on to the graceful lines of a classical structure. And in Preston, Paul Heathcote's new two-hundred-seat brasserie has consciously been given an up-beat metropolitan make-over.

Yet these are still early days in the development of Britain's provincial restaurant scene. Certainly, outside London, these chefs and their colleagues are the bright and confident vanguard driving the new movement. But while the capital has acquired a sophisticated and varied restaurant habit, beyond its boundaries lies a land which is still – as I wrote in 1989 – largely inimical to the pleasures of eating out. It may be improving – but progress is frustratingly slow. As a restaurateur myself, this is an issue that continues to preoccupy me. I see it as an infernal wart on the face of our culture.

Sixty years ago, Edward Bunyard, in his book *The Epicure's Companion*, struggled with the same problem: 'The ear may indulge in music and its orgies go unreproved', he wrote. 'But the palate? Ah! This is mere self-indulgence.' Bunyard even found a problem with the word 'epicure' – 'it is a little battered and now stands as a symbol for self-indulgence and intemperence (sic). Poor Epicurus!' As a word that has been around for over two thousand years, and one which, originally anyway, was based on the philosopher's moral theory, 'epicure' strikes me as a noble and perfectly agreeable expression for someone who has an aesthetic appreciation of food and drink. But, in this age of political correctness, and with its overtones of snobbery and elitism, it has now fallen completely out of favour. In its place we have that utterly banal and very silly word 'foodie' which has slipped like cream into the gullet of the vernacular. Yet even foodie has its problems. Fun is poked at it (rightly so) and it still strikes that gently sneering chord to suggest a person who is, perhaps, a little too obsessed with food. In the end, we have no comfortable word for gastronomic appreciation because our national psyche won't allow it.

To suggest that eating might do more than satisfy the appetite is viewed with deep suspicion. To argue that dining might touch the intellect, even lift the soul, is readily dismissed as pretentious nonsense. At heart we remain unable to embrace the gastronomic arts as one of the richest expressions of a civilized society. As a nation, we are like the two Lutheran sisters in Isak Dinesen's lyrical story *Babette's Feast*. After the great dinner, Babette turns to them and says: 'I am a great artist . . . We have something, Mesdames, of which other people know nothing'.

We have become adept at articulating our ignorance, our disapproval, our cynicism – attitudes which have bred an atmosphere of fear and mistrust. Food scares erupt and subside in hysterical fits. Perfectly healthy foods are declared unhealthy. We are told what to eat, how much to eat and what to avoid. We are not a nation at ease with our food any more than we are a nation at ease with our chefs and their restaurants. Far too many of our commentators – in print, on radio and on television – seem racked by the theme of food as a health medium to the exclusion of the idea of food as an act of celebration.

This debate is not new. It has preoccupied many other writers. In *The British at Table 1940-1980*, Christopher Driver quotes Hannah Wright of the *New Statesman*. Her 'apostrophe' bears repeating here:

> 'There is hardly a degree to be found that cannot be got with first class honours by a person completely lacking in the senses of taste, smell and interior sensation of all kinds . . . If intellectuals, defined by the *Dictionary of Modern Thought* as "the culture-bearers of the nation", continue to consider food and drink an unworthy subject for creative and critical thought, we will have less and less culture to bear for a sadder and sicker nation.'

Later, Driver concludes: 'In a culture, writers depend on readers, composers on listeners and amateur performers, and cooks on eaters who share their "vocabulary" of food and are capable of criticizing their use and extension of it.'

This brings us back to that stern body of eaters – the restaurant critics. They are, after all, today's most influential epicures. We have them to thank for raising public consciousness of the pleasures of the table and for helping to fill our restaurants. But they do not run restaurants, they only write about them – and gradually, very gradually, we are seeing a rising class of epicures who are their readers.

As Christopher Driver has suggested, the relationship between chef and clientele is vital to a dynamic and creative restaurant culture. Yet there is still a link missing – and it is a crucial link. For, while there is a burgeoning growth of talent in the kitchen, the dullards in the chain are those owners and managers of hotels and restaurants who show little interest in food and remain ignorant about eating. We need more epicures and fewer percentage-hungry accountants within the trade itself. This ignorance is particularly apparent in the provinces where the best tables are commonly found in country house hotels run by proprietors who care as much about food as profit. With these notable exceptions, the vast majority are pretty clueless. Invariably, British hotel managers employ perfectly competent chefs in their kitchens, but they cook in a vacuum

– they lack intelligent direction from their bosses and they have little grasp of the link between technical competence and the aesthetics of taste – the palate. The reason Raymond Blanc is such a great chef is because he was taught to eat first. 'I learned the philosophy of food early on at home,' he says. 'I was twenty-seven when I started to hold a frying pan.'

This, in turn, brings us back to the essence of Hannah Wright's dialectic. To a large extent, our intellectual prejudices, enshrined in the attitudes of our educational system, have much to answer for. Unlike music or art, we have no interest in developing an epicurean culture in our schools and colleges. Too often, the best chefs, the best hoteliers, the best restaurateurs are those drawn from the educated classes with no formal background in the catering industry. These people, self-taught like a number of the cooks in this book, are best because they understand the meaning of good taste – a quality woefully absent inside the industry's educational establishment. Instead, the real business of culinary education is left to the great practitioners like Blanc, Mosimann and the Roux – their kitchens are the *Grandes Ecoles* of the trade. They have been the major seed-beds of the rising generation. And we have been the beneficiaries.

The life-stories and work of the eighteen chefs in this volume – like the last – are most emphatically an act of celebration, for epicures and cooks alike, to dip into, to savour, and to enjoy. In the words of England's greatest gourmand-philosopher: 'A tavern chair [is] the throne of human felicity.' Dr Johnson also warned that 'he who does not mind his belly will hardly mind anything else.'

Kit Chapman

February 1995

Rose Gray

——

When our social historians come to reflect on the cultural life of London in the late twentieth century, I suspect they may be impressed by some of the remarkable alliances which have been struck between cooks and leaders in the world of contemporary art and design. These partnerships have transformed dining out from a quotidian social pastime into a fashionable accessory to sophisticated metropolitan living. One immediately thinks of Peter Langan and his patronage of the arts and Sir Terence Conran's expanding empire of restaurants. Their influence has energized the gastronomic culture of the capital and it has produced a creative combustion of some force – one comparable to Richard D'Oyly Carte's partnership with Ritz and Escoffier at the Savoy, where dining in a public place was revolutionized at the end of the last century.

Sir Richard Rogers is the dark horse of this modern movement. Until 1994, his name was generally mentioned in passing as the famous architect husband of Ruthie Rogers who, with her partner Rose Gray, finally killed off the ersatz Italian image of the London trattoria with the vibrant colours and flavours of their *cucina toscana*. Sir Richard is also a partner in the enterprise but when the River Café first opened in 1987, the premises functioned as a workday canteen for his architectural practice and the other studios on Thames Wharf. The acclaim of the place – which

has since inspired an epidemic of imitators – sprang from the earthy brilliance of its cooking. The perfunctory design was incidental.

In the summer of 1994, all this changed when the silent third partner remodelled what a correspondent to *The Good Food Guide* had once described as a 'teachers' dining room of a state secondary school' into what Fay Maschler now concluded was 'sleek and sexy'. But the Rogers' design achieved more for the River Café than a metamorphosis from canteen into London's most exciting new restaurant. He unveiled a stage-set which casually succeeded in projecting the talents of its two leading players and, at the same moment, actively engaged the senses and vanities of their audience. Any good restaurant will encourage a spirit of hospitable interaction, but here Sir Richard has created a setting that artfully magnifies the experience.

> **It is the smell of wood smoke that provides the clue to the heart of the River Café**

The buildings that form Thames Wharf Studios enclose a green and leafy piazza overlooking the river. It is a peaceful retreat from the thunder and mayhem of Hammersmith. Richard Rogers is, of course, the famous father of the visceral school of architecture and in the lobby of his offices, models of his work advertise the style. The Pompidou Centre is there, assembled entirely with Lego bricks, and a giant-miniature of the Lloyd's building is constructed of wood. The same visceral creativity has been applied to the River Café – not by exposing the guts of the place, but by revealing the infrastructure of a smart restaurant that more conventionally remains hidden from public view and then translating it into an extraordinary piece of surreal theatre.

The room – white, silver and blue – is long and fronted by French windows that open out on to a terrace made for summer dining. The stage – fifty feet and shooting the length of the back wall – is a stainless steel clad counter burnished to gleam like polished glass and calculated to flatter the fleeting glances of the wishful Hugh Grants and Elizabeth Hurleys seated at the tables before it.

The real action takes place behind the counter; at the stoves and the char-grill, at the cold section and the sweet service, at the espresso machine, the bar

and the wine dispenser. Then, suspended above, an angled proscenium of opaque glass plates reflects the show beneath and projects it like a piece of soft-focus action on a cinema screen.

But it is the smell of wood smoke that provides the clue to the heart of the River Café. Wafting oak or cherry or ash, a large oven set in the far corner of the room is used for baking and, most particularly, for roasting game, pig and poultry. It is that comforting smell of home and hearth, and a potent symbol of the bond between the three partners, whose ties are less a matter of business synergy and more to do with family, friendship and roots which are deeply Italian. Sir Richard's mother, Dada Rogers – now ninety years old and living in Wimbledon – is Italian. She is also the spiritual matriarch of the River Café. 'Dada,' says Rose Gray, 'basically taught Ruthie and me to cook. She is our inspiration. She is our critic.'

Rose has known Richard since her student years at the Guildford School of Art in the late Fifties. Her best friend, Sue Brumwell, became his first wife. Ruthie, whose background is also highly cultured and artistic, is American, coming from a Jewish family in upstate New York. She came to London in 1967 when she was nineteen and married Richard six years later.

The two families – the Rogers' and Rose's – have shadowed each other almost since birth and some of the children now work at the Café. This is a business bound by the ethos of the Italian family with its innate belief in bringing good food to the table.

To watch Rose Gray at work, these deeper instincts – the love of family and food – are belied by the tall, gangly frame and thoroughbred good looks of an English lady who could pass for a headmistress of a frightfully smart girls' public school. The staff certainly do as they are told and she never has to ask twice. But the stern exterior is softened by her freckled features, an impish smile and a habit of calling everyone darling.

Of herself, she admits to being emotionally quite closed and that as a child her mother never embraced her. Born Rose Swann in 1939, her early life was coloured by tragedy, a strange root-lessness and a family who deliberately kept secret the true story of her father. Shortly before her birth, he died in a fire at their home in Bedford trying to rescue her sister and a nanny who also perished in the blaze. It has taken Rose most of her life to unravel the full truth and her mother, who died in 1985, never really recovered from the trauma.

And so Rose Swann was raised as an only child in Surrey where once her maternal grand-parents had owned a magnificent estate near Box Hill on the River Mole. She never knew her

grandfather, the distinguished botanist Sir William Lawrence who, according to family lore, had died prematurely on account of his heroic appetite for rich food and rare wine. But, while her grandmother's tales of his great dinner parties secretly fascinated her, the other members of the family reacted against his self-indulgence and Rose had little choice but to live as frugally as the rest of post-war Britain.

Although the big house had long since gone and with it its brigade of servants and gardeners, Iris, Lady Lawrence, past-president of the Royal Horticultural Society, continued to mind the fruits and vegetables she loved, albeit in more modest surroundings. As a young girl, Rose would join her grandmother in the greenhouse or the garden where she grew her figs, grapes, tomatoes and some twenty varieties of potato. When the old lady died, 'sitting on a stool pulling weeds from a flower bed', Rose was eleven, but these early memories were to become an important first rehearsal for her obsessive pursuit of good sources of fresh produce thirty-seven years later.

The austere and loveless atmosphere of her childhood and the mystery of her missing father were soon sublimated by the intellectual and emotional stimulus of life at Guildford Art School. Suddenly, she became exposed to a powerful creative milieu which was at the forefront of the modern movement. Through her friend Sue Brumwell, she met Richard Rogers. The many visits she made to his family in Cheam and, not least, the sheer deliciousness of Dada's *millefeuille*, ice creams and almond pastries began to release a zest for life which her own home environment had suppressed for so long.

When Rose left Guildford to teach art at Shoreditch Comprehensive, the importance of kitchen and family on her outlook was again confirmed by a period spent living in a flat attached to the Hampstead home of the famous graphic designer Henrion, who employed her to cook for his children in lieu of rent. Henrion's wife Daphne, a sculptor, was another mid-European mother who believed passionately that good food was the author of all happiness. These early experiences and close friendships were a cathartic influence which set Rose's mind on raising lots of children herself in an atmosphere where there would always be wonderful things to eat. She has four: Ossian, Hester and Lucy – from her marriage to Michael Gray, a film editor, in 1961 – and Dante, her son by David MacIlwaine, an artist, sculptor and director of a London gallery, who has been her partner since 1969.

" Her knack is not simply the product of a creative mind, but one that has translated ideas into dazzlingly successful businesses "

Rose Gray's devotion to her family has marched arm-in-arm with an extraordinarily protean career remarkable for one single quality – its innovation. She has always been first in the ring. Her knack is not simply the product of a creative mind but one that has translated ideas into dazzlingly successful businesses which have subsequently been cribbed by others.

After her marriage to Michael Gray, she started designing and making paper lampshades. The business grew so rapidly that he abandoned the film industry to join her, but when the marriage broke up in 1968, she decided to change tack. On a trip to Brittany, she got hooked on crêpes, imported the equipment, bought proper French flour and set up London's first mobile *crêperies*, which saw service at rock concerts and parties in advertising agencies. Her units even made appearances on the King's and Portobello Roads. But, after a couple of years, this idea was overtaken by another. On one of their buying trips to France, Rose and David picked up seven antique wood-burning stoves. An article in the *Sunday Times* had thirty eager punters knocking on their front door in Maida Vale early the same morning. David returned to the Paris flea markets to buy more and by 1973 they were manufacturing their own range of cast iron and enamel designs which found markets in Italy, Germany and the United States. Such was the success of Home Stoves Ltd that, by the turn of the decade, the company went broke – the consequence of recession at home and a flood of cheaper Taiwan-made copies which wiped out their export trade.

In 1981 they sold up and moved to Tuscany, where they found a hillside house by the village of Pieve di Camaiore near Lucca. David immersed himself in his painting and Rose started a vegetable garden. Dante went to the village school while Lucy pursued her education in Florence with Zad, Richard Rogers' son. For the next four years, Rose became absorbed by the food and life of the region. This was her spiritual homecoming. 'I dropped everything else,' she says. 'From that moment on there was only one way to cook for me and that was the Italian way.'

Pieve di Camaiore soon became a favourite stop for David and Rose's artistic friends. When Nell Campbell, the Australian actress, landed in New York in the mid-Eighties to open a nightclub with the trend-setting restaurateur Keith McNally, she wanted Tuscan pink walls, Florentine mirrors and Rose Gray as her chef. Nell's opened in 1986 and instantly became the Big Apple's hottest nightspot. Rose baked Andy Warhol's birthday cakes, indulged Bianca Jagger's craving for spinach with olive oil and was fêted, as only New York knows how, in fountains of Cristal

champagne. Once again she had scored a first – this time with the rustic simplicity of her Tuscan ingredients served amid the glitter of the city's beau monde.

Rose's principal brief at Nell's was to design the kitchen, write the recipes and mobilize a Chinese brigade of cooks to reproduce her ideas for large numbers. When the job was done she returned to London, by which time Richard Rogers had settled into Thames Wharf. Ruthie immediately asked her to join them in the new enterprise. 'I always knew Ruthie was a brilliant cook,' Rose says. 'Besides, she had Dada breathing down her neck. She had to cook well for this great architect son of hers.' In September, 1987, the Italian kitchen's two adopted daughters opened for business and, in no time at all, items like polenta and bruschetta were appearing on the menus of every other eaterie in the capital.

The pioneering edge to the River Café cuts deeper than the northern Italian leanings of a repertoire which has become something of a Nineties fashion statement. Ingredients, gardening and the sourcing of produce are the big issues here, and Ruthie Rogers is the first to credit Rose Gray's special knowledge in developing lines of supply. Cabalo nero, for example, is a black cabbage grown around Florence. Ruthie and Rose brought the seed back to England and it is now grown for them. They use it in pasta dishes, soups and braised in olive oil and garlic on bruschetta. Now merchants fly the vegetable in from Italy and cabalo nero is available in Covent Garden market.

Cannellini are white beans which have to be imported because they will not grow in a wet climate. They are also available in this country – fresh in their season, or dried. Again, the River Café was the first restaurant to use them. A deeply satisfying soup of fresh cannellini is not presented as a smooth liquidized potage on the French standard. This is more akin to a dense vegetable stew – the beans, parsley and olive oil swirling in a bowl marbled in luxuriant shades of green. Cannellini beans are also matched with a slow-cooked shin of veal, a dish which epitomizes Rose and Ruthie's use of vegetables and aromatic seasonings to deliver their intense primary flavours. The carrots and vine tomatoes, soft and oozing an exquisite sweetness, are grown by Adrian Barran, an off-beat aristocrat whose Suffolk walled garden is shaped like the Campo in Siena. The veal shin's final dressing comes in a generous scatter of gremolata – the traditional Milanese seasoning of chopped parsley, raw garlic and grated lemon zest. When the plate arrives before you, the aromas assail the nostrils and turn the head like a rich herb potion.

A voluptuous, abandoned sensuality pervades this cooking. There are no concessions to presentation. The pleasure of the food – often in its raw state, always unmasked by sauces – is in the smell and taste of marvellous ingredients and their carefully etched seasonings: chillies, lemon, garlic, salted anchovies, capers, herbs and, of course, lots of olive oil. A salad of blue-black figs, mozzarella, rocket and purple basil is lightly bound in olive oil and presented with the fruit in quarters, the flesh exposed: 'a glittering, rosy, moist, honied, heavy-petalled four-petalled flower' wrote D.H. Lawrence in his poem *Figs*. The composition is simple, the effect sweetly carnal.

While the River Café is very evidently a first-division London restaurant, its dishes suggest a dimension which sets it apart from other professional kitchens. The cooking is essentially domestic and the recipes offer ideal inspiration for supper and dinner parties. Pasta is an obvious example, as are puddings like panna cotta – a wonderfully dense crème-without-the-caramel – and an unctuous almond tart which will have guests baying for more. For the show-off, a sea bass – steamed in a bag with thyme, dried porcini mushrooms and sun-dried tomatoes – is easy to prepare and guaranteed to impress as much for the presentation of a whole fish as for the flavours that are beautifully concentrated by the cooking method.

Famous kitchens are notorious fuelling pits for tempers and highly-tuned egos. It is rare to find two chefs in charge of one range. But then the River Café has no peer and the bond between Rose Gray and Ruthie Rogers is palpable and unyielding in its mutual respect, friendship and creative dynamism. The two communicate in a kind of instinctive shorthand and they refuse to fall into the trap of marking off each other's strengths and weaknesses. Like

" A voluptuous, abandoned sensuality pervades this cooking "

twin sisters, they speak as one, think as one. Their families would agree. 'The passion we have for the restaurant,' says Rose, 'is something our families sometimes get quite cross about.' There is a pause in the conversation. The two glance at one another. 'Difficult!' they murmur in unison.

Of one thing Rose Gray can be sure, she is Sir William Lawrence's grandchild. Between the wars, he used to dazzle his dinner guests with the exotic produce he grew at Burford, his Surrey estate. In the Nineties, she is doing much the same for her visitors on the Thames.

Cannellini Bean Soup

___

The new season's olive oil and dried cannellini beans arrive in November – the best time to make this soup.

250 g/8 oz cannellini beans

2-3 garlic cloves, chopped

3 tablespoons olive oil

6 tablespoons chopped fresh flat leaf parsley

sea salt and freshly gound black pepper

Dressing:

extra-virgin olive oil

Soak the beans overnight, cover with cold water, bring to the boil and simmer until tender. Drain, and reserve the liquid.

Heat the oil in a large saucepan and cook the garlic until softened but not coloured. Add the parsley and beans and cook, stirring, until the beans are well coated with the mixture.

Put three-quarters of the beans in a food processor with 250 ml/8 fl oz of their liquid, and briefly pulse (you do not want a purée). Add more liquid if necessary, but it should be thick. Return to the whole beans and season with salt and pepper. If too thick, add more cooking liquid.

Serve, drizzled with a generous amount of extra-virgin olive oil.

Serves 6

VARIATIONS

Escarole: discard the tough outer leaves of 2 heads of escarole. Wash the inside leaves but do not dry. Heat 3 tablespoons of olive oil in a pan and 'cook' the leaves until just wilted. Chop coarsely and add to the soup.

Cavolo Nero or Swiss Chard: heat 40 g/1½ oz butter and 150 ml/¼ pint stock in a pan, add 500 g/1 lb washed and chopped cavalo nero or Swiss chard and braise for about 8 minutes, then add to the soup.

Tomato and Rosemary: Skin, deseed and chop 1 kg/2 lb plum tomatoes. Heat 2 tablespoons olive oil in a pan and fry 1 tablespoon finely chopped rosemary leaves, the tomatoes and 2–3 chopped garlic cloves. Fry gently for about 10 minutes, then add to the soup.

Salad of Figs, Mozzarella di Bufala and Basil

——

6 fresh buffalo mozzarella

12 ripe black figs, quartered

the leaves from 12 sprigs of purple basil

the leaves from 16 sprigs of fresh mint

about 250 g/8 oz rocket leaves

Dressing:

2 tablespoons of lemon juice

6 tablespoons extra-virgin olive oil, plus extra for serving

sea salt and freshly ground black pepper

Combine all the dressing ingredients and set aside. Slice the mozzarella. Pick the stalks from the basil, mint and rocket. Toss the herb leaves with the dressing.

Place half the leaves on each plate, and arrange the slices of mozzarella on top. Sprinkle with coarsely ground black pepper and add the figs. Drizzle with a little olive oil and serve.

Serves 6

Rotollo di Funghi

with Sage Butter

½ quantity fresh pasta (see below)

semolina flour, for dusting

Mushroom or Spinach Filling:

75 g/3 oz butter plus 20 g/¾ oz extra

4 tablespoons olive oil, plus

2 teaspoons extra

875 g/1¾ lb fresh chanterelles, finely sliced,

or 1 kg/2 lb spinach, washed and finely sliced

4 garlic cloves, finely chopped

½ red onion, finely chopped

16 sprigs of fresh marjoram

65 g/2½ oz dried porcini mushrooms,

reconstituted in boiling water to cover

250 g/8 oz field mushrooms, coarsely sliced

about 375 g/12 oz fresh ricotta cheese

65 g/2½ oz Parmesan, freshly grated,

plus extra, for serving

freshly grated nutmeg

sea salt and freshly ground black pepper

Pasta Fresca (Fresh Pasta):

750 g/1½ lb Italian tipo 00 pasta flour

or plain white flour

½ teaspoon sea salt

4 eggs and 9 egg yolks

125 g/4 oz medium semolina flour, for dusting

Sage Butter:

175 g/6 oz unsalted butter

leaves from 8 sprigs of fresh sage

To make the pasta, put the flour, salt, eggs and yolks in a food processor and pulse-blend until they form a loose ball of dough. Dust over your work surface with semolina flour and knead the dough for 3 minutes, or until smooth. (If the mixture is very stiff and difficult to knead, return to the food processor and blend in another whole egg.)

Cut into 2 pieces, briefly knead, wrap in clingfilm and chill for 20 minutes to 2 hours. Use half the dough for this recipe and wrap the remainder in clingfilm for another use.

To make the filling, heat the 20 g/¾ oz of butter and 2 tablespoons of olive oil in a large flat pan, add the sliced chanterelles and quickly fry for just 1 minute, turning once. Add half the garlic, cook until softened, then remove from the pan and set aside to cool. When cool, chop roughly. Alternatively, blanch the spinach for 2 minutes in boiling salted water, drain and cool.

Heat the remaining butter in a pan, add the onion and fry gently until softened but not coloured. Add the marjoram and chanterelles or spinach. Stir to combine the ingredients, season with salt and pepper, then set aside to cool.

Strain the porcini and reserve the soaking liquid. Wash the mushrooms to remove grit. Heat the remaining oil in a pan and fry the remaining garlic gently for a few minutes. Add the field mushrooms, stirring all the time, and cook fast for 5 minutes. Add the porcini and fry gently for 20 minutes, adding a little of the porcini liquid, strained through muslin, from time to time to make the mushrooms moist, not wet. Season, leave to cool, then chop roughly.

Put the ricotta in a large bowl, break up lightly with a fork, then add the chanterelle or spinach mixture, the Parmesan and a generous amount of ground nutmeg. Taste and adjust the seasoning, then set aside.

Place half the fresh pasta dough on a work surface dusted with semolina flour. Roll out, by hand, as thinly as possible into a large sheet about 30 cm/12 inches square – it does not matter if there are a few holes or tears. Cut the edges to straighten. If using a pasta machine, roll out two strips and join to make a square by brushing the edges with water to seal.

Spoon the porcini mushroom mixture along the edge of the pasta nearest to you in a line about 3.5 cm/1½ inches wide. Cover the rest of the pasta with the chanterelle or spinach mixture to a thickness of about 5 mm–1 cm/¼–½ inch. Starting with the dark mushroom edge, gently roll up the pasta into one large sausage, working away from you.

Place the pasta roll on a large, clean tea towel and wrap in the cloth as tightly as you can. Tie up with string every few inches, to hold the roll in shape.

Fill a fish kettle with salted water and bring to the boil. Add the pasta roll, cover and simmer for 18–20 minutes, according to the thickness of the roll.

Make the sage butter just before serving. Gently melt the butter in a pan, then strain off the white buttermilk. Increase the heat, add the sage leaves, and as soon as they sizzle, remove the butter and sage from the heat.

To serve, unwrap the roll, place on a board and cut into 1.5 cm/¾ inch slices. Place 4–6 slices of rotollo on each plate, spoon over the sage butter and sprinkle with extra grated Parmesan cheese.

Serves 4-6

Lo Schinco

Roast Whole Shin of Veal

---

2 tablespoons olive oil

2 shins of veal (ask the butcher to cut them at

each end, to expose the marrow)

1 whole head of celery, tough outer stems removed, finely chopped

2 red onions, finely chopped

1 tablespoon fresh thyme leaves

300 ml/½ pint dry white wine

397 g/14 oz canned peeled plum tomatoes

300 ml/½ pint chicken or veal stock

12 small carrots, sliced

sea salt and freshly ground black pepper

Gremolata:

1 small bunch of fresh flat leaf parsley

grated zest of 3 lemons

3 garlic cloves, finely chopped

Heat the oil in a heavy saucepan, add the veal shins and brown on all sides. Season with sea salt and freshly ground black pepper, then remove from the pan.

Add the celery and onions to the pan and cook for about 15 minutes, until softened but not browned. Add the thyme and cook for a further 5 minutes. Raise the heat, add the white wine, plum tomatoes and stock, and bring to the boil. Lower the heat to a simmer, and return the shins of veal to the pan. Cover with greaseproof paper and the lid and cook gently for 2 hours. Ten minutes before serving, add the carrots to the pan.

To make the gremolata, wash, dry and chop the parsley. Add the grated lemon zest and chopped garlic cloves and mix well.

To serve, carve the shins into medium-thick slices, place on heated dinner plates and pour over the juices from the pan. Knock the shin bone to release the marrow and add a spoonful to each portion. Finally, sprinkle over the gremolata. Serve with wet polenta.

Serves 6-8

Branzino al Cartoccio

Sea Bass Baked in Foil

---

sea bass, about 3-4 kg/6-8 lb, carefully scaled, cleaned and filleted

20 g/³/₄ oz dried porcini, reconstituted in 150 ml/¹/₄ pint of boiling water for 30 minutes

1 tablespoon olive oil, plus extra for brushing the foil

about 125 g/4 oz fresh Italian plum tomatoes, sliced

a few large sprigs of fresh thyme

sea salt and freshly ground black pepper

Place the sea bass fillets on a work surface, skin-side down, and run your hand over them very carefully to check for bones. Pull out any remaining bones with tweezers, then cut each fillet into 3 equal portions.

Drain the porcini, retaining their soaking water, rinse them and pat dry. Fry them in about 1 tablespoon of the olive oil for a few minutes. Strain the soaking water through muslin, then add to the pan. Cook for a few minutes until the porcini are softened.

Make 6 rectangles of doubled foil, dull side out, then brush with oil and sprinkle with salt and pepper. Place 1 fillet, skin-side down, in the middle of one half of each piece of foil. Put 2 slices of tomato, a few porcini and a couple of thyme sprigs on top. Moisten with the porcini juices. Fold the other half of the foil over and seal the edges, making a loose, but leakproof package.

Place the packages on a baking sheet and bake in a preheated oven at 200–230°C (400–450°F) Gas Mark 6-8 for 10 minutes, or 12 if the fillets are very thick. The foil will puff up. Remove from the oven and leave to rest for about 2 minutes before serving.

To serve, place the parcels on 6 heated dinner plates, and snip them open at the table in order to appreciate the fragrance of the fish and the mushrooms. Suitable accompaniments would be braised lentils and steamed spinach or Swiss chard.

Serves 6

VARIATION

Instead of dried porcini and tomatoes, substitute sun-dried tomatoes and *treviso* leaves, and add 1 tablespoon of olive oil to each package.

Animelle e Carcioffi in Padella

Pan-fried Calves' Sweetbreads with Artichokes

---

4 whole calves' sweetbreads, poached

125 g/4 oz plain flour

4 tablespoons olive oil

125 g/4 oz pancetta, thickly sliced

50 g/2 oz unsalted butter

1 small bunch of fresh thyme

6 artichoke hearts (either preserved, or

trimmed and blanched fresh ones)

sea salt and freshly ground black pepper

juice of 2 lemons, and

lemon wedges, to garnish

Slice the sweetbreads diagonally into discs, or lengthways into 12 even slices. Dust with a little seasoned flour.

Heat 3 tablespoons of the olive oil and fry the pancetta over a high heat until crisp. Season and remove from the pan.

Add the remaining oil and half the butter to the pan. When hot, add the sweetbreads and fry until light brown on one side. Sprinkle over the thyme leaves, then add the remaining butter. Turn over the sweetbreads and brown the other side. Add the pancetta and the artichokes and heat through. Season with salt and pepper to taste, then add the lemon juice. Serve with wedges of lemon.

Serves 6

Panna Cotta with Grappa and Raspberries

1.2 litres/2 pints double cream

2 vanilla pods

thinly pared rind of 2 lemons

3 leaves of gelatine

10 tablespoons cold milk

150 g/5 oz icing sugar

125 ml/4 fl oz grappa, plus extra, to serve

3 punnets of raspberries

Pour 900 ml/1½ pints of the cream into a pan, add the vanilla pods and lemon zest, bring to the boil, then simmer until reduced by one-third. Remove the cooked zest and set aside. Remove the vanilla pods and scrape the softened insides into the cream. Rinse and dry the pods and reserve for another use.

Soak the gelatine in the milk for about 15 minutes, until soft. Remove the gelatine, heat the milk until boiling, then return the gelatine and stir until dissolved. Add to the hot cream, then leave to cool.

Whip the remaining cream with the icing sugar, fold into the cooled cooked cream, then add the grappa. Place a piece of cooked lemon rind in each of 6 small dariole moulds, pour in the cream mixture and allow to set for 2 hours.

Turn out on to dessert plates and serve with fresh raspberries and a tablespoon of grappa.

Serves 6

Antony Worrall Thompson

O n the evening of Friday, 4th December, 1987, two hundred guests of the *Académie Culinaire de France* sat down to a gala dinner at the Meridien Hotel in Piccadilly. It was an occasion I remember well. Earlier in the day, my own chef at the time, Gary Rhodes, and five others had been cooking in the finals of the *Meilleur Ouvrier de Grande Bretagne* at Slough College. Modelled on its French equivalent, the *MOGB* is the most exacting test of the creative and professional skills of a chef. To win the title is like receiving a Nobel Prize or joining the SAS.

The MOGB is organized by the British Chapter of the *Académie* – an august body which describes itself as 'the aristocracy of culinary endeavour'. Its spiritual patron is Antonin Carême, the 'Lamartine of the kitchen range' whose employers included Talleyrand, the Prince Regent and Tsar Alexander I.

At Slough, the six finalists had been judged by a distinguished panel led by the great Paul Bocuse. Now, at the Meridien, the moment had come to announce the winners. There were fanfares. There were long and grandiose speeches. There was pomp and there was circumstance. This was an occasion brushed by the *gravitas* of All Souls and sprayed with the tinsel of an Oscar ceremony. Lord Young, the guest of honour and then Secretary of State for Trade and Industry, had to wait

until midnight before presenting the awards. Alas, poor Rhodes had not made the grade. Only three did and each in turn ascended the podium to receive the MOGB medal and embroidered white jacket.

The last to be called was Antony Worrall Thompson, chef-patron of Ménage à Trois, the trendy SW3 eaterie which used *Tatler* to advertise its theme with the slogan: 'Just starters and puddings. No inter-course'. Worrall Thompson, aka AWT, aka Wozza, stood up, grinned defiantly at the assembled guests and raised his right arm saluting the room with two erect fingers. The *Académie* – whose judges sample the work of MOGB candidates 'blind' – was endowing its highest honour on a man whom the culinary establishment considered to be a bit of an upstart, a joker and an iconoclast. That night Worrall Thompson proved to the lot of them that he could cook and he knew it. Intoxicated by the *coup*, he revelled in his triumph.

AWT has devoted a lifetime to sticking his tongue out at institutions to which he has belonged, regardless of the establishment they may represent, and he is a specialist in the art of turning adversity into triumph. One of his most vivid childhood memories is how, as a four-year-old, an imperious governess at his boarding nursery school in Brighton punished him with short spells of incarceration in a coal hole. The last time he suffered this indignity, he built a stack of coal, clambered up it and escaped. Young Wozza spent the next few days in the company of a tramp and when the school eventually caught up with him, his Victorian tormentor had the grace to real-

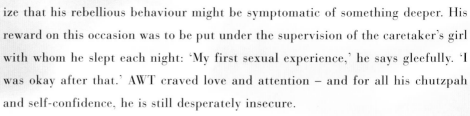

ize that his rebellious behaviour might be symptomatic of something deeper. His reward on this occasion was to be put under the supervision of the caretaker's girl with whom he slept each night: 'My first sexual experience,' he says gleefully. 'I was okay after that.' AWT craved love and attention – and for all his chutzpah and self-confidence, he is still desperately insecure.

In London (or anywhere for that matter), there is no other chef in Worrall Thompson's league who breeds new restaurants with such unassuageable voracity. But in spite of his enormous success and his undoubted public following, AWT's outspoken and pugnacious nature – and not least his priapic tendencies – have caused him, and others, a great deal of grief. In the trade, he is not popular, and in some quarters he is despised. My own attempts to penetrate the higher ramparts of London's culinary establishment for sensible views on his professional standing and the contribution he has made to metropolitan dining were politely, and some-

times not so politely, repulsed. Wozza generates an awful lot of heat.

Extraordinarily, he is a little baffled to understand why, and his feelings that his peers do not always appreciate him are almost endearing in their naïvety. He has even seriously contemplated throwing dinner parties for his detractors at his home on the banks of the Thames near Henley to try to convince them that at heart he is a good egg. In truth, he is not such a bad egg. Deep down he is immensely likeable. But, in the end, one is left wondering what value he places on issues like loyalty and friendship.

Press AWT about his regrets in life and he will mention his two broken marriages and his 'impulsive nature, especially when it comes to relationships'. At the same time, he believes he was 'fortunate' not to have had doting parents 'because it made me into a very strong, independent person'. The pay-off to this side in his character ultimately leaves an impression of human disposability in favour of self-advancement. Towards the end of my interview with him, he told me that he quite liked the idea of becoming more settled. Over dinner two days earlier he had said, 'I'm not ready to settle down yet.' Worrall Thompson does not really know himself any more than he is able to distinguish between his friends and enemies.

Marco Pierre White frequently popped up in our conversations. 'If Marco would allow himself to put his arm around me sometimes,' says AWT, 'then I'd be his friend. But he doesn't trust me. Everybody thinks you are up to something when all you're trying to be is successful.' Again, this begs the question: at what cost to your fellows? Marco and AWT have crossed swords in the past – famously and publicly on Michael Winner's restaurant page in the *Sunday Times*. 'I have no war with him,' says Marco, 'but Antony has questioned our friendship. He forgets. In life we should remember the people who have been kind to us. A few years ago, he was going through hard times and I used to look after him like a brother.'

This is a felicitous simile. In temperament, the two men have much in common. But while Marco Pierre White determinedly distances himself from the restaurant industry's institutions, Worrall Thompson is a joiner who likes to make things happen. He is Vice-chairman of the Restaurateurs' Association of Great Britain and he is active within the *Académie Culinaire de France*. Predictably, AWT is highly critical of both bodies. MOGB notwithstanding, he is currently waging a war of independence within the *ACF* seeking to have its name changed to the Culinary Academy of Great Britain. 'The *Académie* sits on its bum,' he growls. 'The French old school hold it back and they should be deposed.' This is all good swashbuckling stuff but it is part of the same Wozza conundrum. Worrall Thompson wants to belong, to be accepted, to be appreciated – but his terms of engagement are unconditional. The result is conflict.

In AWT's book, 6th May, 1994, may well go down as a date in Anglo-French history as significant as Agincourt in 1415. Eurotunnel

> **ℂ That night Worrall Thompson proved to the lot of them that he could cook and he knew it 𝕁𝕁**

had invited him to join a team of chefs, including Raymond Blanc and Bruno Loubet, to cook for the Queen, the French President and several hundred other guests in Folkestone to mark the inauguration of the Channel Tunnel. Worrall Thompson was quick to advise Eurotunnel that he thought it unlikely the French would be employing English chefs to cook in Calais. The Folkestone party, he felt, deserved to be an all-British show. Eurotunnel took the point. Wozza won an exclusive deal and scooped the glory for laying on a magnificent feast. Back in London, the French grandees of the *Académie Culinaire* were spitting with rage.

For all the bile and controversy sweeping about him, AWT bears not the slightest trace of malice towards his critics. There may be plenty of bluster, but never a hint of ill will – just a little amused bewilderment and pleasure at the fuss he creates. Beneath his shameless triumphalism and undisguised ambition – qualities deeply mistrusted by middle England – there is also great generosity of spirit. He has raised six-figure sums for the Royal Marsden Hospital and he gives time freely to support other pet charities like Whizz Kidz and Honeypot. His extensive teaching assignments, both at home and overseas, include regular unpaid stints at the catering colleges in Lancaster and Scarborough. All are ample evidence of an altruistic side to the otherwise supercharged Wozza whose restless portfolio of commercial activity leaves one gasping for oxygen.

For a full list of credits in the life of AWT, best refer to his interminable entry in Debrett's *People of Today*. The record by early 1995 included directorships of two restaurant companies (Simpsons of Cornhill plc and One Ninety Queen's Gate plc), a restaurant consultancy (Zoë in St Christopher's Place), a rash of television and radio, three books and a recipe column in the *Sunday Times*. Work-in-progress promises more of the same and, at the last count, he controlled and fronted seven restaurants, going on eight and rising. Of these, the AWT-style exemplars are probably Bistrot 190 in Queen's Gate and dell'Ugo in Soho. All of them, including Palio, a less publicized but throbbing neighbourhood diner in Westbourne Grove, have become major hits with the public, in spite of a very mixed bag of notices from Wozza-watchers.

Descended from a landed family of courtiers and generals, Antony Worrall Thompson was born in 1952 to two rising stars of the Royal Shakespeare Company. Richard Burton became a godfather. When he was three, his parents divorced, gradually wasted their promising careers and eventually turned to drink. His grandmother, who paid for his education, had him marked for Eton, but his mother, 'the black sheep of the family', refused and he went to King's School Canterbury where his wickedness showed immense imagination and his cunning saved him from expulsion. He

was bright in the classroom and, although he was small for his age, he competed fearlessly on the playing field. One omission in Debrett's is the distinction of having swum the Channel.

Perversely, AWT probably has his mother to thank for his success as a chef. She was a beautiful woman and he admired her greatly. As early as five years old, he would try to express his unrequited affection by cooking her breakfast, and at seven he had even attempted a duck *à l'orange* (with Kia Ora for the sauce!) But, in spite of his obvious desire to win her approval, she always seemed to let him down, arriving late for his school exeats or after his events on sports day: keen memories which have left their

" Beneath his shameless triumphalism and undisguised ambition there is also great generosity of spirit "

scar. 'I was the little boy standing alone at the gates always waiting for his mother,' he says. 'It used to get to me.' Later, his possessiveness turned to anger and resentment, and it would not be uncommon for him to turf out his mother's boyfriends if he disliked them.

Like the man himself, Worrall Thompson's culinary education may have lacked a certain orthodoxy and discipline, but it was effective, and from his teens he became enthralled by the glamour and excitement of the trade. At school, his early promise as a cook served him well. As a fag, he earned triple rates on the strength of his talent and it soon dawned on Wozza that there was money to be made at this game. On Sundays, he worked at the Duck Inn at Pett Bottom, a short cycle ride from Canterbury. In its day, the Duck was a famous Michelin-starred watering-hole and its owners, John and Ulla Laing, were family friends who became AWT's adopted uncle and aunt. While Ulla drilled and inspired him in the kitchen, the flamboyant Mr Laing impressed the pants off his young charge by returning him to school in his large vintage Bentley.

At the age of sixteen, Worrall Thompson was struck by near tragedy. His head was booted in a rugby brawl, leaving him with a broken top jaw and a crushed face. The incident destroyed his cocky self-confidence, which he only regained five years later after a major operation to rebuild his shattered features. Reconstructed into the Napoleonic cast he bears today, AWT bounced back – losing his virginity at last, then marrying the next girl who so bewitched him he did not believe the beast would ever encounter such beauty again.

In 1971, AWT's formal education ended with a diploma in hotel management from Westminster College. To his grandmother's dismay, he had refused to go to university. His mind was set on a career in catering and for the next six years he cut a swathe through Essex and East London, running restaurants for individuals who appeared to be loosely associated with the criminal classes – from unsavoury elements of the underworld to more 'sophisticated hoods' who specialized in fraud. Almost as a matter of routine, Wozza's departure from each establishment seemed

to be preceded by a punch-up. But he survived, bluffing his way from one job to the next, constantly honing his skills by subscribing to Robert Carrier's *Cookery Course* and by beginning a library which now runs to some 2,500 books.

By the end of 1977, Worrall Thompson eventually found respectability on the Fulham/Chelsea border – at Brinkley's in Hollywood Road. He also discovered Quentin Crewe's *Great Chefs of France*, which swiftly dispatched him on a solo tour of eighteen three-star restaurants in twenty-one days. Filling Crewe's book with their autographs, the chefs made him welcome. Bocuse took him to Lyon market, Guérard allowed him to work in his kitchen for a day and, after a night out in Roanne with the *frères* Troisgros, he returned to his bedroom to find that his hosts had arranged a warm surprise between the sheets.

Back in London, AWT's cooking changed gear and in the process he drove John Brinkley close to ruin. *Foie gras*, truffles and all manner of gustatory extravagance appeared on the menu. When he moved to Dan's in Sydney Street in 1979, Dan Whitehead suffered in much the same way. 'A brilliant chef,' sighs Mr

" As in life, so in the kitchen . . . he has no fear. Some couplings misfire . . . some are brilliant "

Whitehead. 'Antony put us on the map and filled the place – but he also cost us a fortune.' Meanwhile, Worrall Thompson had embarked on a clandestine affair with Annie Foster-Firth, a 'hooray girl' who, with her husband Donald, owned a bistro across the road from Brinkley's. In 1981, the two lovers persuaded Don to arrange the funding for a property in Beauchamp Place, and in November the three opened their restaurant under the mischievous moniker Ménage à Trois. It was not long before its secret was blown and the partnership disintegrated in a state of acrimony and litigation, ultimately leaving AWT in charge.

Neatly exploiting the *nouvelle* craze and helped by the occasional patronage of the Princess of Wales, Ménage à Trois made Worrall Thompson famous – establishing him as a trendsetter, innovator and publicist on the back of his ingenious theme of promoting an eclectic menu of starters and puddings but no main courses. His clever artifice – designed for ladies who lunch – captured the mood of the times and he managed to export the idea to Bombay, New York and Melbourne.

In 1988, AWT sold Ménage à Trois for £700,000 – ten times the sum of its original purchase price. But once again his personal life was in turmoil.

His second marriage to Militza Jane Hamilton Miller, the daughter of a wealthy Australian doctor, and the mother of his two sons, Blake and Sam, collapsed when he fell hopelessly in love with a beautiful Japanese-American girl, Ronda Kamihira. Worrall Thompson bought and created a delicatessen in Wandsworth for his new paramour and he called it the KWT Food Show. Six days before the opening, she left him. Devastated by the shock of losing the greatest love of his life, embroiled in divorce, and stuck with a business he did not want, AWT withdrew into himself. His debts mounted and finally KWT was declared bankrupt. To his good fortune, he was rescued by Roy Ackerman, the well-known London restaurateur, who invited him to open 190 Queen's Gate in 1989. From that moment, the AWT meteor lit the atmosphere and has, to date at least, remained in the ascendant.

Antony Worrall Thompson's greatest gift as a chef-restaurateur is his sharp instinct and a natural feel for his metropolitan audience. 'I'm not after a Michelin reputation,' he says. 'I'm after a reputation with my customers.' (*Pace* Bocuse, Guérard, Troisgros, et al.) He is quick to recognize the fickleness and restlessness of fashionable eating and he trades on it. Like his thematic approach at Ménage à Trois in the Eighties, AWT remains a concept man – except that today his formulas are dressed up to look as if they are nothing of the kind. In the past, he has described himself as the 'tart of the industry' – a typically gauche throwaway line – but if it is reasonable to ascribe a sobriquet for the colours he is flying in the Nineties, it might be the 'Thinking Foodie's Pizza Merchant'.

In tune with the rise of cultural populism and greater informality in our lifestyles, Antony Worrall Thompson is in the business of creating atmospheres which are fun and affordable. The food – big portions, big flavours – is novel and polyglot, with a bias towards the current passion for the Mediterranean. He has made olive oil a personal trademark, placing bottles or saucers of it on his tables instead of butter. Dell'Ugo and its sister, Café dell'Ugo near London Bridge, are named after his favourite Umbrian oil.

It is almost impossible to talk definitively about AWT's cooking – his repertoire breeds so prolifically that it lacks any real permanence. As in life, so in the kitchen – some of his compositions are immune to potential dissonance, because he has no fear of taking risks, indulging wilfully in fits of cross-ethnic, cross-ingredient promiscuity. Some couplings misfire, but when they succeed, the results are brilliant.

This buccaneering, pioneering approach to food makes Worrall Thompson one of the most exciting and imaginative cooks of his generation. His focaccia (or *pugliese*), hollowed out and stuffed with vegetables, mozzarella, tapenade and pesto, is an

exuberant celebration of just about everything the Mediterranean has to offer, sandwiched in a loaf of bread. A Thai casserole flirts merrily with Italian bread gnocchi. Monkfish and herbs wrapped in pancetta sit on *skordalia* (a Greek garlic confit). Peruvian and Thai ingredients (*ceviche* and *nam pla*) embrace in a salad of scallops and green mango. A spicy Moroccan stew of lamb shanks is ornamented with a tomato and chilli salsa, parsley and mint infused couscous, and a silky, mousse-like confection of aubergine. Plump oily sardines are a perfect match for a salad of chickpeas and avocado.

These samplings serve only to hint at Worrall Thompson's prodigious output and creative energy. Whatever his detractors may think, he has made London a more thrilling destination for eating out, and he has knocked the élitist stuffiness out of smart dining. Fay Maschler, the *Evening Standard's* restaurant critic, is an admirer who has followed AWT's progress from the beginning. 'He does spread himself thinly and his judgement does not always keep up with his invention,' she says. 'But there is no doubt that he can cook, he reads widely and sometimes he is extraordinarily prescient. Without him London would be a duller place.' Marco Pierre White echoes Maschler's encomium. 'The public's interest in cuisine is greater today than ten years ago,' he says. 'Antony has done a lot to create that interest. The catering industry could do with more people like him.'

Antony Worrall Thompson's vision of his future is characteristically bullish: 'I want to build Simpsons of Cornhill into the most powerful restaurant chain outside fast food.' High ambition from a man who has come unstuck too often in the past – but, equally, Wozza has spent a lifetime leaping out of coal holes and surprising the world.

More philosophically, he is keen to emphasize the importance of restaurants as places of pleasure. 'I want people to enjoy rather than worship in a gourmet temple,' he says. 'I hate hushed whispers in restaurants. I like people to laugh and have fun, and I don't think you can do that in Le Gavroche very easily.' Here, there is a pause for a moment's reflection. 'Having said that, I had my stag night at the Gavroche.'

Cod in Horseradish Crust with Beetroot Juices

———

6 tablespoons unseasoned fresh breadcrumbs

2 teaspoons unsalted butter

2 tablespoons grated white horseradish

3 spring onions, finely chopped

½ tablespoon chopped fresh rosemary leaves

1 tablespoon chopped fresh flat leaf parsley

1 tablespoon chopped fresh thyme leaves

300 ml/½ pint dry white wine

4 cod fillets, about 175 g/6 oz each

salt and freshly ground black pepper

Beetroot Sauce:

5 beetroot, peeled, chopped and juiced in a centrifugal juicer

1 tablespoon fresh lime juice

4 tablespoons unsalted butter

3 teaspoons snipped fresh chives

To garnish:

50 ml/2 fl oz vegetable oil, for frying

1 beetroot, thinly sliced on a mandolin, dried 1 hour at room temperature, then dusted with flour

4 small beetroot, peeled, cut into wedges and brushed with oil

To make the garnish, heat the oil in a pan, add the floured beetroot slices, fry until crisp, then drain on kitchen paper. Brush the beetroot wedges with oil, and roast in a preheated oven at 200°C (400°F) Gas Mark 6 for about 1 hour, until tender. Set aside.

To make the beetroot sauce, boil the beetroot juices until reduced by half, add the lime juice and stir in the butter. Season and keep warm. Add the chives just before serving.

Mix the breadcrumbs, butter, horseradish, spring onions and herbs in a food processor, add 3 tablespoons of wine and process to a paste. Spread the top of each cod fillet with the mixture, then place in a roasting tin with the remaining wine and bake in a preheated oven at 200°C (400°F) Gas Mark 6, for 10 minutes. Brown under the salamander or a very hot grill, and season to taste.

To serve, place the cod on heated dinner plates, spoon the beetroot sauce around, and garnish with the roasted beetroot wedges and fried beetroot crisps.

Serves 4

Pan-fried Scallops

with Carrot Purée and a Julienne of Preserved Ginger

—

12 scallops, with corals

3 tablespoons unsalted butter

Carrot Purée:

10 carrots

2 celery sticks

5 cm/2 inches fresh root ginger

1 teaspoon fresh lime juice

4 tablespoons unsalted butter

To garnish:

sprigs of chervil

pickled ginger, cut into

fine julienne strips

To make the carrot purée, juice the carrots, celery and ginger, place in a saucepan, add the lime juice and whisk in the butter. Bring to a boil and keep warm.

Heat the butter in a ridged pan and fry the scallops over a medium-high heat for about 30 seconds on each side. Blanch the scallop roe for 30 seconds, then dice.

To serve, place 3 scallops, close together, on 4 heated dinner plates. Spoon the carrot purée beside them, and place a julienne of pickled ginger on top of the scallops. Garnish with sprigs of chervil and the diced scallop corals.

Serves 4

Mediterranean Sandwich

—

1 pugliese loaf (Italian round country bread)

1 garlic clove, halved

olive oil (see method)

1 tablespoon tapenade

150 g/5 oz sliced aubergine, char-grilled

150 g/5 oz sliced courgette, char-grilled

1 red pepper, skinned and char-grilled

1 yellow pepper, skinned and char-grilled

30 large basil leaves

150 g/5 oz sun-dried tomatoes

4 tablespoons pesto

425 g/14 oz buffalo mozzarella, thinly sliced

125 g/4 oz pitted black olives

50 g/2 oz red onion, thinly sliced

50 g/2 oz rocket leaves

1 tablespoon balsamic vinegar

50 g/2 oz spinach leaves

salt and freshly ground black pepper

Cut a lid off the top of the loaf and hollow out the bread, leaving a 2.5 cm/1 inch crust all the way round. Rub the cut surfaces with the garlic, then drizzle with olive oil. Spread the tapenade in the base, then layer up all the ingredients in the order shown above, seasoning each layer with salt and pepper. Pour on the vinegar between the rocket and spinach. Replace the lid and wrap the loaf in clingfilm. Refrigerate overnight, heavily weighted.

Serve in wedges with a salad of frisée.

Serves 12

Spicy Sardines

with Chickpea and Avocado Salad

———

8 sardines

25 g/1 oz unsalted butter

1 fresh red chilli, diced

2 shallots, diced

¼ bunch of flat leaf parsley, finely chopped

¼ bunch of fresh coriander, finely chopped

3 garlic cloves, crushed with a little salt

1 tablespoon extra-virgin olive oil

juice of 1 lemon

Chickpea and Avocado Salad:

250 g/8 oz dried chickpeas

1 bay leaf

yolk of 1 hard-boiled egg, sieved

4 tablespoons olive oil

2 tablespoons red wine vinegar

1 tablespoon finely chopped onion

1 garlic clove, crushed

2 tablespoons chopped fresh flat leaf parsley

1 tablespoon small capers

1 ripe avocado, chopped into chunky dice

salt and freshly ground black pepper

Soak the chickpeas in cold water overnight. Next day, transfer to a large saucepan, with the soaking water, bring to the boil, add the bay leaf and simmer, adding more water if necessary, for 1½–2 hours. Drain and cool.

Place the yolk in a bowl, beat in the oil and vinegar and stir in the onion, garlic, parsley, capers, chickpeas and avocado. Season to taste.

Scale, gut and dehead the fish, flatten and pull out the backbones. Wash thoroughly.

Heat the butter in a small pan, add the chilli and shallots and cook until softened but not coloured. Combine the parsley, coriander, garlic, chilli, shallots, salt, pepper and olive oil and spread over the flesh side of the fish.

Char-grill for 2 minutes on each side. Place in a dish and drizzle with oil and lemon juice.

To serve, place a pile of salad on each plate and put the fish on top, with the spicy side up.

Serves 4

Green Mango Scallops

———

8 raw diver scallops, thinly sliced horizontally

2 tablespoons clear honey

2 tablespoons nam pla (Thai fish sauce)

2 tablespoons of lime juice

2 green mangos, peeled and finely diced

(if unavailable, use tart green apples)

2 tomatoes, skinned and finely diced

1 bunch of spring onions, finely sliced

2 tablespoons finely chopped coriander

2 tablespoons finely chopped lemongrass

1 teaspoon finely chopped garlic

1 teaspoon finely chopped red chilli

sprigs of coriander, to garnish

Place the scallops on 4 chilled plates. Mix all the remaining ingredients together and add to the plates. Serve, garnished with coriander.

Serves 4

Tagine of Lamb

with Raisins, Almonds and Sweet Tomatoes

——

8 lamb shanks, *piqued* with garlic, anchovies
and pickled lemons

2 teaspoons saffron strands

3 teaspoons ground ginger

3 tablespoons paprika

1½ teaspoons freshly ground black pepper

1 tablespoon ground cinnamon

olive oil for frying

10 garlic cloves, peeled and diced

3 cups grated onion

250 g/8 oz blanched whole almonds (not flakes)

3 cinnamon sticks

900 ml/1½ pints tomato juice

900 ml/1½ pints chicken stock

1.5 kg/3 lb tomatoes, skinned, deseeded
and roughly chopped

125 g/4 oz raisins

4 tablespoons clear honey

500 g/1 lb small new potatoes, peeled,
but left whole

6 tablespoons chopped fresh coriander

To garnish:

peel of pickled lemon, diced

fresh or pickled coriander leaves

Trim the fat from the lamb, toss the meat with the saffron, ginger, paprika, pepper and ground cinnamon, and marinate overnight. Heat the oil in a large pan and fry the lamb until brown all over. Add the garlic, grated onion, almonds and cinnamon sticks, cover with tomato juice and chicken stock, bring to the boil and simmer for 1½ hours.

Remove the meat and set aside. Add the tomatoes, raisins, honey and potatoes to the pan. Cook until the tomatoes break down, the sauce thickens and the potatoes are tender.

Poached Figs

with Blackberries in Red Wine

---

750 g/1½ lb ripe, undamaged blackberries,

washed

juice of 2 lemons

juice of 1 orange

175 g/6 oz caster sugar

1 bottle Zinfandel red wine

16 firm, ripe, fresh figs

75 ml/3 fl oz crème de mure (blackberry

liqueur) or crème de cassis

(blackcurrant liqueur)

1 tablespoon finely chopped fresh mint leaves

Place the blackberries, lemon and orange juice in a liquidizer or food processor, and blend until smooth. Strain through a fine sieve into an enamel or stainless steel saucepan, and discard the pips.

Add the sugar and red wine. Bring to the boil over a medium heat, then reduce the heat, simmer, and skim when necessary. When the sugar has dissolved, poach the figs, 4 at a time, for 4–5 minutes depending on ripeness. Remove the figs to a glass bowl as they finish cooking.

Bring the blackberry purée to the boil and reduce to about 450 ml/¾ pint. Allow to cool, then add the liqueur and the mint. Pour over the figs. If possible, prepare this dish 24 hours ahead, and turn the figs in the liquor from time to time. Delicious unadorned – or you could serve with a rich vanilla ice cream.

Serves 8

Remove the cinnamon sticks, return the lamb to the sauce, stir in the coriander and season.

Garnish with pickled lemon peel, fried in oil, and fresh or pickled coriander leaves. Serve with *tabbouleh* (salad of parsley and cracked wheat) and an aubergine purée.

Serves 8

Stephen Bull

S tephen Bull is a devilishly clever chap. In a notoriously precarious trade, he is one of the few restaurateurs I know never to have made a loss – not from the day of opening each of the five restaurants he has owned. Indeed, there appear to be only two moments in his life when he has made a fool of himself. The first was at Oxford when he sat before a grave panel of dons at his viva in 1965. By the end of the interview, his left leg had gone to sleep and when he got up to leave, he fell over. The second embarrassment came a few years later when he was lunching a client of his advertising agency at San Frediano – a fashionable Chelsea haunt of media types and Sloanes in the Seventies. He ordered an artichoke vinaigrette and attempted to eat the leaves.

These comic incidents happened a long time ago but they suggest the presence of a more vulnerable persona behind the façade of today's successful chef-entrepreneur. Bull is scared stiff of failure – his diffidence sometimes betrayed in the rapid, clipped speech of the bashful academic and by a tendency to understate everything he has done. You get the feeling that he is slightly bewildered by his success but at the same time you realize that success would never have come unless the man possessed a keen sense of his own self-worth stoked by a determination to win against all odds. His staff say he can be quite tyrannical and he admits that occasionally he has to be tough to maintain the momentum behind his three London restaurants. Each one opened to great critical acclaim. All demonstrate a creative and individual mind whose ideas have been acquired without any real points of reference other than the ones Bull has himself evolved. As both cook and restaurateur, he is almost entirely self-taught.

But to pin Stephen Bull's success purely on his commercial nous – and he does have an extraordinary knack of sensing the trends and tastes of the moment – is to do an injustice to a deep and complex personality. In an industry which revels in gossip and its own incestuous sociability, Bull is a loner and confesses to being unclubbable, but he is also a man who enjoys civilized company and he believes passionately that good food and wine should be life-enhancing pleasures in a cultured society. It is this philosophy that really explains the reason he is in the restaurant business at all.

> **" Bull came to food late and he was already in his late thirties when, in 1980, he hit the gastronomic jackpot "**

Bull came to food late and he was already in his late thirties when, in 1980, he hit the gastronomic jackpot at Lichfield's, his restaurant in Richmond, by winning the double distinction of a star in the *Michelin Guide* and a pestle-and-mortar in *The Good Food Guide* – an eccentric symbol attached 'grudgingly' to a curt register of top restaurants selected by Christopher Driver, *The GFG's* editor at the time. But, while Lichfield's was Bull's proving ground as a craftsman, it was not until he had sold it in 1987 and subsequently opened his eponymous restaurant in Blandford Street, followed by Stephen Bull's Bistro in Smithfield and, finally, Fulham Road in March, 1994, that we see the charm of his touch and the very real contribution he has made to the advance of good eating in the capital. Gifted as a cook he may be, but Bull differs from other more

self-obsessed chefs in that he is neither possessive nor egocentric about his talents. He likes to present menus that people want to eat, at prices they are willing to pay and in environments that echo the spirit of the times and the demands of their location. The approach with each of his three outlets has been the sum of his imagination and instinct coupled to a well-honed intellect – an attribute which, typically, he prefers to play down.

Towards the end of the Eighties, and a good two years before the onset of recession, Bull had already anticipated a mood swing in public attitudes to dining out. People were beginning to tire of pretension, elaboration and the excesses of a decade of *nouvelle cuisine*. They were also reacting against the assumption

"Fulham Road was Bull's biggest test of nerve. He went out on a limb, launching the place against the will of his partners"

that high prices were the automatic penalty you paid to eat well. Bull's response – first in Blandford Street and then even more aggressively at his Bistro which opened in 1992, at the bottom of the economic trough – was to devise a formula that offered Michelin quality on a more populist ticket. Luxury ingredients were abandoned, flavours went big and bold, and menus had to be simple but exciting. Harnessing his flair as an ex-advertising man, he packaged his product in spaces that were bright, modern and 'pleasingly spare'.

The opening of Fulham Road in 1994 marked a subtle but distinct shift of emphasis. On a rising market, Bull bagged a site that was perfectly situated to mine the gilt seam of the Kensington-Chelsea residential axis. He did not change his strategy of simplicity, taste and value – rather, he adapted it to suit a very different location. Items like lobster and *foie gras* reappeared but were mixed with resolutely bucolic pieces like ox cheek and faggots. The setting became more upholstered – the Bistro's hard edges, designed to appeal to ambitious city traders, were replaced by more flatteringly feminine curves in a whimsical retro-theme reminiscent of the post-war New Look era.

Fulham Road was Bull's biggest test of nerve. He went out on a limb, launching the place against the will of his partners – a battle, he says, that was painful and very tough. But once again the old magic paid off, and handsomely.

It took him almost thirty years to decide what he wanted to make of his life and it was only then that he discovered this tenacious side to his nature – in itself a measure of his self-belief in spite of the doubts that often haunt him. Not that success passed him by before he celebrated what he likes to describe as his 'epiphany', a suitable enough metaphor for the eventual realization of his chosen career. Before that happy moment, he did very well for himself without really trying.

Born in December, 1943, Stephen Bull grew up in Abergavenny. From his bedroom window he would look out towards the Black Mountains, a part of South Wales to which he remains deeply attached. His mother was a teacher and his father, a miner's son, had stood valiantly but unsuccessfully as a Tory candidate in two Labour strongholds before joining ICI as an industrial chemist. At the age of ten, Bull won a scholarship to Monmouth and in 1962 he went up to St Catherine's College, Oxford, to read English.

In his second term, his father died suddenly of a massive heart attack. He was only 52. Bull had worshipped him and he was heartbroken: 'I was close to my father,' he says. 'He was a charismatic chap – warm, affectionate, funny and interesting. Sadly, he never really found his niche and he could have shone in various areas, but he just didn't. I am sure he would have got into parliament eventually if he had the resources.'

The tragedy cast a shadow across Bull's Oxford years – which, he says, were fairly aimless – and he graduated with an undistinguished degree. But his profound impressions of the father he admired so much probably account for his fear of failure and the dogged will to succeed in his own chosen niche.

After leaving Oxford, Bull took up a career in advertising, principally because it sounded glamorous and appeared to pay well. By his mid-twenties, he was travelling first class, dashing around town in an Austin Healey and on a fast track to an early directorship. For a time he worked with Peter Mayle – 'a very civilized chap' – before the adman-turned-author retired to Provence to write books which in themselves became the most potent campaign ever conceived for a holiday destination. Mayle rated the young suit for his 'intellectual approach to problems' but, after seven years of it, the glamour was beginning to fray. Bull may have been good at thinking, but he was no hustler – a necessary quality in a famously abrasive profession.

The years in advertising were not wasted. One of Peter Mayle's accounts was Olivetti and Bull made several trips to the company's offices in Ivrea, near Turin, where his clients preferred to conduct business over lunch and dinner in some of the region's finest restaurants. 'The food we ate was a revelation,' Bull says. 'I had never heard of white truffles and suddenly I saw these things being shaved over a risotto and smelling wonderful. It struck a chord which had never been there before.'

In 1972, and at the age of twenty-eight, Stephen Bull turned his back on a high-flying career in advertising with nowhere to go. He

> **❝ By his mid-twenties, he was travelling first class, dashing around town in an Austin Healey and on a fast track to an early directorship ❞**

bought a second-hand Renault 16 and took off round Europe for three months to think. When he returned, he answered a job ad for a waiter at Odin's, Peter Langan's restaurant in Devonshire Street. Langan took him on and, conscious of his humbler circumstances, Bull immediately grew a beard to provide his self-esteem with a little protection from the inevitable taunts of old colleagues

who frequently ate there. The foil worked and after five months he had grasped the rudiments of a trade which he reckoned had to be pretty straightforward if his boss could make it work in the wake of the epic binges that left him slumped on the floor each night for the early shift to scoop up the following morning.

With £3,000 and the support of his bank manager, Stephen Bull retreated into obscurity. If his plan were to fail, he did not want too many people to know about it. For the next five years, a Victorian terraced house on the edge of the village of Llanrwst in North Wales became his home-in-exile. While a local builder set about restoring the place, Bull schooled himself on the first volume of Julia Child's great classic, *Mastering the Art of French Cooking* and, by the time Meadowsweet opened in the autumn of 1974, he had mastered a repertoire of sixty dishes. At the end of his first year in business he was appalled by the size of his tax demand.

Inevitably, the price of isolation was a gap of some years before the critics eventually discovered that good food was to be found in this remote corner of Britain. But when they did arrive, both Egon Ronay and Christopher Driver were quick to note the assertiveness, skill and originality of the chef-patron. Mr Driver's only irritation seems to have been one beyond Stephen Bull's control. 'The donkey across the road needs a mute,' remarked the curmudgeonly editor of *The Good Food Guide*. Mr Ronay, on the other hand, appeared to be more concerned about the staff who, he felt, were 'sometimes unwisely overworked'.

Soon after the restaurant critics' long trek to the foothills of Snowdonia, Bull started to plan his return from the wilderness. He was now ready for a more sophisticated audience and in August 1978, he opened Lichfield's in Richmond. In spite of his self-apprenticeship, his innate diffidence again got the better of him and for the first four months he hired a professional chef until he realized that he knew more about cooking than his employee. Even after he had resumed command of his kitchen, he felt something of an impostor, consciously refusing to wear whites, the traditional chef's uniform, making do with a striped apron instead. 'I think I knew what I was doing,' he says, 'but I still saw myself as a jumped-up amateur.'

Michelin and the *Good Food Guide* disagreed and, when they endowed Lichfield's with their honours two years later, Stephen Bull's credentials were finally established as a professional of the first rank. The endorsement of these powerful authorities also gave Bull the confidence he had been lacking and, as his cooking matured, it developed into a grinding ambition for a second Michelin star – an attempt which contributed to the break-up of a five-year marriage and the sale of the business in 1987. But, in the end, Bull's long run in Richmond was, for all its glory, much like a suburban fringe show in rehearsal for its move to the West End. Along with others at the time, he went through a phase of playing with period novelties like raspberry vinegar, but many of the themes which made his name as a cook still have their place on his menus today – particularly in Blandford Street and at the Bistro.

These culinary themes defy any cogent definition but the threads tend to be pan-European with modern British accents and a particular liking for offal and the cheaper cuts – a contemporary trend which he has success-

> **" Jane Grigson . . . he believes, will be recognized historically as a more important figure than Elizabeth David "**

fully fuelled. Sources of ideas have evolved principally from his reading, which has included the books of all the great French chefs. But the author who has impressed him most is Jane Grigson who, he believes, will be recognized historically as a more important figure than Elizabeth David.

While simplicity with innovation and the primacy of flavour have been the governing principles for Bull's three restaurants, their menus are leavened by a reassuring timelessness. The best dishes are the old favourites. The recipe for a *bourride* of plaice and mussels began service in Llanrwst and twenty years on it

is a regular fixture at Stephen Bull's city eaterie. The aïoli is whisked into the stock to make a light and creamy broth for the fish, which leans casually on a mound of mash in the centre of its bowl. It is perfect nourishment for the rush of thirtysomethings in sharp suits and loud ties who storm the place at lunchtime.

Another Stephen Bull classic dish (this one ex-Lichfield's) is his chicken liver parfait – Tuscan pink, bitter-sweet and as smooth as clotted cream. One forgets how meltingly delicious these familiar confections can be when perfectly done.

Some of Bull's more imaginative ideas are not only examples of his powers of invention, but also evidence of an inventive frugality – hence his consistent ability to turn in profits. In Richmond, one of his more outlandish dishes was a *millefeuille* of duck where the crisp, defatted skin of the fowl was used as a pastry substitute to sandwich a mix of chopped meat and lime. There has been no reincarnation of this gastronomic wonder in central London but its ghost lives on refreshingly in a salad of leaves, oranges and walnuts where crispy duck skins make an alternative to lardons. The result is a simple starter – crunchy, zesty and wonderfully reviving on a warm summer's day.

The remains of fine cheeses are another area of potential waste which Bull deftly mitigates in his 'twice-cooked' soufflés. Tangy goats' and blue cheeses are ideal for the purpose and his method – economic and efficient in itself – is to pre-cook the mix in moulds coated with crushed hazelnuts and breadcrumbs, turn them out and then re-cook them to order. The effect is to add a textural dimension to the soufflé – a deliciously crisp coating to contrast with its light fluffy interior.

As he darts between his three restaurants in his Alfa Romeo, a briefcase permanently by his side, Stephen Bull's routine is very different these days. The shots of adrenalin which fired him at his stoves – especially in Richmond – have been replaced by the problems of managing a complex modern business: an inadequate extraction system, a power failure, a basement flood, legal issues, battles with planners, staff matters. There is always a problem demanding his attention and he makes little secret of the fact that at times he finds it pretty tiresome. 'I miss the creative buzz of the kitchen,' he says. ' It's so much more satisfying. As a cook, I wanted to be as good as possible and, deep down, I regret that I did not win that second Michelin star at Lichfield's.' Certainly, Bull prefers to work on his own terms and he is not at ease with the inevitable constraints imposed by the interests of shareholders.

In 1992, he married the music journalist, Anne Inglis, and they now have a young family which has changed his perspective on life. He has come to dislike London with a passion – 'an unpleasant, dirty, violent, noisy place to live' – and he often dreams of returning to Wales. Meanwhile, he refuses to discount the addition of a fourth restaurant to his portfolio if ever the opportunity arose. Stephen Bull may be a country lad at heart and he may hate the big city. But he hates the idea of losing even more.

Twice-cooked Goats' Cheese Soufflé

900 ml/1½ pints milk

1 onion, finely sliced

1 small bay leaf

1 sprig of thyme

10 black peppercorns

75 g/3 oz butter

75 g/3 oz flour

50 g/2 oz or more fresh goats' cheese, and

50 g/2 oz blue or mature goats' cheese, softened

3 eggs, separated

hazelnut oil (see method)

grated Parmesan cheese, for sprinkling

salt and freshly ground black pepper

Hazelnut Breadcrumbs:

25 g/1 oz finely grated stale bread, mixed

with 12 finely chopped roasted hazelnuts

Sauce:

béchamel mixture (see method)

50 g/2 oz goats' cheese

(a different variety if possible)

50 g/2 oz Gruyère cheese

¼ teaspoon grated nutmeg

Paprika Oil:

1 teaspoon paprika

2 tablespoon groundnut oil

Pour the milk into a saucepan, add the onion, bay leaf, thyme and peppercorns. Bring to the boil, allow to infuse, then strain. Make a blond roux béchamel with the butter, flour and strained milk. Pour one-third of the béchamel into a separate pan, mix in the two cheeses, heat gently, then stir in the beaten egg yolks. Beat the egg whites until stiff and fold in. Add seasoning and more cheese, if necessary, as the cheese flavour must be strong. Line straight-sided cups or ramekins with hazelnut oil and hazelnut breadcrumbs and fill two-thirds full with the mixture. Bake in a *bain-marie* at 190°C (375°F) Gas Mark 5, for 20 minutes. Cool, then turn out.

To make the sauce, add the goats' cheese to the remaining béchamel. Stir in the Gruyère, nutmeg, salt and pepper and cook until smooth.

To make the paprika oil, mix the paprika with the oil, allow to settle for 20 minutes, then pour off the oil. Set aside.

Reheat the soufflés for about 5 minutes in a hot oven, 230°C (450°F) Gas Mark 8. Pour over the cheese sauce, then sprinkle with the Parmesan and brown under a hot grill. Serve, drizzled with paprika oil.

Serves 4

Cod with Rocket
and Hazelnut Butter

———

4 fillets of cod, about 175 g/6 oz each, skinned

a large handful of rocket leaves

12 roasted hazelnuts, chopped

25 g/1 oz butter

salt and freshly ground black pepper

chopped hazelnuts, to garnish

Hazelnut Butter:

25 g/1 oz roasted hazelnuts, ground

125 g/4 oz unsalted butter, softened

Beurre Blanc:

50 m/2 fl oz dry white wine

12 ml/½ fl oz white wine vinegar

25 g/1 oz chopped shallots

1 tablespoon double cream

125 g/4 oz cold butter, cut into 4–5 pieces

To make the hazelnut butter, mix the roasted, ground hazelnuts and softened butter together until evenly blended, roll into a cylindrical shape about 2.5 cm/1 inch in diameter, and chill in the refrigerator until hard.

To make the *beurre blanc*, place the dry white wine in a small saucepan, add the wine vinegar and chopped shallots, bring to the boil and reduce until almost evaporated. Add the double cream, bubble for a few seconds, then add the pieces of butter. Raise the heat and boil the butter and cream together, stirring constantly, until the sauce has a smooth consistency. Strain, taste and adjust the seasoning, then set aside and keep warm.

Season the cod fillets, and fry gently in butter over medium heat in a covered pan until just cooked. Remove and keep warm. Throw the rocket leaves into the pan, and stir around in the remaining butter for a minute or so, until the leaves have just wilted. Season.

To serve, divide the rocket leaves between 4 heated dinner plates, place the fillets of cod on top, and pour the creamy sauce over. Top each portion with a slice of hazelnut butter and scatter with chopped hazelnuts.

Serves 4

Duck Skin, Orange and Walnut Salad

—

1 large orange

16 walnuts

skin trimmings from the carcass of a duck

4 large handfuls of mixed salad leaves

walnut oil or hazelnut oil

salt and freshly ground black pepper

Peel the orange over a bowl to catch the juice, and remove any pith or membrane. Cut out the segments, then cut each segment into three pieces. Reserve the orange juice in the bowl.

Roast the walnuts for about 15–20 minutes in a preheated oven at 190°C (375°F) Gas Mark 5. Rub in a clean tea towel to remove the skins, and chop the nuts roughly.

Place the duck skin trimmings in the oven and cook until crisp, pouring off the fat from time to time. (Keep this for roasting or frying potatoes.) This crisping process will take anything up to an hour. Remove from the oven, sprinkle lightly with salt and drain on kitchen paper. Pick over carefully and remove any hard bits of meat or cartilage.

Mix together the leaves, walnuts and oranges. Dress with a lightly seasoned mixture of oil and the reserved orange juice. Add the crisp duck skin, then serve immediately.

Serves 4

Mixed Livers

with Lentils and Vinegar

—

250 g/8 oz green lentils, washed and

picked over

1 carrot, finely diced

1 leek, finely diced

1 celery stick, finely diced

900 ml/1½ pints chicken stock or water

2 bay leaves

pancetta trimmings or

2 rashers streaky bacon, diced

4 duck livers

4 chicken livers

4 pieces lamb's or calf's liver

25 g/1 oz butter

balsamic or red wine vinegar

salt and freshly ground black pepper

chopped fresh flat leaf parsley, to garnish

Put everything except the livers, butter, vinegar and parsley into a large saucepan, bring to the boil, skim and cook until the lentils are tender – about 25–30 minutes. Strain, keeping the cooking liquid for another use. Season lightly and keep hot.

Remove any veins or tubes from the livers.

Heat the butter in a large pan, season the livers and sauté quickly, until lightly browned but still pink in the centre. Divide the lentils between 4 plates, place the livers on top, and sprinkle with the vinegar. Scatter with the chopped parsley, then serve.

Serves 4

Bourride of Plaice and Mussels

25 g/1 oz butter

1 shallot, finely chopped

2 leeks, finely sliced, blanched and refreshed

2 garlic cloves

1 sprig of thyme

150 ml/¼ pint dry white wine

150 ml/¼ pint fish stock

1 kg/2 lb cooked mussels (250 g/½ lb shelled
weight), cooking liquid reserved

1 kg/2 lb plaice fillet, cut in 5 cm/2 inch pieces

2 tablespoons double cream

salt and freshly ground black pepper

paprika or parsley, to garnish

Aïoli:

2 garlic cloves, blanched and mashed

2 egg yolks

lemon juice

175 ml/6 fl oz olive oil

Heat the butter and cook the shallots, leeks and garlic until softened. Add the thyme, wine, stock and mussel liquid and cook for 10 minutes. Add the plaice and mussels, poach for 5 minutes, remove and keep hot. Reduce the liquid to one-quarter; remove the garlic, add the cream, simmer and remove from the heat.

Make the aïoli, then whisk 6 tablespoons into the cream mixture to form a thick sauce. Reheat for 30 seconds, season, then pour over the fish and sprinkle with paprika or parsley.

Serves 4

Roast Rump of Lamb

1 lamb chump, well trimmed and seasoned

lamb stock (see method)

1 onion, chopped

1 fat garlic clove, crushed

1 sprig of rosemary, bruised

mixture of red wine and water (see method)

butter and olive oil, for browning

1 tomato, skinned, deseeded and diced

a walnut-sized knob of cold butter,
cut into pieces

a pinch of sugar (optional)

salt and freshly ground black pepper

Make a small quantity of stock from the browned lamb trimmings, onion, garlic and rosemary, with half red wine and half water, to cover.

Heat the butter and oil in a roasting tin, add the seasoned lamb and brown on all sides. Roast in a preheated oven at 200°C (400°F) Gas Mark 6 for about 20 minutes.

Set aside to rest for 5–10 minutes in a warm place.

Reduce the stock to a couple of spoonfuls and use to deglaze the roasting tin. Strain, add the diced tomato and swirl in the butter. Add salt and freshly ground black pepper, and a pinch of sugar if needed. Pour over the lamb.

Serve with a crisp potato galette or rösti and sliced courgettes well seasoned and dressed with olive oil.

Serves 1

Chocolate Brownie Thins
with Chocolate Praline Ice Cream

———

300 g/10 oz butter

125 g/4 oz cocoa powder

4 eggs

500 g/1 lb caster sugar

125 g/4 oz plain flour

¼ tablespoon vanilla essence

150 g/5 oz hazelnuts, roasted, skinned and crushed

Chocolate Ice Cream:

375 g/12 oz bitter chocolate, broken into pieces

¾ teaspoon instant coffee granules

175 g/6 oz caster sugar, plus 2 teaspoons extra

175 ml/6 fl oz water

600 ml/1 pint whipping cream

vanilla essence

Praline:

175 g/6 oz sugar

6 tablespoons water

a few drops of vanilla essence

175 g/6 oz almonds, blanched, skinned, flaked and dry-fried until golden

To make the praline, melt the sugar with the water in a pan over high heat. When bubbling, add the vanilla. Mix in the almonds, then spread over a greased baking sheet and cool.

To make the ice cream, melt the chocolate in a bowl over hot water. Dissolve the coffee and 175 g/6 oz of the sugar in the water, bring to the boil, then stir in the chocolate. Leave to cool. Whip the cream with the remaining sugar to soft peaks, add a few drops of vanilla, then mix in the praline. Combine with the cooled chocolate mixture and freeze in a sorbetière.

To make the brownies, melt the butter in a pan with the cocoa, beat the eggs and sugar together, then combine the two mixtures. Add the flour, vanilla and nuts and pour into 2 Swiss roll tins lined with buttered baking paper, then cook in a preheated oven at 180°C (350°F) Gas Mark 4 for about 15–20 minutes. Cut into triangles and serve with the ice cream.

Serves 10-12, with about 32 brownies

Sally Clarke

By the age of ten, Sally Clarke had discovered Elizabeth David and was ticking her mother off for buying margarine instead of butter. In her early teens, the blueprint for the restaurant that now bears her name was already drafted in her mind. At seventeen, on her first morning at catering college, she stubbornly declined to crown her grapefruit segments with a maraschino cherry. A spray of mint would do better, thank you. Two years later, she had moved on to the Cordon Bleu School in Paris. Here she felt that her course in advanced cookery was not adequately testing. So she headed for Le Grand Véfour, one of the noblest addresses in Parisian gastronomy, walked in and, without the comfort of an appointment, asked to see its distinguished patron. M. Raymond Oliver was impressed and duly installed her at his son's restaurant, the Bistro de Paris in the *septième*.

In her mid-twenties, Sally Clarke had landed in southern California. At Michael's in Santa Monica, haunt of Hollywood egos, she managed the tables. When there were none, movie moguls bellowed and bullied her. She stood her ground and disarmed them with her smiles.

In 1984, at the age of thirty, she realized her teenage dream and opened Clarke's on Kensington Church Street. Against the loud advice of the good and the great, she broke the first law of all serious metropolitan restaurants by refusing her customers the pleasure of choice on the

evening's menu. One of the most famous aphorisms of the Eighties – 'There Is No Alternative' – became Sally Clarke's battle cry.

John Whitley, restaurant critic for the *Daily Telegraph*, labelled Clarke's a 'TINA-diner' and reckoned that her approach made 'Mrs Thatcher's cabinet discussions seem open-minded to the point of anarchy'. The essential difference between the two women, of course, is that the Blessed Sally is still firmly in power – so much so that her constituency now extends to a bakery and a food shop.

However, there is more to Clarke than chutzpah, conviction politics and the energy it takes to win. There is an English blush to her cheeks, she has sparkling eyes and looks which belie her age by at least ten years. She has this winning smile and an elfin charm, which conceal her wilfulness and blinding clarity of intent – both needed to persuade a seasoned and sophisticated public that they can enjoy her restaurant without the usual benefit of choice. The risk she took does not make her a reckless gambler. The joys of dining out are as much a function of place and personality as they are of good food and Sally Clarke is, quite simply, a brilliant hostess who cooks brilliantly.

These two qualities in her nature – this rare mix of steely will and feminine charm – are manifest in the way she organizes her work. She cooks by day, hosts the evenings. Sixteen hours a day, five days a week and a 'full day *plus*' on Saturdays, chasing neglected paper in the restaurant's office and minding the shop next door.

At midday there is a perceptible edge to the atmosphere in the basement's open-plan kitchen – an air of controlled tension, a distinct sense of urgency. The fringes of the long service counter separating cooks from the sweep of impeccably laid tables are decked with wicker baskets bulging exuberantly with good things; flowering rhubarb, huge knobbly bulbs of Egyptian garlic, thick bunches of herbs and a cascade of bread loaves – sourdough, raisin, green olive, black rye and onion. Behind the counter, Clarke – tousled, pencil lodged behind her right ear – looks sharp and earnest, her crisp whites covering lime green and pink polka dot leggings. She is flanked by her two senior lieutenants. The telephone rings incessantly. She answers, whisks, ladles and directs all at the same time. A waiter hands her a typed draft of the day's lunch menu. She scrutinizes it, her face contracting in an expression of fierce concentration.

" Sally Clarke is quite simply a brilliant hostess who cooks brilliantly "

Shortly before 12.15, the waiters – striped shirts, white aprons – muster round the counter. On the quarter hour precisely, they line up before *la patronne* for The Menu Reading – a formal ritual which proceeds thus. The head waiter, in a crisp and clear voice, recites each dish in turn. Clarke responds. Speaking rapidly, precisely and in great detail, she describes the dish, its constituents, the provenance of the ingredients and how they are composed. Where appropriate, she gives the origin of the recipe: it may be Elizabeth David or, in the case of a bitter chocolate soufflé, Bernard Pacaud, the three-star wizard of L'Ambroisie in Paris. 'We always undercook our soufflés,' she says. Yes. And the result is rich, liquid and wicked. The French have a word for places like Clarke's for which there is no equivalent idiom in English. It is *sérieux*. Clarke's is seriously so.

When lunch is at full tilt – the tables filled upstairs and down – she leaves the service to her deputies and sets about the *mise-en-place* for the evening; shelling peas, stoning olives, stripping thyme from its twigs, each task ticked off against a checklist. After service, the preparation for dinner continues. It is done without a break save, perhaps, for a cup of tea or a bowl of something at the work bench. Silently, relentlessly through the afternoon, the only sounds are of chopping, slicing, scraping, picking as the three women quietly work their way down the list. There is no badinage. Just devotion to the task of the moment. Heart and mind in tune with the raw materials.

At 6.00 p.m. she leaves for home. At 7.30 she returns transformed – made up and elegantly dressed – the perfect Kensington hostess. Sally Clarke's guests fall for her as much as her table and the bright, hospitable surroundings. When they leave, they have not just eaten well, they have spent an evening in the company of Sally Clarke.

For the driven few, endowed with the power of self-belief, life seems strangely predestined. Almost from the beginning, it was written that Sally Clarke would become a restaurateur of her own making and be fashioned in the image of her ministering spirit, Alice Waters, the celebrated proprietor of Chez Panisse in Berkeley, just across the Bay from San Francisco.

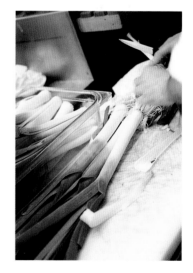

Contrary to popular myth, Sally never worked at Chez Panisse, but she did visit the restaurant frequently in the four years she spent on the West Coast. The seed for her Big Idea was sown much earlier – in France. On summer holidays as a child, the family would break their journeys at remote wayside inns where *madame* would announce the dinner she had cooked using ingredients picked from the garden or bought that day from the

❝ She has an artist's eye and her finished plates have the look and liberation of an impressionist painting ❞

local market. 'It made so much more sense to me,' says Sally. Vast restaurant menus invited imperfection and, besides, the personal touch and a feeling of home struck her as the proper way to run a good restaurant.

In England, Sally's formative years were touched by another remarkable woman who was signally responsible for inspiring and shaping the course of her education in the trade. This was Jean Alexander, bespoke caterer to Home Counties society, whose company was based in Guildford where Sally grew up. In between schooling at Guildford High, singing in the choir and playing lacrosse for Surrey ('Oh! I was *very* good at lacrosse!') she cooked or waitressed for Alexander in grand houses, marquees and St James's Palace. Sometimes she worked until two or three in the morning to the dismay of her devoted father, who felt she was being used as child labour. But Sally loved every moment.

In 1973, and now nineteen, Sally Clarke arrived in Paris for her course at the Cordon Bleu where she fell in with a lively group of ambitious American students. The leader of the pack was a larger-than-life character 'with an enormous ego' called Michael McCarty who boasted that one day he would open the best restaurant on Malibu Beach and change the face of gastronomy in Southern California. At weekends, they would scour the Paris markets in the morning, repair to McCarty's apartment to cook all afternoon and throw dinner parties for twenty-five in the evenings.

These were exciting times, but for Clarke not exciting enough. She wanted to see kitchens at the sharp end and, to do it, she was prepared to skivvy for nought. After Raymond Oliver's introduction to the Bistro de Paris, she moved on to two other restaurants working during the day. Young and attractive, she was the only woman in the kitchen and the butt of cruel pranks which

only the chauvinist French could devise. But they soon learned to reckon with her English grit. At night, to keep body and soul together, she cooked supper for a banker's family in the *seizième* in return for a room and her keep.

Her education complete, Clarke eventually returned to London to work for Prue Leith and, shortly after, to teach at Leith's cookery school. Then, in 1978, she took a call from Los Angeles. It was McCarty crackling hype down the wire telling her to fly out immediately. When she arrived, she was welcomed by a forest of tinsel but no town. Her old student chum had not even found the premises for his new restaurant in Santa Monica and another year elapsed before Michael's was up and running.

Sally Clarke's years in California were a rehearsal for many of the routines and methods she adopts in London today. At Michael's she cooked by day, greeted and seated by night. However, in her kitchen, the only stylistic import is her charcoal grill. It was Jonathan Waxman, McCarty's head chef, who taught her the subtle science of manipulating food on the grill. But, more importantly, she has Waxman to thank for introducing her to Chez Panisse, where he had worked before his move to Santa Monica. Her first visit in 1979 was a revelation. Alice Waters presented a no-choice, five-course dinner. Baskets of wildflowers, like hedgerows, adorned the restaurant. The kitchen was open to view. Breads tumbled warm from the oven and were sliced at table. 'At last,' enthuses Clarke, 'this nutty idea I'd had on my mind for so long suddenly made sense. This woman had been doing it successfully for ten years and more perfectly than I could have possibly imagined.' Sally had found her spiritual beacon and she and Alice Waters became as sisters.

By 1983, Sally Clarke was primed to make her move. Besides, she wanted to come home. Her decision was emphatic, clear, determined. There was no deference to the wise counsel of family and friends: 'I wanted to do it my way. Equally, I wanted to do it in my land, with my people. Also, I had to raise the money myself and, if necessary, lose the money myself.' She did. And she did not lose her shirt.

Like the cook, so the food. Sally Clarke has a highly individual style. Her compositions are at once precise and beguiling. When you see them on the plate, they are unmistakably hers. But there is also an odd dissonance of place and presentation here, like an enchanting deceit. What you get is strangely removed from what you might expect in a smart cosmopolitan city restaurant. Instead, the freshness and luminosity of her dishes have a way of transporting you to some *jardin fleuri* in Provence or Tuscany. She has an artist's eye and her finished plates have the look and liberation of an impressionist painting. Lunching at Clarke's puts you in mind of Manet's famous picnic.

Perhaps it is her way with herbs and greens. These garnishes – integral to each dish – have become a bold trademark and she uses them generously in large sprays rather than meek sprigs, as in a warm salad of wild salmon where the foamy whiteness of the crème fraîche on the fish is diffused by a branch of flowering chervil. Similarly, a plate of deep-fried baby artichokes and English curly parsley with tartare sauce is dressed with a thick bunch of Kentish-grown mustard leaves. A sunny and crusty pizza of spiced lamb and aubergine is set on a rush mat of bright green rocket supplied by the walled garden of a Suffolk manor house. Like everything else she does, Sally is meticulous about the sourcing of her growers.

The absence of refined sauces is another Clarke hallmark. She dislikes methods which require a lot of 'sieving and mucking about'. In the mid-Eighties, she was one of the first London restaurateurs to popularize the Latin passions which grip us still in the Nineties; olive oils, balsamic vinegars, pesto, sun-dried tomatoes, salsas and the rest. These are themes which still feature in her repertoire. However, her favourite means of lubrication is the liberal but carefully judged use of virgin olive oils; a standard oil for cooking vegetables or as a soup base, another for marinating, a more fruity extra-virgin oil for dressing salad leaves, and a top-flight product like Colonna for drizzling over a plate of baby fennel or spring asparagus with Parmesan. The same oil will also be used as a final moistening agent for a char-grilled halibut with a salsa of mint, orange and chilli or to a grilled breast of chicken filled with basil and served with salad leaves, aubergine and lightly toasted focaccia.

There is a simplicity and purity about all these compositions, but they obscure a complexity and an intelligence deep in the detail of each plate which, ultimately, makes Sally Clarke's cooking so exciting. She has such a keen understanding of how to bring together her various ingredients that, in the end, they create dishes where the sum of the parts exceeds the whole. There is also a gentleness, a feminine grace and allure about her food. So it is not surprising to discover that her kitchen is all-female and that she prefers it this way. 'Women,' she says, 'are more careful. Ninety per cent of our work is in the preparation. And because we buy so carefully, care in the preparation is paramount.' Who can argue when the results are so blissfully seductive?

Sally Clarke is the outstanding woman in this generation of chefs. But for all her remarkable drive and self-will, there is not the slightest trace of the hauteur and arrogance which seems to affect some of her male contemporaries. Clarke's self-confidence is checked by an equal measure of humility and a wonderfully giving nature. Beneath the public persona, she is an intensely private person, supported by a loving family and a small circle of close friends. And, as for those hotly-held convictions about her mission in life, there are moments when she is equally emphatic in self-doubt. Alice Waters may be her mentor but, she says, 'I am not as much of a perfectionist as Alice, and would never get anywhere near. Never ever!' Some might argue. But, with Sally Clarke, there's no point.

Salad of Buffalo Mozzarella

with Anchovies, Olives, Black Grapes and Capers

—

8 salted anchovies, rinsed, filleted and drizzled with olive oil, or

16 tinned anchovy fillets in oil, decanted and

remarinated in fresh olive oil and fresh thyme leaves

1 teaspoon chopped fresh thyme leaves

150 ml/¼ pint extra-virgin olive oil

4 handfuls of rocket leaves,

carefully picked, washed and spun

3 large balls of buffalo mozzarella,

quartered, sprinkled with salt and pepper,

then drizzled with extra-virgin olive oil

1 small bunch of grapes, halved and deseeded

4 tablespoons baby capers

16 black olives, pitted and roughly chopped

1 tablespoon picked and washed fresh coriander leaves

1 tablespoon picked and washed fresh flat leaf parsley leaves

1 teaspoon balsamic vinegar

salt and freshly ground black pepper

8 breadsticks, to serve

To prepare the anchovies, place them on a flat plate, drench with 4 tablespoons of olive oil and sprinkle with chopped thyme.

Toss the rocket gently in about 4 tablespoons of the olive oil, seasoned with salt and freshly ground black pepper, then arrange on 4 individual salad plates. Place 3 pieces of mozzarella on to each 'nest' of leaves.

Mix the grapes, capers, black olives, coriander leaves, parsley leaves, salt, pepper, balsamic vinegar and the remaining 2 tablespoons of the olive oil in a bowl.

Spoon the grape mixture over the mozzarella, arrange the marinated anchovies attractively and serve immediately with breadsticks.

Serves 4

Grilled Breasts of Corn-fed Chicken,

with Basil, Various Leaves, Marinated Aubergine Salad and Focaccia

———

4 breasts of corn-fed chicken

8–12 basil leaves

salt and freshly ground black pepper

Marinated Aubergine Salad:

5 large aubergines, halved

1 tablespoon chopped fresh thyme leaves

150 ml/¼ pint olive oil

3 tablespoons basil, roughly chopped

2 tablespoons chopped fresh flat leaf parsley

2 garlic cloves, crushed with salt and olive oil

grated zest of 2 lemons

To serve:

mixed salad leaves

good extra-virgin olive oil

4 slices grilled bread

lemon wedges

To make the aubergine salad, criss-cross the flesh of the aubergines with a small, sharp knife without piercing the skin. Sprinkle with salt, pepper, thyme and olive oil. Place in a roasting tin in a preheated oven at 200°C (400°F) Gas Mark 6 and cook until soft and golden. Remove, cover with foil and allow to steam until cool. When cool, cut into large cubes of about 3.5 cm/1½ inches, and place in a bowl with the remaining ingredients. Toss gently and allow to infuse, adding extra oil if necessary.

Lift the skin of the chicken breasts along one edge and push 2–3 leaves of basil flat against the flesh. Pull over the skin to seal. Season both sides with salt and pepper. Grill or pan-fry until tender and juicy.

Meanwhile, toss the salad leaves in olive oil, salt and pepper, and arrange on 4 dinner plates. Place a scoop of aubergine salad and a slice of grilled bread beside. Slice the chicken breasts in 2–3 pieces diagonally, arrange on the plates, drizzle with oil and serve with lemon wedges.

Serves 8

Stew of Lamb Shanks

with Green Olives and Orange Peel

—

8 tablespoons inexpensive olive oil

4 lamb shanks (from leg, not shoulder)

1 large carrot, cut into chunks

4 celery sticks, cut into chunks

1 fennel bulb, cut into chunks

1 onion, cut into chunks

½ leek, cut into chunks

4 garlic cloves, crushed

½ bottle hearty red wine

250 ml/8 fl oz orange juice

250 ml/8 fl oz lamb or chicken stock

1 sprig of thyme

1 sprig of rosemary

1 sprig of sage

4 bay leaves

salt and freshly ground black pepper

To serve:

20 green olives

8 pieces of orange peel, without pith (peeled using a potato peeler)

Heat the olive oil in a large, heavy-based pot and fry the shanks until brown on all sides. Remove to a plate and add the vegetables to the pan, stirring over high heat until golden. Add the garlic, wine, orange juice, stock, herbs and shanks and bring to the boil. Season with salt and freshly ground black pepper, cover, leave to simmer on very gentle heat for 50–60 minutes, or until tender.

Remove the shanks to a plate and cover. Strain the vegetables out of the stock and use for an informal supper dish with pasta. Strain the stock through a sieve and allow to settle. Skim off excess fat. Boil rapidly to reduce and thicken slightly. Add the olives and orange peel, then taste and adjust the seasoning as necessary. Place the lamb shanks in a serving bowl and spoon over the sauce.

Serves 4

Pizza of Spiced Lamb Sausage, Aubergine and Rocket

250 g/8 oz lamb shoulder, minced

1 garlic clove, crushed with salt

1 small red chilli, chopped very finely

1 bunch of coriander leaves, chopped roughly

grated zest of 1 orange

½ teaspoon fennel seeds, lightly toasted

¼ teaspoon cumin seeds, lightly toasted

2-3 tablespoons fine cornmeal

Pizza Dough

200 g/7 oz plain flour

75 g/3 oz rye flour

40 ml/1½ fl oz olive oil

25 ml/1 fl oz milk

15 g/½ oz fresh yeast

about 150 ml/¼ pint warm water

Topping:

aubergine salad (see page 80)

2 onions, finely sliced

4 tablespoons olive oil

1 small red chilli

1 tablespoon chopped fresh coriander leaves

4 handfuls of rocket leaves

salt and freshly ground black pepper

Mix the first 7 ingredients together, cover tightly and leave to marinate overnight in the refrigerator.

Make the aubergine salad as described on page 80 and set aside.

Next day, make the pizza dough. By hand, mix all the ingredients with a generous pinch of salt to form a soft, smooth and elastic dough. Kneading will take approximately 10 minutes. Alternatively, use a mixing machine, with a dough hook, on the slowest speed. Allow to rise in a warm place in a covered bowl.

To make the topping, cook the onions in the olive oil until golden, season with salt, chilli and chopped coriander leaves. Set aside to cool.

Pick over the rocket, wash and spin. Set aside in a plastic bag in the refrigerator.

Sprinkle cornmeal generously over 2 baking sheets. Cut the dough into 4, and roll into thin, flat discs, approximately 15 cm/6 inches across. Lay 2 on to each prepared sheet and spread with the onion mixture, leaving a rim of at least 2.5 cm/1 inch around the outside. Cover with clingfilm and leave to prove gently for about 10–15 minutes.

Scatter walnut-sized piles of the lamb and similar amounts of the aubergine salad over the top of the pizza. Bake in a preheated oven at 200°C (400°F) Gas Mark 6 for about 10–12 minutes, or until the dough is crisp. Remove from the oven.

Meanwhile, make a salad of half the rocket leaves, tossed in olive oil, salt and freshly ground black pepper.

Scatter the remaining rocket over the pizza, sprinkle with salt, drizzle with olive oil, and return to the oven for 1 minute until wilted.

Remove the pizza from the oven and serve immediately with the rocket salad.

Serves 8 as starter, 4 as main course

Bitter Chocolate Soufflé

Adapted from a recipe by
Bernard Pacaud

melted butter and caster sugar,

for soufflé dishes

125 g/4 oz bitter chocolate, chopped

75 g/2½ oz unsalted butter

25 g/1 oz good-quality cocoa powder

4 eggs, separated

50 g/2 oz caster sugar

icing sugar, for dusting

150 ml/¼ pint double cream, whipped,

for serving

Brush 4 individual soufflé dishes with melted butter, then sprinkle with sugar.

Melt the chopped chocolate and the butter in a bowl over a pan of simmering water.

Cool slightly, then add the cocoa powder, followed by the egg yolks. Stir until smooth. Whisk the egg whites to the soft peak stage, then fold into the chocolate mixture.

You can now cook the mixture immediately, or let it stand for up to 3 hours before cooking.

Spoon the mixture into the soufflé dishes and cook in a preheated oven at 200°C (400°F) Gas Mark 6 for about 5–6 minutes. They should be quite runny – the runnier the better.

Dust the soufflés with icing sugar, and serve immediately, with a bowl of whipped double cream on the side.

Serves 4

Summer Berry Trifle

1 punnet of strawberries

1 punnet of raspberries

1 punnet of blackberries

1 punnet of blackcurrants

sugar and lemon juice, to taste

8 sponge fingers or

equal weight of Genoese cake

300 ml/½ pint crème anglaise

150 ml/¼ pint double cream,

lightly whipped

1 tablespoon roughly chopped

pistachio nuts

Reserve half the fruits from all the punnets for serving (choose the best ones). Place the remaining fruit in a liquidizer or food processor and purée with the sugar and lemon juice to taste. Pass through a sieve.

Chill 4 soup plates. Cut the sponge into 1 cm/½ inch cubes and arrange in a ring in the bottom of each soup plate.

Toss the reserved fruits together with the fruit purée and place carefully in the centre of the sponge cubes.

Mix the *crème anglaise* with the lightly whipped cream and pour carefully over the sponge cake.

Sprinkle the chopped nuts over the cream and serve immediately.

Serves 4

Adam Robinson

People are not the only customers to dine at the Brackenbury. As twilight gathers over the terraces of Brackenbury Road in West London, chimney stacks like a row of broken teeth silhouetted against the evening sky, a black cat pauses beneath the awning where animated tables spill on to the pavement. The cat purrs, its nostrils wet with expectation and, like a regular, strides confidently into the restaurant. Moments later, Gaby appears with the remains of a black bream. Expertly, she serves her feline guest in a discreet corner beyond the honeysuckle and jasmine trellises enclosing the street tables.

Gaby is a waitress and a member of the Brack-pack. Inside, the others go about their work with immense good humour. They obviously love what they do. Clive, the manager, slaloms gracefully between chairs spreading an easy charm. He's been with the Brack since Adam and Katie Robinson opened the place in 1991. Before that, Clive's career was pretty chequered. He was fired from Kensington Place. Fired from The Eagle. And fired from Charles Fontaine's Chop House – 'which I'm very proud of', says Adam Robinson.

Around the bar, Mini is dispensing wine and singing as she pours. Suddenly, a bevy of friends descends on her. They are all ex-staff and, for several minutes, there is an awful lot of hugging and kissing going on. Meanwhile, centre stage – all mountain green and bright terracotta – the players are plundering one another's plates or diving into a communal dish of savouries, a variegated Brack set-piece which might include olives and toasted almonds, chorizo, crostini of grilled vegetables, vegetable fritters, lambs' brains, roasted fennel and couscous salad. The one fixture is a boiled egg in its shell, served with a spicy salt – an idea adopted by the Robinsons after their honeymoon in Central Africa where these eggs are sold to passengers at bus stops.

Eating at the Brack – like working there – is a shared experience in good fun. A celebration in the simple joys of everyday living. This is not a place for display or best behaviour. The folk who come tend to be locals, professional types mostly, who prefer to dress down. For the Brack is London's arch-specimen of the neighbourhood café – an old concept, perhaps, but one which has acquired a new respectability in the Nineties, with its absence of chic trimmings and slick service. The Brack has become the anti-hero of the city's smart eating-out scene.

Restaurants often shape and colour the images of particular areas – Soho, Chelsea, even Docklands thanks to Sir Terence Conran. This is not, however, the traditional remit of a neighbourhood eaterie. It is the singular achievement of the Robinsons that they have artfully coloured in the map of an obscure quarter of London no one had ever heard of before.

Their restaurant is sandwiched between a chippy and a hardware store in a remote urban village within a labyrinthine cluster of nondescript streets somewhere between Shepherd's Bush and Hammersmith. Indeed, Brackenbury Road is so remote that veteran cabbies reach for their street atlases to find it.

The unbuttoned sociability about the tables turns to unbridled frenzy below stairs where our anti-hero presides over a kitchen smaller than a ship's galley. In full flight, Robinson and two red-bloods dish up a hundred meals a session on second-hand burners spitting wild flames of blue, crimson and orange. They work with their check trousers rolled half-way up their calves. Now and then, one of them will jerk a bottle to his lips, tilting it high and downing the water in one long draught. For three hours or more, these boys play a thrilling, throbbing gig in an airless pit relieved only by an open door to the garden at the back of the house. But this is the Brack, so for 'garden' read 'overgrown urban plot'. Still, it has its uses. Robinson is keen on his herbs and he grows chives and tarragon, mint, horseradish, sorrel and sage. Most prolific of all is a rich colony of nettles by the boundary wall. These, however, are not harvested. Remember – the village includes a lively community of cats.

The Brackenbury's phenomenal success is akin to a piece of fringe theatre that triggers a nerve in the public psyche and suddenly goes mainstream. Adam Robinson has the spirit of John Osborne running through his soul – he is an

iconoclast. When the Brack opened at the turn of the decade, he won tremendous critical acclaim for his cooking. 'A truly talented chef,' noted Jonathan Meades. 'A great discovery,' wrote Fay Maschler. But Robinson had achieved more. He had established the credentials of an idiom which was hitherto alien to the values usually attributable to first-division restaurants. At a stroke, he finally dismantled all the gastronomic preconceptions of the Eighties – a process which Alastair Little had already begun in Soho. This was not calculated. The eccentric romanticism of the Brackenbury's remote location, the peasant accents which characterize its cooking and the laid-back culture of the place reflect the nature of its owners.

" One of the defining spirits of his age . . . who has shaped the gastronomy of the Nineties "

What the Robinsons are doing here is not far removed from their own attitude to life. Rebellion and a social consciousness are part of their make-up. On their extended travels, they have been deeply affected by the simple beauty of the peasant food they ate. Hence, their middle-class backgrounds are liberally tinted by gypsy instincts.

Born in 1959, Adam Robinson grew up in a large house on the banks of the River Ouse at Great Barford near Bedford. He was a dutiful and conscientious boy until he won an army scholarship at the age of fourteen. His father was very keen and it seemed like a good idea at the time. But although he probably had the brain to become Chief of the Defence Staff one day, Adam regretted the decision almost immediately and it took another six years before he dared to tell his parents. In the meantime, private resentment turned to open reaction.

Bedford, his public school, was quietly relieved to see the back of him but he came away with super-grades in fifteen O Levels and four A Levels, including a brace at S Level. With the army's blessing, he went on to read philosophy at the London School of Economics, where he discovered the student bar, punk and pot. He acquired all the usual accessories; earrings, a cropped head, pale skin and a mean, thin figure. By the end of his second year, and now twenty years old, his tutors were complaining about his indolence. So he dropped out and spent three months in Morocco doing what students are expected to do in Morocco – 'I lay on my back and got really stoned'.

On his return, he made his confession at last, shattering his parents'

illusions about their son's future career. The army, not unnaturally, demanded its money back. While his father took care of the school fees, Robinson agreed to pay the £3,000 debt on the wasted years at LSE. This he did with ease by taking a well-paid job as a cocktail barman at Zanzibar, a trendy rendezvous in Covent Garden owned by Tony Mackintosh, and by assuming the ascetic existence of a squatter in Kings Cross.

The debt cleared, he was off again. Robinson has a wanderlust that even now is not sated. The mysticism of writers like Hermann Hesse move him and he sees travel as a parable for the inward journey. This time it was Egypt and a job teaching English in Cairo.

His father's death in the winter of 1980 brought him home again. They had never been close but the moment was the turning point in his life. The dizzy, turbulent carousel finally came to a halt. Robinson found purpose, direction and his métier. Through the Eighties, three key figures laid the foundations for the *chef-patron* in Brackenbury Road today. Alastair Little became his inspiration and culinary soul mate, Guy Mouilleron at Ma Cuisine in Walton Street taught him classical technique, and Tony Mackintosh was to become his mentor, a surrogate father and a partner in his business.

In 1981, Robinson settled into his new squat in Islington – a lifestyle he favoured in those days – and he found a waiter's job at L'Escargot in Soho. But it was the kitchen that fascinated him and it was here that he first encountered Alastair Little, who was happy to let him swap his role as a well-tipped waiter for that of a badly paid *commis*. Like Little, Robinson has an immensely fertile and inquisitive mind – so, for the novice, L'Escargot offered the creative stimulus to fire his imagination. On his days off, he spent all his money eating out in good restaurants and he began to hoover his way through the corpus of the great cookery writers. Jane Grigson's *Charcuterie and French Pork Cookery* was consumed in one sitting: 'Just the most brilliant book,' he insists.

Mouilleron came next and, in Robinson's words, the experience was his 'making', even though he hated the man with a passion. 'Nobody has reduced me to tears like he has. I used to cry every Monday morning before going to work.' Mouilleron's style, it seems, was to humiliate and ridicule his *commis*. Still, it was a method of education that appears to have worked a perverse magic on Robinson, who learned the nuts and bolts of his craft from the vile lip of this woodcutter's son from the south-west of France.

In the spring of 1983, Adam rejoined Alastair Little who had moved to 192, another madly fashionable Mackintosh investment in Notting Hill. He stayed three years, breaking the time with occasional sabbaticals to work for William Black, the fish merchant, the Roux brothers' Boucherie Lamartine and the *frères* Troisgros in Roanne. When Little left to open on Frith Street, Robinson

" His food is real 'Back-to-Basics' stuff and the restaurant wears its low prices like a badge of honour "

took the helm and moved into experimental overdrive by doing things with goat, for example, or steaming calves' liver with soy – his 'awful dish of the century'.

It was at 192 that Adam met and fell in love with Katie, a spirited woman who, so her beloved alleges, 'was expelled from seven schools'. In 1986, they took off for two years to travel through Latin America, a seminal pilgrimage which would underscore the mood and ethos of their work at the Brackenbury. In New England, they bought a pick-up truck, put a bed in the back and drove it down to Tierra del Fuego.

On the beaches and in the fishing villages in Mexico, they feasted on the most wonderful seafood. In Peru, they ate *ceviche* – raw scallops, monkfish and other white fish marinated in hot chillies and limes. On the high Andean plains, historical source of the potato, where the dry heat of the day falls to freezing at night, they discovered *chunos*, naturally freeze-dried tubers in dozens of varieties. The peasants rehydrate them in pots which they carry from village to village – they taste delicious and redolent of chestnuts. In southern Chile, these two English nomads gorged themselves on huge clams, salt pork and potatoes cooked in hot stones by locals who plied them with fiery spirits.

They loved walking and camping in the wilderness. They loved the simplicity of life and the culture of these ancient peoples. And they loved the striking landscapes which awakened a quiet animistic spirituality within them. However, the day inevitably came for them to return home.

The transition was difficult. In South America they had gone native. They had lost all touch with the habits and regulation of everyday London life. But with the help of their former employer and friend, Tony Mackintosh, Adam and Katie readjusted and they were soon caught up in the fever of the restaurant scene in the late Eighties. Alastair Little had become the media's number one heart-throb. The hottest tables in town were to be found at Bibendum and Kensington Place. And all the people at the sharp end of the movement were their chums.

In 1990, Adam and Katie were married. They took three months off to travel to Zambia and Malawi and, by the time they had returned, they were set on finding their own premises. A year later, their daughter Adelaide was born and the Brack opened for business breezily oblivious of recession at home and war in the Gulf.

As a chef, Adam Robinson is the icono-clast who unwittingly made the Brackenbury a

Right: The Brack set-piece of antipasti, which can vary according to the season. The boiled egg, served with spicy salt, is a traditional dish from Central Africa.

Nineties' icon. Cooking of his deceptively hick complexion did not exist in the Eighties and is a style which is almost a knee-jerk reaction to the meanness and prissiness of cutesy *nouvelle cuisine*. His food is real 'Back-to-Basics' stuff and the restaurant wears its low prices like a badge of honour. It is saying, 'Look at me. I'm classless' – but of course it is not. Like the rest, it is still pretty much a middle-class show but, in this example, the cooking is classically-primed peasant-inspired food eaten largely by the bourgeoisie of W6.

In the words of a review in the *Spectator*, there are 'no namby-pamby arrangements on the plate'. Fingers of smoked herring are scattered over a loose mound of beetroot cubes the size of Lego bricks, the whole dish tingling with the zing of horseradish: it looks like an unassuming lunchtime gap-filler. In fact, the food nourishes, tastes big and brightens your afternoon.

Another very satisfying, and satisfyingly English, characteristic of Robinson's method lies in his use of vegetables which are made equal partners, rather than side issues, on a plate. Green beans, with the points left untrimmed, long carrots, celery and whole leeks are integral to a dish of poached capon, ox tongue and salt beef moistened with a wonderfully aromatic parsley sauce. This intelligence and imagination in balancing bold components are a strong suit and they provide a rich seam to Robinson's dynamic repertoire. Broccoli with anchovy fillets and generous shavings of Parmesan is one brilliant example and a grilled chump of lamb with aubergines, tomatoes and courgettes – the vegetables spiked with twigs of thyme – is another. And a soft poached egg, hidden beneath the deep saffron of a thick Andaluçian garlic soup, again demonstrates his cunning sleight-of-hand.

The intriguing question about the Robinsons, and the spotlight that has been cast on this obscure corner of West London is, 'What next?' The Brackenbury is enjoying its moment of fame, but for how long? Adam Robinson is one of the defining spirits of his age, a leading player who has shaped the gastronomy of the Nineties. But for him, and for Katie too, there is another side. 'I love cooking,' he says, 'but there is more to life.' And on his contribution to the body politic he adds, 'In a Marxist way, we are a function of history, not a maker of history.'

One thing seems clear – theirs is an unfinished journey. They are dreamers, romantic adventurers who see themselves leaving London one day to introduce Adelaide to some of the wonder and magic of their past experiences in the wild. Ultimately, they dream of settling in a place far, far away from Brackenbury Road.

'Part of the reason we yearn to be somewhere beautiful and uncrowded comes from our two years in South America. Whenever we get fed up, we talk about going back to Chile and buying a remote farmstead in the lakes and setting up a restaurant there. It's a dream. But we may go and live in the Pyrenees. Or the west coast of Scotland. Or the West Country. Somewhere very remote, quiet and beautiful.'

Broccoli with Warm Anchovy Dressing

——

1 large head of broccoli per person

Anchovy Dressing:

300 g/11 oz tinned anchovies in olive oil

6 garlic cloves

2 teaspoons fresh thyme leaves

2 tablespoons fresh basil leaves

2 tablespoons Dijon mustard

2 tablespoons red wine vinegar

1 litre/1¾ pints good (but not over-fruity) virgin olive oil

1 medium-strong red chilli, finely chopped

To garnish:

freshly ground black pepper

shaved Parmesan cheese

12 marinated anchovy fillets

To make the anchovy dressing, place all the dressing ingredients, except the red chilli, in a liquidizer and whizz. It does not have to emulsify. Add the chilli.

Cut the broccoli into smallish florets and cut crosses in the stalks. Peel the large stalks and slice them thinly. Blanch in salted water and drain well. Divide between 4 heated plates.

Dress with 1 tablespoon of the anchovy dressing per person (or more, according to taste). Add a little ground pepper and some shaved Parmesan and serve, together with some freshly marinated anchovies.

Serves 4

Andaluçian Garlic Soup

——

2 tablespoons olive oil

4 slices stale ciabatta bread

4–6 large garlic cloves

a pinch of saffron powder

about 1.2 litres/2 pints chicken stock

4 fresh free-range eggs

50 ml/2 fl oz white wine vinegar

Oil a roasting tin, add the bread and garlic and roast until the garlic is cooked and the bread is dry. Purée in a food processor with the saffron and enough chicken stock to reach the consistency you prefer, then taste and adjust the seasoning. Do not sieve.

Poach the eggs in about 600 ml/1 pint unsalted water with the vinegar then place in 4 heated soup bowls. Reheat the soup, pour it over the eggs and serve.

Serves 4

Deep-fried Salt Cod Cakes with Aïoli

—

3 kg/6 lb potatoes

1.5 kg/3 lb salt cod, soaked

9 eggs

12 garlic cloves, finely chopped

lots of coarsely chopped flat leaf parsley

freshly ground black pepper

Aïoli:

3 garlic cloves

6 saffron threads

2 egg yolks

1 dessertspoon Dijon mustard

about 600 ml/1 pint olive oil

lemon juice

salt and freshly ground black pepper

To serve:

lemon wedges

deep-fried parsley

Poach the potatoes and salt cod in unsalted water. Remove the cod, flake and debone. Put the potatoes through a *mouli* into a bowl, beat in the eggs, then add the cod, garlic, parsley and pepper. Deep-fry small, egg-sized blobs of the mixture at about 170°C (335°F).

To make the aïoli, purée the garlic, saffron, egg yolks and mustard, then add the oil, a few drops at a time, as in making mayonnaise. Add lemon juice, salt and pepper to taste.

Serve the cod cakes with a wedge of lemon, large sprigs of deep-fried parsley and aïoli.

Serves 12

Smoked Herring and Roast Beetroot Salad

—

4 smoked herring fillets (preferably French Saur herring), or jugged kippers

1.5 kg/3 lb raw beetroot

300 ml/½ pint soured cream

tops of 1 bunch of spring onions, chopped

2.5 cm/1 inch fresh horseradish, grated

salt and freshly ground black pepper

Marinade:

100 ml/3½ fl oz light olive oil

2 shallots, thinly sliced

freshly ground black pepper

Slice the smoked herring fillets into 3 or 4, and place in a glass dish. Mix the marinade ingredients, spread over the fish and set aside to marinate overnight.

Roast the beetroot in a preheated oven at 190°C (375°F) Gas Mark 5 for 2–3 hours, or until done. Peel, chop coarsely and mix with the soured cream, spring onion tops, horseradish, salt and freshly ground black pepper.

To serve, place the beetroot on the plate, with the marinated smoked herring arranged around or on top.

Serves 4

Poached Capon, Salt Beef and Ox Tongue
with Mustard and Parsley Sauce

———

We salt our own beef, but butchers also have good salted beef and salted ox tongue.

1 small salted ox tongue

1.5 kg/3 lb salted brisket

12 onions, chopped

14 large carrots

14 celery sticks

4 leeks

2 faggots of herbs, e.g. bay leaves and sprigs of thyme and parsley, tied with string

24 peppercorns

1 capon or, if unavailable, 1 large chicken

smoked bacon trimmings

6 fat garlic cloves (optional)

125 g/4 oz French or runner beans, blanched, to serve

Mustard and Parsley Sauce:

15 g/½ oz butter

2 shallots, finely chopped

150 ml/¼ pint white wine vinegar

300 ml/½ pint white wine

300 ml/½ pint double cream

400 ml/14 fl oz capon stock (see method)

1 tablespoon Dijon mustard, or to taste

leaves from 1 bunch of fresh flat leaf parsley

Desalinate the ox tongue and salted brisket by soaking in a bowl of cold water overnight, changing the water at least once. Drain and place both meats in a large stockpot with 1 chopped onion, 2 carrots, 2 sticks of celery, 2 leeks, a faggot of herbs and 12 peppercorns, with water to cover. Bring to the boil, reduce the heat and poach slowly for about 2½ hours, until done. The ox tongue is ready when it slips off a carving fork (don't forget to peel it after it's cooked) and the salt beef is ready when it's tender to a carving fork.

Place the capon in a deep pan, cover with water, add the bacon trimmings with 1 chopped onion, 2 chopped carrots, 2 chopped sticks of celery, 2 chopped leeks, a faggot of herbs and 12 peppercorns. Bring to the boil, uncovered, simmer for 5 minutes, then remove from the heat. Cover. When cool, remove the capon from the liquid and remove the legs and breast. Replace the bones in the liquid, simmer for about 45 minutes, then strain the stock into a rinsed pan and discard the solids. Poach the remaining vegetables in the stock until tender.

To make the sauce, heat the butter in a pan, add the shallots and cook until softened but not coloured. Add the vinegar, bring gently to the boil and reduce until dry. Add the white wine and reduce to a quarter, then add the cream and 400ml/14 fl oz of the capon stock. Bring to the boil, taste and adjust the seasoning, then whisk in the mustard to taste (not too strong). Add the parsley, place in a liquidizer or food processor and purée until smooth.

Reheat the meat, vegetables and French or runner beans in capon stock, reheat the sauce without boiling, and serve.

Serves 10

Pan-fried Skate Wings, Lentils and Salsa Verde

—

1 tablespoon duck fat

125 g/4 oz Puy lentils

a mirepoix of 50 g/2 oz each of carrot, onion and celery, all finely diced

a few rinds of smoked bacon

6 bay leaves

4 fat, fresh skate wings about 200 g/7 oz each

flour (half polenta, half plain flour), for dusting

mixture of butter and oil, for frying

50 g/2 oz butter

500 g/1 lb spinach

Salsa Verde:

15 g/½ oz garlic, crushed

12 green peppercorns, crushed

125 g/4 oz shallots, finely chopped

75 g/3 oz capers, coarsely chopped

2 sprigs of tarragon, chopped

500 g/1 lb (2 bunches) fresh flat leaf parsley, chopped

2 dessertspoons Dijon mustard

300 ml/½ pint olive oil

salt

To cook the lentils (they must be Puy), melt the duck fat in a pan, add the mirepoix and cook gently until softened but not coloured. Add the lentils and cook gently for about 5 minutes. Add water to cover, the bacon rinds and bay leaves, bring to the boil and simmer gently for about 30 minutes to 1 hour, depending on the age of the lentils, until tender (neither *al dente* nor mushy).

Mix together all the ingredients for the *salsa verde* and set aside.

Season the skate wings and toss in the flour mixture. Heat the butter and oil in a large pan, add the wings and fry gently on both sides until golden brown and the flour has formed a crisp crust. If they are good and fat, they may need to go into a hot oven for 5 minutes first.

Heat the butter in a large pan, add the spinach and cook until wilted. Reheat the lentils. Place the skate on heated dinner plates, add the lentils and spinach, and dress with the *salsa verde*.

Serves 4

Crostini of Lambs' Brains with Salsa Verde

——

1 set of lambs' brains per person

1 tablespoon white wine vinegar

1 bay leaf

1 sprig of thyme

1 sprig of parsley

6 peppercorns

1 shallot, chopped

1 garlic clove

salt

salsa verde (see previous recipe)

To serve:

5 slices of baguette

1 clove of garlic, halved

Make the *salsa verde*, as in the previous recipe and set aside.

Put the lambs' brains in a bowl under a dripping cold tap for about 6 hours, or until the blood has disappeared.

Place in a pan, cover with water, add the vinegar, bay leaf, thyme, parsley, peppercorns, shallot, garlic and salt. Bring to the boil, remove from the heat, allow to cool in the liquid, then remove and slice.

To serve, toast the slices of baguette, rub with garlic, top with the sliced brains and dress with *salsa verde*.

Serves 1

Buttermilk Pudding with Caramelized Blood Orange Salad

——

400 ml/14 fl oz double cream

1.2 litres/2 pints buttermilk

1 vanilla pod

250 g/8 oz sugar

thinly peeled rind of 1 lemon

7 leaves of gelatine, soaked

Caramelized Blood Orange Salad:

9 blood oranges

200 g/7 oz sugar

Whip half the cream and mix with the buttermilk. Place the vanilla pod, sugar, lemon rind and the remaining cream in a saucepan and bring to the boil. Add the gelatine, allow to cool, then fold into the whipped cream mixture.

To make the blood orange salad, remove the peel from 3 blood oranges using a peeler, cut into it small julienne strips, blanch twice, then cook slowly with 50 g/2 oz of the sugar.

Remove pith and peel from all the oranges, holding them over a bowl to catch the juice. Cut them into thin slices and add the cooked peel. Dissolve the remaining sugar in water and boil until it forms a light caramel. Deglaze with the reserved orange juice, then add the oranges. Place the orange salad on chilled plates with large blobs of buttermilk pudding.

Serves 9

Rowley Leigh

F or the first thirty years of his life Rowley Leigh did not believe in manifestos. At Cambridge he was an anarchic situationist – an outfit so loonily extreme it toppled off the left-hand edge of the political stage. By definition, situationists did not belong to parties. They were in the game of ridiculing and mobbing up the proliferation of leftist factions (there was nothing active on the right) that swept the politicized world of student unrest in the late Sixties. Remember Paris – *les Evénements*? Grosvenor Square?

But that was another time. Another Rowley Leigh. By 1987, he had had a dream and he translated it into a 'very clear manifesto'. With eight years' experience of highbrow cooking under Albert Roux, Leigh wanted to open a brasserie. It had to be big and lively and it had to be democratic: there would be no bookings. Most revolutionary of all, he wanted to bring the pleasures of *haute cuisine* to the widest possible audience, but at prices that were comfortable. In November, Leigh saw the realization of his vision in all its essentials. But, like any draft manifesto, the final version had been honed and the restaurant which opened at the top of Kensington Church Street was the result of a unique piece of alchemy between two restaurateurs, Nick Smallwood and Simon Slater, the chef they persuaded to join their partnership, and designer Julyan Wickham.

In the mid to late Eighties, restaurant development in London was already shifting gear. Alastair Little and Simon Hopkinson were blowing holes in the cult of *nouvelle cuisine*. In Hammersmith, Rose Gray and Ruthie Rogers were spearheading an Italian movement which subsequently gripped the capital. A new and fresh diversity in eating out was beginning to excite metropolitan palates. But, with the arrival of Kensington Place, Smallwood, Slater & Co. began to drive a wedge in the notion of top-notch dining as an exclusive recreation for the well-heeled. More, they finally cracked the aura of hushed worship which too readily accompanied perceptions of serious restaurants. Suddenly, the ideas of good food and good fun were conjoined – and, with it, Kensington Place paved the way for the spread of gastronomic populism in the Nineties and the ascendancy of other pioneering spirits like Terence Conran, Stephen Bull and Antony Worrall Thompson, who applied their own interpretations on the theme of good food at accessible prices set in vibrant spaces. In prophetic voice, Jonathan Meades was the first commentator to feel the ripples of this New Wave. Writing about Kensington Place and its founders in *The Times* in January, 1988, Meades noted: 'What they have created is something that suggests London is coming of age as a city to eat in . . . It will become an institution'.

Like Rowley Leigh, Messrs Smallwood and Slater – two talented and keenly instinctive operators who had made their name with Launceston Place – wanted to open a large brasserie. But at first chef and restaurateurs came at the common proposition from different directions. 'Rowley blew away all our preconceptions. His initial input was to redefine the concept,' says Nick Smallwood. 'Once he had put together a menu, we virtually shouted hallelujah! That, coupled with Julyan Wickham's design, struck us as the obvious way to go.'

Although Leigh insists there are parallels, the higher aspirations of his published menu and Wickham's brilliant set barely coincide with a purer definition of the tag 'brasserie'. Even if something of the spirit of the idiom is present, Kensington Place achieves more in the sense that it is unique – a first – and, as such, deserves to stand in its own right without recourse to generic labelling. Besides the sophistications of the menu, Wickham's design is also light years away from the raffishness and aesthetic distress one tends to associate with great names like Lipp or Coupole in Paris, or even Langan's in London. But it is the casualness and functionalism implicit in the word 'brasserie' which appeal to Leigh, whereas restaurant is a term for which he cares little. 'For me it is a negative word,' he says. 'Restaurant means soft furnishings, a blanketing of sound.' Kensington Place is famous for its gaiety and din – it is in a perpetual state of party – and it is this extraordinary union of form and function, inspired by its people, the space and the food,

❝ It is the casualness and functionalism implicit in the word 'brasserie' which appeal to Leigh ❞

which has made it into such an admired and loved institution. To lapse into a dreadful fit of cliché, in the classless Nineties – anyway in a post-recession era where conspicuous consumption is disparaged – Kensington Place is a fantastic advertisement for the acceptable face of hedonism. Its vast expanse of plate glass along the street and its brightness within have the effect of drawing the life of the city into the room and grafting the room on to the everyday social vigour of the city. Passersby are positively incited to gatecrash the party. This affinity with the street is reasserted inside – the milk and pale blue scheme, colours of cloud and sky, lending an air of breezy abandon. The furnishings, too, send their signal – simple wood tables and clownishly coloured chairs inviting you to laughter and play.

An atmosphere of democracy and good humour also pervades the kitchen in spite of the pressures on a brigade of young cooks who deliver up to four hundred meals a day. Given the standards he has set, Leigh's achievement is remarkable. 'Rowley has a terrific ability to inspire people,' says Smallwood. 'He makes them want to excel at what he does so well.' While Leigh is not especially active within the institutions of the restaurant industry, he is universally liked and respected. And his kindness and commitment to encouraging young people is rare in its generosity. 'If they've got the motivation and curiosity,' he says, 'I will employ anybody who comes to me for a job.'

Rowley Leigh is not a chef to nurse a high profile. For all his easy sociability, he is also a very private man who guards his weekends for his family. But, as the success of Kensington Place has shown, Leigh's quiet influence on the development of eating out in London has been immensely significant. Far more than he would care to admit, he possesses a sparklingly potent intellect. Nick Smallwood describes his vision as incisive, adding that, if Leigh had been less lazy and disruptive as a young man, he could easily have ended up as a don at Cambridge. Who can tell? But a glance at his library at home at least indicates his taste for the cerebral. *Inter alia*, one bookshelf alone packed in Amis, père et fils, Peter Carey, Anthony Burgess, Umberto Eco and Saul Bellow.

Certainly, a brief history of the educating of Rowley Leigh reveals protracted periods of sloth, rebellion and turbulence. Learning was not really the issue. His behaviour was – but, with one exception, Leigh's biting criticisms of the establishments he attended also suggest that most of his tutors were simply incapable of harnessing the mind of such a bright young chap.

Born of an Irish Catholic mother and Jewish father on St George's Day, 1950, Leigh spent much of his childhood in Northern Ireland. The third of four children, his family lived in a grand Victorian house set in twenty acres of land, eight miles from Belfast. Father was an Oxford scholar turned businessman, who won the Military Cross 'for something in Greece'. Indeed, such was Robert Leigh's heroism that the grateful people of Igoumenitsa named a street after him.

In spite of the privileges of home and the advantages of being raised in a literate household, Leigh's difficulties with authority began from the moment he stepped into a classroom. In disgrace, he spent most of one term at his desk facing the wall. In 1959, the family returned to England and Rowley's peripatetic schooling continued in Bedford. 'A very backward prep school – I was the only boy in five years to get the eleven plus.'

At fifteen, Leigh was expelled from Clifton College in Bristol and, as his parents had moved to Kingston-upon-Thames, he entered Tiffin Boys', the local grammar school. 'It was a very bright place,' he says, 'and the headmaster was quite clever at coping with public school drop-outs.' While there was no attempt to reform his anarchic tendencies, for the first time in his life,

> **" Kensington Place is a fantastic advertisement for the acceptable face of hedonism "**

he took a more positive interest in his work: 'I got motivated and I was well taught in English.' But, in the end, Leigh's appalling record earned him a pile of rejection slips from all the universities to which he had applied through UCCA. His response was to sit the Cambridge entrance exam and win an exhibition to Christ's College without really trying.

Throughout his education, there was a blasé but fundamental conviction that nobody could teach him anything. Cambridge, he thought, would be different. 'But I wasn't very impressed!' he chuckles. 'The English faculty was pathetic and I think any serious intellectual history would agree that the school was in a pretty feeble state. It was insular and unrewarding.' Leigh stuck it for two years and came away with an ordinary degree. In that time he immersed himself in a syllabus of his own construction – 'structuralist stuff, anthropology, psychoanalysis, everything except English really' – and he assuaged his anti-Establishment Furies through his political activism. It was at Cambridge that he also met Alastair Little – 'through dope, I think' – and the two have been close friends ever since. Indeed, it was Little who ultimately brokered the partnership between Leigh, Nick Smallwood and Simon Slater.

For a while Leigh remained in Cambridge – attempting a novel, translating French structuralist texts and drawing the dole. In 1972, temporarily suspending his state of malaise, he joined his father's dairy farm in Sussex where he entered a period of bucolic contentment living in a cottage with his girlfriend, growing vegetables in the garden and dipping into the recipes of Elizabeth David in the kitchen.

By 1975, the novelty had worn off and Leigh settled in Fulham where he became 'an afternoon man.' Now twenty-five, he confesses that an element of self-justification was also creeping into his life. He resumed his pose as a novelist and succeeded in writing forty pages – demonstrating, at least, a measure of serious

intent. 'It is only when you start to doubt your own self-esteem that you need to justify yourself or deliver something,' he says. 'I have huge elements of arrogance but I also have huge elements of self-doubt.'

The turning-point in Leigh's progress came two years later and it had nothing to do with his state of mind, or the fulfilment of some intellectual ambition, or any foggy search for direction. The reason Rowley Leigh became a cook was practical and the result of the circumstances in which he found himself. In 1977, he was struck off the dole. He had to find a job.

A small-ad in the *Evening Standard* led Leigh to Joe Allen, the American diner in Covent Garden, where he became a grill chef. 'I loved it!' he declares, describing the drama, pace and

" Albert Roux succeeded where a parade of school masters and university tutors had failed "

excitement of the kitchen. 'I was dropped in way beyond my depth and I swam.' Rowley Leigh spent eighteen months at Joe Allen where he also met Sara, daughter of the author Peter George, whom he married in 1982. At the same time, his culinary curiosity was aroused and he started reading widely. His substantial cookery shelves at home still include both hefty volumes of *Mastering the Art of French Cooking*, which Kensington and Chelsea's Central Library hoped might

be returned by 9th January, 1978.

By the summer of 1979, Rowley Leigh was in a mood to return to school and be very serious about it. He applied to Roux Restaurants, accepted a two-thirds cut in his wage packet and began work as a junior at Le Poulbot in the City. Three weeks after starting, he was fired. The restaurant had been short-staffed that day and Albert Roux himself came in to assist on the busy lunchtime service. This was the great master's first encounter with Leigh and what he saw was an incompetent cook who was not even capable of turning a potato. After the service Roux left without a word except to instruct his head chef to sack the new recruit. Leigh protested and demanded a personal interview with the boss who reluctantly agreed, insisting there could be no reprieve. Albert Roux still remembers that famous meeting. 'Rowley had tears in his eyes,' he said. 'He was right to tell me I was unfair. The boy had great determination and I had to give him a second chance.' Roux immediately transferred him to Le Gavroche and suddenly he found himself installed in London's *Grande Ecole* of cuisine.

Leigh could not believe his good fortune and for the next two years Albert Roux succeeded where a parade of school masters and university tutors had failed.

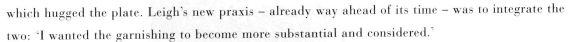

To this day, Rowley Leigh still has a deep respect – even veneration and love – for the man who taught him a craft in all its classical detail. 'He was my teacher,' he says. 'A strong and charismatic person, you hung on his every word. If you got any praise, you felt ten feet tall. But most of the time you were living in fear.'

The regime may have been tough, but reflecting back on his protégé, Roux regards Leigh as one of his most outstanding pupils. After a stint in Wandsworth where he ran the patisserie, butchery and buying arms of the business, Leigh's reward came in 1984 when he ended up as head chef of Le Poulbot – a prodigal's return which thrilled him. Then, in 1986, his triumph was crowned with a double coronation. First, the new *Gault Millau Guide* to London awarded him two toques and a score of sixteen out of twenty – one point higher even than Le Gavroche – and, second, *The Times* made Le Poulbot its Restaurant of the Year.

With a free rein from his mentor, Leigh's years at Le Poulbot laid the foundations for the evolution of his menu at Kensington Place. 'When I wasn't cooking,' he says, 'I'd spend my time in an armchair planning and thinking.' The style that emerged came through a process which Leigh describes as his 'intellectual conundrum'. In the Eighties, the widely accepted habit was to serve vegetables as an incidental appendage to the main event – often on twee, crescent-shaped dishes which hugged the plate. Leigh's new praxis – already way ahead of its time – was to integrate the two: 'I wanted the garnishing to become more substantial and considered.'

This harmonization of main course elements on one plate has now become a standard in London (the provinces are, predictably, another story). But, at Kensington Place, one of the most striking features of all Rowley Leigh's compositions is his subtle ability to judge precisely the interaction of the ingredients he brings together – something he dismisses self-deprecatingly as plain good cooking. The point about Leigh is that he has perfect pitch and that is rare. This acuity of palate is a gift he shares with Paul Rankin – a very different cook – but, of course, another distinguished Roux graduate. While Rankin is pantheist, Leigh's parish is squarely European.

A chicken and goats' cheese mousse – topped with chopped olives, floating on a pool of butter, marbled with a red wine reduction – is so smooth and delicate it quivers like blancmange. This is a Leigh original and fascinating for the incongruity of its invention: matching northern butter and cow's cream with the southern flavours of goats' cheese and olive. It is a classic example of Leigh's finely tuned approach. The dish is at once gentle and seductive, and the savoury edge of the cheese lends the mousse a clear and assertive character. It also defines Leigh's Englishness within the French tradition. 'We paint with a far broader brush,' he says. 'I use more garlic than Albert would. We like our flavours to stand out more.'

This emphasis on flavour approaches combustion in KP's *tarte tatin* which, for me, is quite the best I have ever eaten. The purity and sheer intensity of Cox's apple, the balance of acidity and sweetness, leave a clean, fresh after-taste which purrs comfortingly around the gills between pudding and coffee. This effect is achieved by stacking the fruit tightly to allow the caramel to come from the sugar in the apple as well as the syrup in the pan.

While Leigh's menu bristles with the product of his own thinking – scallops with a split pea purée and mint vinaigrette are another sublime original – he is equally clever at adopting the ideas of others and making them his own. The provenance of KP's famous griddled *foie gras* with sweet-corn pancake was inspired by Michel Guérard and the baked tamarillos are 'a straight lift' from Comme Chez Soi in Brussels.

With main courses, Leigh's keen understanding of the ingredients he assembles is manifest. There are no duff notes; dishes are carefully judged, perfectly balanced, beautifully crafted, full of contrast and colour. Well-hung fallow deer, modulated by a seasoning of pineapple, sultanas, pine nuts and capers, makes an ideal match for the ferrous quality of its spinach garnish. Leigh's turbot in beer (an idea first mooted by Jonathan Meades) is a triumph of daring. A deep white bowl is filled with potatoes and cabbage and onion and roughly hewn chunks of carrot. There is an

" Leigh has perfect pitch . . . a gift he shares with Paul Rankin. But while Rankin is pantheist, Leigh's parish is squarely European "

exquisite sweetness to the beer gravy – a light and distinctive liquid to lubricate the meatiness of the fish without overwhelming it. The effect is dazzling – evidence again of the sleight-of-hand of this craftsman.

The intellectual conundrum which so absorbed Rowley Leigh, the craftsman, is also the inherent enigma in the man himself. Where Academe failed to engage the gifted brain of a young man, a kitchen finally provided the fulfilment he sought. The juxtaposition of these two spheres of life makes for a bizarre paradox, but so what? The beneficiary has been the catering industry and Leigh's legacy to it will endure.

At the end of the nineteenth century, César Ritz and Auguste Escoffier revolutionized eating out in London with their innovations at the Savoy. Ritz hired Johann Strauss to 'cover the silence which hangs like a pall over an English dining table'. White linen was stripped from the tables which were relaid with pink. 'My best dishes,' said Escoffier, 'were created for ladies.'

A hundred years on – and in the spirit of their age – Nick Smallwood, Simon Slater and Rowley Leigh have given London another shot in the arm.

Griddled Foie Gras

with Sweetcorn Pancake

———

65 g/2½ oz plain flour

½ teaspoon baking powder

2 eggs

milk (see method)

250 g/8 oz tinned sweetcorn, drained

a little groundnut oil

1 foie gras

salt and freshly ground black pepper

To make the pancake batter, mix the flour, baking powder and eggs in a bowl and add milk, a little at a time, to give a thick pouring consistency. Allow to stand for 1 hour, then add the sweetcorn and season well.

Heat a small blini or pancake pan until very hot and add a film of oil. To make the pancakes, drop spoonfuls of mixture on to the pan and spread very thinly to about 5 mm/¼ inch thick. Cook 1–2 minutes on each side.

Cut the *foie gras* into long escalopes, about 5 mm/¼ inch thick, or 75–125 g/3–4 oz each. Season well and sear in a very hot, dry frying pan for about 20 seconds on each side.

Serve the *foie gras* escalopes on the pancakes, absolutely plain.

Serves 6-8

Noisettes of Venison

with Sweet and Sour Sauce

———

75 g/3 oz sugar

200 ml/7 fl oz white wine vinegar

75 ml/3 fl oz orange juice

sauce poivrade, made with venison trimmings

1 teaspoon redcurrant jelly

1 teaspoon lemon juice

15 g/½ oz butter

salt

12 noisettes of venison

To garnish:

2 tablespoons pine nuts

50 g/2 oz sultanas

125 ml/4 fl oz white wine, boiled for 5 minutes

50 g/2 oz fresh pineapple, cut into julienne

150 ml/¼ pint sugar syrup

50 g/2 oz capers

Place the sugar in a pan and cook gently to a dark caramel. Add the vinegar and reduce until syrupy. Add the orange juice and reduce again. Add the sauce poivrade and reduce until dark and glistening. Stir in the redcurrant jelly, lemon juice, salt and butter.

To make the garnish, toast the pine nuts; soak the sultanas in wine for 20 minutes. Cook the pineapple in the syrup until translucent. Drain.

Sauté the noisettes in a non-stick pan quickly but fiercely, until rare. Rest briefly. Add the garnishes to the sauce. Coat the noisettes, adding a few pieces of candied pineapple.

Serves 6

Turbot in Beer

---

25 g/1 oz butter

2 shallots, chopped

1 celery stick, chopped

1 carrot, chopped

1 garlic clove, crushed

2 teaspoons sugar

1 teaspoon tomato purée

75 ml/3 fl oz white wine vinegar

1 whole turbot, filleted,

with the bones reserved for the stock.

2 bottles of Belgian wheat beer

3 juniper berries

cracked peppercorns

1 sprig of thyme

1 bay leaf

Heat the butter in a small pan. Add the shallots, celery, carrot and garlic. Cook gently until softened and lightly browned. Add the sugar and continue cooking over a low heat, shaking the pan from time to time, until the vegetables are caramelized.

Add the tomato purée and vinegar and reduce until dry. Add the turbot bones and 1 bottle of Belgian wheat beer. Add the juniper berries, cracked peppercorns, thyme and bay leaf. Cook for about 45 minutes on a gentle heat. Strain, taste and adjust the seasoning and reserve.

Pour the remaining wheat beer into a turbot pan or large roasting pan and bring to the boil. Add the turbot fillets and poach gently for about 10 minutes, until tender.

Serve with baby potatoes, carrots and lightly steamed Savoy cabbage with plenty of the dark, bitter-sweet sauce poured around.

Serves 4

Griddled Scallops with Pea Purée and Mint

—

3-5 scallops per person,

cut in half if large

Pea Purée:

50 g/2 oz butter

1 onion, sliced

1 small lettuce, shredded

2 mint leaves

250g/8 oz peas, fresh or frozen

½ teaspoon sugar

125–150 ml/4–5 fl oz dry white wine

150 ml/¼ pint double cream

1 teaspoon lemon juice

salt and freshly ground black pepper

Mint Vinaigrette:

leaves from 3 sprigs of mint, finely chopped

1 teaspoon sugar

about 50 ml/2 fl oz boiling white wine vinegar

150–200 ml/5–7 fl oz light, clean-tasting oil,

e.g. sunflower or groundnut

salt and freshly ground black pepper

To make the pea purée, heat half the butter in a casserole, add the sliced onion and cook until softened but not coloured. Add the lettuce, mint, peas, sugar, salt, pepper and white wine. Cook very gently for 30 minutes, or until the peas are tender. Boil off any excess liquid, and then add the cream and reduce again. Purée the mixture with the remaining butter and the lemon juice.

To make the mint vinaigrette, place the chopped mint in a bowl, add the sugar and a generous pinch of salt, then cover with the boiling vinegar. Infuse for a few minutes, then add salt and pepper to taste and whisk in the oil.

To finish, sear the scallops and place around the outside of the plates. Add a good scoop of the pea purée in the middle and drizzle 2 teaspoons of vinaigrette around the scallops.

Serves 10

Baked Tamarillos

with Vanilla Ice Cream

——

6 tamarillos (1½ per person)

icing sugar, for dusting

Raspberry Sauce:

1 punnet of raspberries

125 g/4 oz icing sugar

1 teaspoon lemon juice

Vanilla Ice Cream:

500 ml/17 fl oz milk

1 vanilla pod

8 egg yolks

125 g/4 oz caster sugar

250 ml/8 fl oz double cream

To make the ice cream, pour the milk into a saucepan, split the vanilla pod and scrape the seeds into the milk, add the pod and bring to the boil. Remove from the heat and set aside to infuse for 20–30 minutes.

Whisk the egg yolks and the sugar in a large bowl. Bring the milk back to the boil, remove the vanilla pod, and pour into the egg yolk mixture, whisking continuously. Return to the heat and, stirring constantly with a wooden spoon, cook until the custard thickens enough to coat the back of a spoon. Set aside to cool.

Whip the double cream to a light ribbon, and fold into the cooled custard mixture. Churn in a sorbetière, then freeze.

To make the raspberry sauce, macerate the raspberries and sugar for about 15 minutes, then press through a sieve.

Cut the tamarillos in half lengthways and sprinkle with plenty of icing sugar. Place under a very hot grill, or in an equally hot oven, until the sugar starts to caramelize.

To serve, place pools of raspberry sauce in 4 wide soup plates, add the hot tamarillos and top with a large quenelle of vanilla ice cream.

Serves 4

Rick Stein

———

'When low tides drain the estuary gold . . .' The ribbed and herring-boned prints in the dunes near Rock drag, as links in a chain, round Brea Hill and Betjeman's pilgrims follow those 'Paths, unfamiliar to golfers' brogues', to St Enodoc. The church's wonky, rough-hewn spire, like some upturned ice cream cone, prods the sky between the eleventh and fourteenth tees and, in the churchyard, when I was there in the spring of 1994, a few wilting bluebells filled a jam jar by the side of the laureate's ornate slate headstone.

In high summer, the pursuits of visitors to this magical stretch of north Cornwall are altogether more prosaic. But they would still furnish Betjeman with plenty of raw material for his gentle, satirical wit. For the strip that sweeps from Constantine round Trevose Head to Padstow Bay and the River Camel is a curious socio-geographical blip which neatly sends up the cliché of the English seaside as the customary destination for the proletarian holiday. In July, when the schools break, this small pocket of the Cornish coast suddenly becomes a gilded ghetto, a maritime playground for the middle classes of London and the Home Counties who pour across the Tamar in their Mercedes Estates and Range Rovers, re-enacting their childhood progress west with a new generation of 'young' in the back seats. Their capital town is Rock, SW3-on-Sea, where the air is thick with the indistinguishable noises of seagulls wailing and plummy mums screeching at wayward Henriettas and Camillas. By day, they parade in wet suits, deck shoes, Fair Isles and frilled-necks (shellsuits and trainers holiday in Newquay, a safe distance downwind). And by night, they will be found fresh-faced, spruce and in full cry at the Seafood Restaurant in Padstow. They know a good thing when they see it. The Seafood is the best fish restaurant in Britain.

More, they are at home here. The place feels good. It's bright and modern and full of fun. The walls sharp white, decked with colourful prints and huge polished mirrors which flatter and reflect an abundance of green foliage. The hardwood floors amplify the chatter, bounce the high spirits off the ceiling and around the room. The atmosphere, the vitality of the place, has all the vigour and animation of a fashionable metropolitan restaurant. Not only is the food terrifically good, but Rick and Jill Stein also know how to entertain, excite and amuse. 'I come from the same background as our customers,' says Stein. 'So I would not set up in Newquay.' And his rugged, dappled features break into a wicked smile.

Sheepishly, Stein confesses to being a bit of a snob, a trait he mitigates by his own gravelled dialect of estuary English. His accent, of course, is more Camel than Thames. But it is, perhaps, the audible product of a life story of one Sixties' rebel who reacted to his charmed and highly cultivated upbringing with some zeal and, at moments, not a little anguish. However, at the time, the arrival of new icons – John Osborne, the Stones, grass – challenged the old conventions of upper middle class society and, in the spirit of the age, young Richard 'two-fingered the whole bizz'. The result was a wildly eccentric route to the quayside in Padstow and the creation of a celebrated restaurant which cleverly mixes bourgeois aspiration with a dollop of rock 'n' roll.

Born in 1947, Rick Stein spent a blissful childhood on the family farm in Oxfordshire. But the social atmosphere of the home – a large Cotswold stone house surrounded by hills – was not remotely akin to its idyllically pastoral environment. Indeed, it was something of an

❝ Wildly eccentric . . . a restaurant which cleverly mixes bourgeois aspiration with a dollop of rock 'n' roll ❞

intellectual hothouse. His father, the son of wealthy German immigrants, was head of the Distillers Company. Mother was an English graduate from Newnham College, Cambridge. And of the five children, John, Rick's elder brother by six years, won a scholarship to Oxford, emerged with a first in medicine and is now a

don at Magdalen College. At weekends, the family would entertain their circle of friends from the world of the arts and Academe, including the artist, Michael Ayrton, and his wife Elizabeth, the novelist and cookery writer.

Inevitably, high academic honours were expected of the Steins' younger son, but he did not deliver and culturally he much preferred the sounds of Elvis Presley and Eddie Cochran. Deep down, he longed to hang out with the leather jackets in Chipping Norton, but he couldn't because he didn't speak like them. The accent had yet to be honed. Still, he more than made up for it at Uppingham where he played gigs in school as the bass guitar for his rock band, Lightning Strikes. Rock 'n' Roll and sweaty adolescent fumblings with a Liverpudlian housemaid were so much more fun than Sunday luncheon in Oxfordshire.

It is hardly surprising, then, that the happiest and most vivid memories of his boyhood years were of the family's summer holidays in Cornwall. In the mid-Thirties, his father and uncle had built a magnificent Odeon-style villa on Trevose Head. All white, bow-fronted, large windows, the house looked out across Mother Ivey's Bay to Stepper Point. Each year, they would travel down in their Jaguar, the rich odour of the leather upholstery inducing bouts of car sickness in the children. But once there, those golden balmy days were spent fishing for mackerel and bass and eating crabs and lobsters, freshly boiled, with mayonnaise. 'To me,' says Stein, 'that's what English food is. Good materials, simply turned out.' These times in the Fifties and early Sixties were the seminal foundation for his restaurant today.

While food and cooking inspired no practical interest in his youth, there was one other experience which was to touch his latent enthusiasm. In his mid-teens, he and his younger sister were packed off to a grand château near Cambrai in northern France for a little cultural and linguistic burnishing – although the benefits enjoyed by the two

> **" This chef is a showman who knows that his diners like a bit of theatre on the plate "**

children probably did not coincide with the educational return expected by their parents. For a start, the châtelaine's son was a prig who fancied himself as a show jumper and 'strutted around in a red coat and jodhpurs, and really made us very cross.' Instead of dutifully cheering him on at his wretched shows, the two young ravers escaped to the car park and the family's huge old Plymouth where they tuned in to Elvis on the American Forces Broadcasting Network.

However, it was the sumptuousness of the château's table which made a big mark on the impressionable palate of Rick Stein. The food, served by butlers from grand sideboards, was unlike anything he had ever tasted; thick cuts of beef cooked beautifully pink, served with a garlic gravy and frites, wonderful salads, creamy soups, rabbit stews, bowls of enormous cherries and, to drink, pitchers of dry fizzy cider from the orchards on the 3,000-acre estate. Every meal was a celebration performed with a *joie* and a style he had never experienced. But he was to wait another fifteen years before he would begin to spin his own brand of gastronomic brio on his guests in Padstow.

In 1965, tragedy struck the family when Stein's father, who suffered from manic-depression, took his own life. The trauma was complicated for the young eighteen-year-old who had now left school, had lost direction and was passing through a crisis of identity. He had scraped a few A levels, flunked a job with BP and, more out of desperation than desire, he had embarked on a management traineeship with British Transport Hotels. After six months in the Orwellian kitchens at the Great Western Hotel in Paddington, he quit. The psychological freight of family expectation weighed on him. 'I was depressed. I thought I was a failure academically. I had not got into university. I couldn't get a decent job. And I didn't like catering. So I decided to go away.'

The next two years of his life had the terse, unsentimental texture of a Hemingway novel. In Australia, he lived in the desert near Alice Springs, working for a while on a railway maintenance gang and learning to survive with the hoodlum exiles of the Sydney underworld. From New Zealand, he worked his passage to New York as a greaser on a German cargo vessel. In the United States he was propositioned by weird men in Greyhound bus depots. And in Mexico he briefly fell in love with a French-Canadian girl before returning home via Montreal.

The experience was Stein's catharsis. There had been good times. But there were also moments of acute loneliness, hunger, fear and near-penury. Back in England, emboldened, self-confident and free of the old familial pressures, he set his sights on Oxford entrance and won his place at New College to read English. After three years of merry-making, mischief, girls and grass, he came away with his degree. Just. His finals and, perhaps, the delayed shock of his father's death brought him close to a nervous breakdown.

At Oxford he edited the *Cherwell* by day and ran a mobile disco at night. Both suggested future careers. But, characteristically, he was quick to reject journalism and advertising in favour of his decks and speakers. Besides, the disco was making good money. And there was the abiding allure of Cornwall. The prodigal son ached for his perpetual summer home.

By 1974, with the support of a partner and a £10,000 bequest from his great-uncle Otto, the mobile disco had found a fixed address with a late licence by the harbour in Padstow. It was a disaster. At closing time, the town's fishing fraternity tipped out of the pubs and into the new nightspot. Mayhem ensued and Stein could not control it. If he wasn't being carried off to casualty

" The system may appear casual, but it makes damn good sense – the fish are still wriggling on delivery – and the benefits end up on the tables two hours later "

himself, he would be hosing the blood of others off the terrace. Eventually, the police called it a night and removed all the club's licences. Except one. The restaurant licence to the steak bar at the top of the building.

There can be few chefs whose conversion to the *métier* was so sublime and dramatic. The irony of this tale is that the fishermen who caused his downfall and brought him close to bankruptcy became his angels of fortune. Many of those young Seventies ruffians supply him today. Revenge may be sweet, but redemption is sweeter.

After his marriage to Jill in 1975, the fight for survival quickly evolved into a fresh start with a shared vision of the future. They ate out a lot and a favourite seafood bistro in Falmouth provided the blueprint for the new restaurant which was relocated on the ground floor two years later. Jill already had catering experience, so she managed the front while Rick taught himself to cook and submitted to tuition at the local tech. 'I was cooking to save my life,' he recalls. But the struggle to revive the business took another seven slow years. The break came in 1984 when the Seafood Restaurant won a competition in the *Sunday Times*. The national publicity made their reputation 'almost overnight' and they have been filling their tables ever since.

For most of his life, Rick Stein had been searching, testing, reaching out. Never quite sure where he was going, he was always trying to reconcile his back-

ground with what he might want to be. There had never been a grand plan. This uncertainty and the unpredictability of his own passage have made him sensitive and sympathetic towards the upbringing of the three young sons to whom he and Jill are devoted. The same thoughtful attitude pervades his restaurant kitchen which – even in the heat of a busy service – is calm, smooth and uncommonly devoid of tension. It is democratic too, with Stein rostered to move around the different sections along with all the other chefs in his team.

This unconventional style – the product of an independent mind unwarped by conventional training – turns positively eccentric in his dealings with suppliers. He operates a kind of negative ordering system by actively encouraging the local fishermen to drop off the pick of the day's catch on their return each evening. If there is anything he doesn't want, an injunction is posted on the fridge by the back door: 'No lobsters! No velvets!' for example. The system may appear casual, even unbusinesslike, but it makes damned good sense. The fish are still wriggling on delivery and the benefits end up on the tables two hours later.

Drew Smith, as the editor of *Taste* magazine, once wrote that Stein's was a 'kitchen in love with its subject.' The evidence is palpable. He came late to cooking, and then by an accident of circumstance, so the fervour he feels for his subject is like that of a convert to a new religion. But his way of winning you over is to charm rather than to preach. Nevertheless, he admits to his proselytizing tendencies and his menus read like a canticle to seafood and its consumption. On Dover sole, the menu states: 'The sole is seasoned with sea salt and cooked un-skinned on a grill, the skin being very pleasant to eat when crisply cooked in this way.' In fact, 'pleasant' is hardly the right word. The ozone freshness of the fish is brilliantly magnified by the crispness of the skin and the crunch of its seasoning.

While simplicity, freshness and big piscine flavours are the principles which underscore Stein's gastronomic propaganda, the chef is also a showman who knows that his diners like a bit of theatre on their plates. So, here and there, oriental spicing, herbs and other flavourings are applied with judicious restraint. A generous pile of blue-black mussels woven with ribbons of leek sit in a saffron tinged, curry-spiced soup the texture of liquid silk. The garlic broth over a plate of hot shellfish is speckled with the green of parsley and the red of mild chillies. A slab of grilled hake is dressed with a clever fumet, the sweetness of the *mirepoix* mitigated by the peat of Laphroaig and the earth of morels. It is a class act.

Pitched across the last forty years of big names, Rick Stein is cast in the mould of swashbuckling cooks like George Perry-Smith and Kenneth Bell in the early generation and Alastair Little and Shaun Hill in this. Stein's coming took time but since his big break in 1984, he has been unstoppable; a prize-winning book on seafood cookery, the addition of new premises in Padstow, a deli and a bistro, and the promise of television and more writing.

These are, however, by-products of his fame. In the end, his heart is with his Cornish kitchen: 'The smell of mullet cooking is like the smell of hot sand on Constantine Bay.' It could be Betjeman.

'Here Petroc landed, here I stand today.'

Mouclade with Leeks

———

25 g/1 oz butter

80 mussels, washed, scraped, debearded and washed again

125 g/4 oz leeks, white and pale green parts only, thinly sliced

50 g/2 oz onions, chopped

1 garlic clove, finely chopped

1 tablespoon Cognac

a good pinch of saffron strands

50 ml/2 fl oz dry white wine

150 ml/¼ pint crème fraîche

1 teaspoon beurre manié, made with

1 teaspoon of butter kneaded with ½ teaspoon flour

salt, to taste

Curry Spice:

1 teaspoon turmeric

¾ teaspoon coriander seeds

¾ teaspoon cumin seeds

¼ teaspoon fenugreek seeds

½ teaspoon paprika

¼ teaspoon cayenne

½ teaspoon black peppercorns

To make the curry spice, heat a small pan and roast the spices until they start to jump. Grind in a spice grinder, and use ½ teaspoon here and reserve the remainder for other uses.

Melt the butter in a pan big enough to take all the mussels, add the leeks, onions, garlic, Cognac, saffron and curry spice and cook, covered for 5 minutes, or until the onions are softened but not coloured. Add the white wine and cook gently, covered, for a further 5 minutes. The dish may be completed to this stage, and the mussels added just before serving.

When ready to serve, put the mussels, crème fraîche and *beurre manié* in the pan, return to a high heat, place the lid back on the pan and steam the mussels open, turning them occasionally with a big spoon. Taste and adjust the saltiness of the sauce – it should be a little on the salty side.

To serve, place the mussels in 4 heated dishes, spoon all the sauce over, then serve.

Serves 4

Roast Cod with Aïoli,

with a Spicy Sauce, Butter Beans and Fennel

——

50 g/2 oz dried butter beans,

soaked overnight in cold water to cover

2 hard-boiled eggs, shelled and halved

1 bulb of Florence fennel, finely sliced

4 cod fillets,

about 175–200 g/6–7 oz each,

with skin left on

melted butter, for brushing

sea salt and freshly ground black pepper

Spicy Sauce:

50 g/2 oz butter

250 g/8 oz mirepoix of finely chopped

carrot, leek, celery and onion

1 tablespoon Cognac

5 g/¼ oz dried mushrooms

1 tablespoon balsamic vinegar

¼ fresh red chilli

2 tablespoons olive oil

1 teaspoon fish sauce

600 ml/1 pint fish stock

⅓ teaspoon salt

4 basil leaves, finely sliced

Aïoli:

8 garlic cloves

2 egg yolks

1 tablespoon lemon juice

salt

350 ml/12 fl oz olive oil

To make the sauce, melt half the butter in a small pan, add the *mirepoix* and cook until softened but not coloured. Add the Cognac, bring to the boil, then add the remaining sauce ingredients except the basil. Simmer for about 30 minutes, then pass through a fine sieve. Return to the rinsed pan, bring to the boil and simmer until reduced to about 150 ml/¼ pint.

To make the aïoli, place the garlic cloves, egg yolks and lemon juice in a liquidizer or food processor and blend for about 10 seconds. Slowly add the oil to form a thick mayonnaise.

If using a mortar and pestle, first crush the garlic to a purée, then beat in the salt, egg yolks and lemon juice. Beat in the oil, adding it in a slow, steady drizzle.

Place the butter beans in a pan with salted water to cover, then simmer gently until very soft. Keep warm in the cooking liquid. Cook the fennel in salted water, drain and keep warm.

Brush the cod fillets with melted butter, then season with salt and pepper and place in a shallow roasting tin brushed with more butter. Place in a preheated oven and roast at 230°C (450°F) Gas Mark 8 until just cooked through (8–15 minutes, depending on the thickness of the fillets).

To serve, place the cod on 4 warmed dinner plates. Add a spoonful each of butter beans, fennel and aïoli, followed by the halved boiled eggs. Bring the sauce to the boil and whisk in the remaining butter, then add the basil leaves. Pour the sauce over the butter beans, boiled egg and fennel.

Serves 4

Meurette of Plaice
and Lemon Sole with Beaujolais

---

1 kg/2 lb fish fillets, 2 varieties,

e.g. plaice and lemon sole

Beaujolais Sauce:

2 slices white bread

2 tablespoons groundnut oil

65 g/2½ oz butter

250 g/8 oz mirepoix of finely chopped carrot,

celery, leek and onion

1 tablespoon brandy

1.2 litres/2 pints chicken stock

½ bottle good red wine, e.g. Beaujolais

1 bay leaf

1 sprig of thyme

24 shallots

¼ teaspoon sugar

1 rasher rindless smoked bacon, sliced

250 g/8 oz button mushrooms, quartered

beurre manié, made with 25 g/1 oz butter

mixed with 15 g/½ oz flour

salt and freshly ground black pepper

Persillade:

1 small bunch parsley

1 small garlic clove

Using a round biscuit cutter, cut discs of bread, 2.5 cm/1 inch in diameter. Heat the groundnut oil and 15 g/½ oz of the butter in a small pan and fry the bread croûtons until crisp and golden.

Melt 30 g/1 oz of the butter in a saucepan, add the *mirepoix* and cook gently until the vegetables are just beginning to catch. Add the brandy, boil off the alcohol, then add three-quarters of the chicken stock, all the red wine, the bay leaf and thyme. Bring to the boil and simmer for about 30 minutes.

Meanwhile, heat a further 15 g/½ oz of the butter with the sugar in a shallow pan, add the shallots and cook until brown. Add the remaining chicken stock, bring to the boil and simmer gently until the shallots are tender, then increase the heat and reduce the cooking juices to a shiny brown glaze.

Heat the remaining butter in a small pan, add the bacon and fry gently for about 1 minute.

Add the button mushrooms, fry gently, season with salt and black pepper, set aside and keep warm.

To make the *persillade*, chop the garlic and parsley together until very fine.

Strain the red wine stock into a shallow pan and boil rapidly until reduced by half. Add the fish and poach very gently until just cooked – about 5 minutes.

Remove the fillets from the pan and divide the two varieties of fish between 4 heated dinner plates. Break up the *beurre manié*, add to the pan and stir well until dissolved. Add the shallots and mushrooms, then the *persillade*. Taste and adjust the seasoning.

To serve, spoon the sauce over the fish, add the croûtons and serve immediately. Suitable accompaniments are boiled new potatoes and French beans.

Serves 4

Hot Shellfish with

Olive Oil, Garlic and Lemon Juice

——

A selection of shellfish and crustacea, e.g.

8 whelks

40 winkles

24 mussels

12 small clams

12 oysters

4 crab claws or 1 small lobster

8 langoustines or Mediterranean prawns

75 ml/3 fl oz extra-virgin olive oil

4 garlic cloves, finely chopped

1 tablespoon chopped fresh flat leaf parsley

½ fresh red chilli, deseeded and finely chopped

1 tablespoon lemon juice

Place the whelks in a pan of well-salted water, bring to the boil and simmer for 4 minutes. Remove the whelks and set aside. Bring the winkles to the boil and drain at once.

Place the mussels in a large saucepan and cover with a lid. Place the pan on a fierce heat, and as soon as the mussels open, remove from the heat, strain off the juice and reserve. Repeat with the clams and oysters. (Oysters take longer and will not open fully – lever them open with a short, thick-bladed knife or oyster knife.) Save all the liquor from the oysters and clams.

Bring a large pan of water to the boil, add the crab claws and the langoustines, boil for 4 minutes, then remove. If using lobster, boil for 15 minutes, then remove. Crack the claws, cut the body in half lengthways, then cut each half in half again to produce 2 portions consisting of the head and a quarter of the tail, with 2 further portions consisting of the rest of the tail. For equal portions of lobster meat, serve the head sections and claws to 2 people and the tails to the other two. If serving as a first course, serve half these quantities per person.

When cooked, arrange the seafood on 4 plates. Pour the juice from cooking the shellfish into a small pan and add the olive oil, garlic, parsley, chilli and lemon juice. Bring to the boil and pour over the seafood on the plates. Serve with plenty of French bread and Italian white wine.

If serving as a first course, omit either the langoustines or the crab claws – or the lobster.

Serves 4 as a main course

Poached Quenelles
of Gurnard with Lobster Sauce

——

25 g/1 oz butter

150 ml/¼ pint milk

50 g/2 oz fresh white breadcrumbs

375 g/12 oz gurnard fillets, skinned and boned

1 egg, size 2

1 tablespoon lemon juice

⅛ teaspoon grated nutmeg

½ teaspoon salt and ground white pepper

125 ml/4 fl oz double cream

Lobster Sauce:

1 small lobster, preferably a hen with coral

75 g/3 oz butter

2 teaspoons flour

1 small onion, chopped

1 small carrot, chopped

1 tablespoon brandy

1.2 litres/2 pints fish stock

50 ml/2 fl oz dry white wine

1 teaspoon tomato purée

1 egg yolk

25 ml/1 fl oz double cream

To make the quenelles, melt the butter, add the milk and breadcrumbs to form a *panade*. Chill the *panade* and the remaining ingredients. Purée all the ingredients except the cream in a food processor, then pour in the cream over a period of 10 seconds.

Halve the lobster, remove the claws and crack open. Separate the head section from the tail. Remove the dark green coral (if any) and the light green tomally and mix with 50 g/2 oz of the butter. Make a *beurre manié* with the flour and 2 teaspoons of softened butter.

Heat the remaining butter in a pan, add the onion and carrot and cook until softened and lightly coloured. Add the lobster and any juices, turning the shells in the pan until they turn red, then pour on the brandy and boil. Add the stock, wine and tomato purée, bring to the boil and simmer for 10 minutes. Remove the claws and tail sections, cool rapidly under cold water, extract the meat, return the shells to the stock and simmer for about 15 minutes more. Slice the lobster meat and keep warm.

Strain the stock into a shallow pan and reduce to about 300 ml/½ pint. Stir in the *beurre manié* and let it thicken on the heat. Remove from the heat and keep warm.

Bring a shallow pan of lightly salted water to the boil, reduce to a simmer and place under a hot grill. Mould the quenelle mixture into lozenge shapes using serving spoons, dipping them in hot water periodically to achieve nice smooth shapes. As you form the quenelles, drop them into the lightly simmering water and poach for about 5 minutes.

Remove with a slotted spoon and place on a clean tea towel to dry. Place the quenelles in 4 warm gratin dishes with the lobster around.

Whisk the yolk and cream, add to the warm sauce, together with the lobster coral butter. Warm over a low heat but don't allow to boil. Pour over the quenelles, place the dishes under a grill to brown. Serve immediately.

Serves 4

Poached Pears

with Crème Brûlée Ice Cream

———

4 pears

150 g/5 oz caster sugar

275 ml/9 fl oz port

1 cinnamon stick

1 vanilla pod

150 ml/¼ pint water

Crème Brûlée Ice-cream:

50 g/2 oz caster sugar

5 egg yolks

600 ml/1 pint double cream

½ teaspoon vanilla essence

Peel the pears. Place all the other ingredients in a saucepan which will fit the pears tightly, bring to the boil, then simmer for 10 minutes. Add the peeled pears and, if necessary, top up with a little water, just to cover them.

When the pears are soft, carefully remove them from the saucepan, using a slotted spoon. Continue simmering the cooking liquid until it is reduced to a syrup. Remove the cinnamon stick and the vanilla pod.

To make the ice cream, whisk the caster sugar and egg yolks together in a bowl. Place the cream in a saucepan, add the vanilla essence, bring to the boil and remove from the heat. Have a second pan of boiling water ready into which the bowl will fit.

Pour the hot cream on to the mixture of egg yolk and caster sugar, whisking all the time. Place the bowl over the boiling water and stir the custard till it begins to thicken. (The level of heat required to thicken a custard is precisely the temperature which feels uncomfortably hot when tested with your little finger.)

Pour the custard into a shallow tray and leave to cool and set. Sprinkle the top of the set custard generously with caster sugar and place under a preheated grill until the sugar caramelizes.

Cool the crème brûlée, break up the top into small chunks and freeze in a sorbetière.

To serve, place the pears on 4 small plates or bowls, spoon over the syrup and add 2 scoops of crème brûlée ice cream.

Serves 4

Phil Vickery

O ur first meeting was not propitious and would, most likely, have been our last had we not found ourselves in a state of mutual despair. I found him pushy, defensive and rather too eager to demand a swift decision. He left the interview convinced that I had just graduated from a school for neo-Nazi *Gauleiters*. My problem was that I had a kitchen in turmoil and a reputation to defend. Gary Rhodes had left me rather too abruptly for comfort, snatched by a predator who carried him off to London and a new career which was to set him on his road to stardom. Like my kitchen, Phil Vickery's life had also hit a patch of turbulence. His employer's handsome Regency pile near Taunton had just welcomed the receiver, and now he was left wondering how he was going to service the hefty mortgage on his pretty Victorian terrace in Wellington.

So it was raw need and the lucky coincidence of these unhappy circumstances which eventually conspired to throw us together. Five years on, we still rib one another about that early acquaintance. Today he sits on the Castle's Board, the first cook to be appointed a director of the company and the best head chef in our forty-five-year history as a family firm.

Vickery's road to the top, by contemporary standards anyway, was not fast-track. He is now thirty-four. Certainly, he has always been ambitious and competitive, but when you engage him in

conversation, you are not immediately conscious of the driven man. Rather, it is the kindness and warmth in his eyes which engage the attention. Ambition is modulated by restraint and modesty set in the values of his Catholic up-bringing and dictated more by craft than career.

It is at first curious and then instructive to reflect that, for one so keen to get on, Vickery never cared much about working abroad: neither did he attempt to join one of the kitchens of the super-chefs. He chose his places almost casually from the job ads in *Caterer and Hotelkeeper*. Such a transparently haphazard method of charting a future rarely sets markers for high honours later on. But Vickery was different. The wellspring of his singular spirit comes from the creative mind of a gifted amateur artist, an obsessive curiosity about food and a passion for self-instruction which began before the child had even hit double figures. The didactic rigour of the schools of Roux or Mosimann were not his bag. He did not want to be brainwashed. He did not want to be cloned. Instead, he preferred a gentler route; through books and home experiment, through country houses and their kitchen gardens. To these aesthetic and scientific instincts add Vickery the sportsman and you discover the source of the man's driven edge. At fourteen, he was British Schools Judo Champion and for several years he ran sub-three-hour marathons.

Inevitably, the shaping of such a well-honed character – the self-discipline, the single-mindedness, the clarity of purpose – has infected the atmosphere of the Castle's kitchens. A stranger below stairs might be forgiven for believing that the place was run by some evangelical. The Word of Vickery – expressed through the aphorisms and one-liners of others as much as his own – is pinned to boards and blu-tacked to walls. One from the writer John Whitley reads: 'Imaginative and able cooks should be prouder of creating exciting food from cheaper ingredients than of charging a fortune for showing off with curlicues of spun sugar or hand-carved cherry tomatoes.' Another – 'Don't retaliate. Re-evaluate. Some suggestions are worth listening to' – contrasts poignantly with 'A food critic is a legless man who teaches running'. Metaphorical confusion perhaps. But thus spake Marathon Chef.

Creating exciting food from cheaper ingredients has been a culinary nostrum for Phil Vickery since the early years of his childhood.

" Such a transparently haphazard method of charting a future rarely sets markers for high honours later on. But Vickery was different "

Although he was born and raised in Folkestone in Kent where his father worked as a post office engineer, he felt more naturally at home in Lancashire where his maternal grandparents lived. They once owned a fish and chip shop in Blackburn and the grandchildren – three boys – spent their long summer holidays in Blackpool. Young Phil's earliest memories are of his grandmother's table, with wonderful stews, cow heels, trotters and slabs of tripe with black pepper, vinegar, raw onions and tomatoes. To finish, there might be a whimberry pie made from tiny purple berries picked by the lads in the Forest of Bowland.

Family life back in Folkestone was happy and well ordered – directed by the devotion of strong Catholic parents and seasoned by the tenets of church and school. Vickery himself does not subscribe but, he says, the Faith has provided him with 'a certain morality'. At a more secular level, his upbringing was also grounded on the notions of the work ethic and the need to achieve. But at school, he found learning a problem and while his academic elder brother sailed through grammar school and university to embark on a career in tropical medicine, he failed his eleven-plus and, at O Level, passed only in Art – a subject he loved.

This gap in familial achievement in the classroom has left a scar on his self-worth. He refuses to regard himself as 'intelligent', once confiding in a friend: 'I don't want people to say I'm a brilliant chef but that I'm a bit dense'. The non sequitur in these words still leaves him unconvinced in spite of all his success. However, it was the blunt wisdom of Vickery's father who, sensing the emotional struggle within his second son and conscious that he might too readily fall for the easier option of copping-out, reassured his boy of his own special gifts by adding, 'When

the going gets tough, you just give up'. The criticism stuck. The boy got going. And he hasn't looked back.

Although the boy's mother used to say that his favourite toys were pots and pans, it was the caretaker of the church hall who first ignited Vickery's interest in food when he gave him a fusty old book which had been left lying around. Vickery was nine at the time and the book – *Warne's Everyday Cookery*, published in 1937 – was packed with step-by-step illustrations of how to perform basic kitchen tasks. Before long, he had mastered the technique of filleting fish. More books followed from doting aunts and by the time he was fourteen he was making choux buns and *millefeuille*, and fashioning *pastillage* churches – 'because they were such a nice shape'. At fifteen, he had bought his own sugar thermometer, made fondant and taught himself to temper chocolate. The confectioner's kitchen became more than just an alternative art studio. The work was challenging, difficult. And it came to symbolize his personal proving ground.

So, when the time came to leave school, he entered Folkestone College with a grossly unfair advantage over his fellow students and emerged two years later with a roll call of distinctions and a job in the kitchens of the town's only four-star hotel.

In 1980, and now nineteen, Vickery packed up his knives, bought his father's old Allegro and headed north-west for the English Lakes and Reg Gifford's Victorian mansion, Michael's Nook, in Grasmere. He stayed four years and the experience was salutary, perhaps less for the shaping of his craft and more for the profound effect it had on his attitude to leadership in the years to come. The head chef was a barrack-room bully with the infelicitous name of Nigel Marriage, who subsequently left – to Vickery's immense relief – to work with Raymond Blanc at the Quat' Saisons in Oxford. On one famous occasion, Marriage booted his young charge in the stomach, a vicious and gratuitous act which still lives in the mind of a man whose inbred sense of justice and tolerance had been outraged.

The culinary disciplines absorbed in the latter half of the Eighties really anchored his technical ability as a cook. From Grasmere, he returned south where he did two eighteen-month stints at that paragon of the country house hotel genre, Gravetye Manor, sandwiched between a spell with Ian McAndrew in Canterbury.

These were the years when *nouvelle cuisine* was still the accepted currency but, for Vickery, it was also a time to learn as much about gardening as kitchen technique. At Gravetye, Peter Herbert – the *eminence grise* of the brotherhood of British country house hoteliers – had set about the restoration of William

Robinson's great gardens. The fecundity of the soil, augmented by 150 square metres of glass, continues to produce fruits, vegetables and herbs in prodigious quantities and varieties for a kitchen blessed like no other. McAndrew in contrast

❝ To know how to cook was one thing, but the way to cook well was quite another and above all demanded a deep knowledge of his raw produce ❞

was unlanded, but sharing Herbert's passion for the home-grown, he devoted his free afternoons to persuading the yeomen of Kent to dig for his restaurant. The correspondence of the pot and the hoe taught Vickery a fundamental lesson. To know how to cook was one thing, but the way to cook well was quite another and, above all, demanded a deep knowledge of his raw produce.

By the turn of the decade, Vickery was head chef of the ill-fated Mount Somerset – the comically grandiloquent name ascribed to Henlade House, perched atop a mump rather than a mount beside the village of that name east of Taunton. Long before our famous first meeting, I had eaten there a few times to gauge his form as Gary Rhodes's close competitor. Certainly, there was little to fault in his cooking. Indeed, his gift as a craftsman was immediately apparent, even though his food was clearly derivative and devoid of any discernible personal identity.

For a while, this amorphous line to his repertoire persisted after his arrival at the Castle. An asparagus mousse would be fringed with immaculately cut triangles of red, green and yellow peppers. Perfectly turned vegetables would be colour co-ordinated on to main plates. Little crosses of rhubarb might decorate puddings.

This was not what the Castle was about but, before long, Vickery had assimilated his new brief and the cooking began to change gear. In the London *Evening Standard*, Fay Maschler described his baked egg custard tart with nutmeg ice cream as a 'profoundly satisfying confection, seemingly the synthesis of the land of rich, buttery cream'. Geography, a sense of provenance and agricultural heritage are the principles that, for me, define the gastronomic backbone of a hostelry which has been feeding travellers in Somerset for eight hundred years. Local waters, our meadows and uplands offer a prodigious source of goods for the larder. Besides, and given our background, it seems almost impertinent to me that we should rob an honourable culinary tradition of its nobility and, indeed, its excitement.

Vickery – to a far greater extent than any of his predecessors – has developed the neo English theme beyond the more prosaic strand of professionally-worked superior home cooking, now enjoying a minor revival in some British restaurants. His is pioneering stuff. The thinking may be rooted in the home tradition but the execution is unmistakably refined, high-church, incidentally eclectic and always underpinned by restraint and a classical simplicity of presentation. Good old-fashioned spices, dried and candied fruits – so prevalent in the seventeenth and eighteenth centuries – recur in many of his dishes.

Braises dispel the myth that slow cooking methods do not work successfully in restaurants.

A braised shoulder of lamb is so tender, so deeply flavoured, it recalls childhood memories of well-hung mutton. Lightly perfumed with garlic and thyme, it sits in a bowl scattered with vegetables, the abundance of the English kitchen garden meeting the windswept uplands of Exmoor.

Vickery's preserved dishes hark back to the first Elizabethan Age. His potted pigeon and duck is packed into a forcemeat, seasoned with mace and nutmeg, and sealed with clarified butter and soft herbs. The wedge cut from the pot is served with sweetly spiced pears to foil the rich meatiness of the fowls. But the pitch of this repertoire is not like some culinary anachronism. It is not some parody of Olde English Fayre. To borrow from Jonathan Meades: 'Vickery's a Guscott, a wonderfully subtle operator with the lightest of touches'.

At the end of 1994, Meades's annual honours list in *The Times* was headed by Marco Pierre White, the River Café and the Castle. For Vickery, this was the moment of final recognition in a period which had brought him a stream of awards, including the *Egon Ronay Guide's* Dessert of the Year for his baked egg custard tart. He had arrived.

While 1994 was the year of Phil Vickery's apotheosis, the alchemy of the man is what it has always been: a strange instinctive potion of restless curiosity fortified by single-mindedness and rigid self-discipline. The result today is a brand of cooking which bears its own unique identity and one which is reassuringly English. For me, what began as an uncertain partnership has now blossomed into a rare friendship with a supremely talented artist.

❝ The thinking may be rooted in the home tradition but the execution is unmistakably refined, high church ❞

Potted Duck

with Spiced Pears

——

4 duck legs

75 g/3 oz sea salt

2 tablespoons chopped fresh thyme leaves

500 g/1 lb tinned duck or goose fat

2 large chicken breasts, skinned

300 g/10 oz pork back fat

6 small shallots

3 garlic cloves

1 smoked duck breast, skinned and cut into

2.5 cm/1 inch dice

1 teaspoon ground mace

salt and freshly ground black pepper

Spiced Pears:

250 g/8 oz sugar

3 teaspoons mixed spice

2 teaspoons whole coriander seeds

600 ml/1 pint water

grated zest and juice of 2 lemons

4 ripe Williams or Red Bartlett pears,

peeled and cored

To make the spiced pears, place the sugar, spices, water, lemon zest and juice in a pan, bring to the boil, simmer for 5 minutes, then cool. Add the pears, bring to the boil, cover with greaseproof paper and simmer for 2–6 minutes, until done. Cool in the syrup, preferably overnight. To serve, lengthways into 4.

Place the duck legs in a non-metal bowl, mix with the salt and thyme, cover with cling-film and chill for 24 hours, turning occasionally.

Next day, rinse, pat dry with kitchen paper and pack into a small casserole dish. Melt the duck or goose fat and pour over the duck legs. Cover and cook in a preheated oven at 140°C (275°F) Gas Mark 1 for about 3–4 hours or until a skewer can be pushed through the thigh. Remove from the oven, cool and chill overnight.

Mince the chicken breasts, back fat, shallots and garlic finely in a mincer or food processor. Mix in a bowl, then add the smoked breast. Remove the duck legs from the fat and wash under warm water. Pull off all the meat from the legs, taking care not to break the thin bone on the drumstick, then cut away and discard all the skin. Cut into large chunks and add to the mixture. Season with salt, pepper and mace.

Pack into a small, buttered casserole dish or terrine and cover with 2 layers of foil. Seal well. Place the dish in a *bain-marie* (a roasting tray filled halfway up the dish with hot water) and cook in a preheated oven at 150°C (300°F) Gas Mark 2 for about 2¼ hours. To test whether the potted duck is cooked, remove from the oven, take off the foil and pierce with a skewer. The juice should run clear. Take out of the *bain-marie* and place a small plate or saucer on top, ensuring it fits tightly. Put a small weight on the plate, cool, then chill overnight.

To serve, remove the foil and place the mould in a bowl of warm water to loosen the fat. Turn out on to a chopping board and cut into wedges. Serve with the spiced pears, salad leaves dressed with walnut oil, and crusty brown toast.

Serves 8-10

Seared Salmon

with Roasted Spices, Watercress and Spring Onion Crème Fraîche

———

4 x 125 g/4 oz salmon fillets,

all bones removed

50 ml/2 fl oz vegetable oil

8 sprigs of watercress

black caviar, to garnish (optional)

Roasted Spice Mixture:

2 tablespoons whole coriander seeds

1 tablespoon whole cumin seeds

3 tablespoons whole black peppercorns

1 teaspoon green cardamom pods

2 teaspoons ground cinnamon

2 teaspoons whole cloves

2 teaspoons freshly grated nutmeg

2 teaspoons mustard seeds

Spring Onion Crème Fraîche:

300 ml/½ pint crème fraîche

6 spring onions, finely chopped

50 ml/2 fl oz white wine vinegar

1 tablespoon chopped fresh chives

a pinch of sugar

salt and freshly ground black pepper

Couscous:

125 g/4 oz couscous

250 ml/8 fl oz boiling fish stock

1 red pepper, finely diced

50 ml/2 fl oz olive oil

salt and freshly ground black pepper

To make the roasted spice mixture, roast the spices in a hot, dry frying pan, making sure not to burn them. Grind in a coffee grinder and store in a sealed jar.

To make the spring onion crème fraîche, combine the crème fraîche in a bowl with the spring onions, vinegar and chives. Add salt, pepper and sugar to taste, then chill.

Place the couscous in a bowl and pour over the boiling fish stock. Cover with clingfilm and leave for 10 minutes – the couscous will swell and absorb all the stock. Stir well, then add the diced pepper and the olive oil. Season to taste with salt and freshly ground black pepper, then set aside.

Sprinkle the salmon on a tray with salt and a generous amount of the roasted spice mixture. Heat the oil in a non-stick frying pan until it starts to smoke. Gently lower in the salmon pieces, spice-side down, and season with salt.

Slightly reduce the heat (the salmon should colour, but not burn) and cook for a few minutes until white liquid starts to run from the fish, and the top is still raw but warm. Remove from the heat and set aside in a warm place for about 10 minutes. The salmon will just start to fall apart when pressed.

Pile the couscous in the middle of 4 heated dinner plates and put the sprigs of watercress on top. Carefully turn the salmon over and place, crust-side up, on top of the couscous. Spoon over the crème fraîche mixture and serve immediately, garnished with a spoonful of caviar, if using.

Serves 4

Braised Shoulder of Lamb

---

1 shoulder of English lamb, boned

1 whole head of garlic

1 tablespoon chopped fresh thyme leaves

1.2 litres/2 pints lamb stock

4 carrots, chopped

2 celery sticks, chopped

4 onions, chopped

2 leeks, chopped

3 fresh plum tomatoes, peeled, deseeded and diced

1 tablespoon chopped fresh basil

1 tablespoon chopped fresh parsley

1 tablespoon chopped fresh tarragon

salt and freshly ground black pepper

Open the shoulder and trim away any excess fat. Chop 2 cloves of the garlic (or more if you like a strong garlic flavour) and mix with the thyme. Rub the mixture into the meat and season well with salt and pepper. Tie the lamb into an even shape and place in a saucepan. Cover with the stock and vegetables.

Cut the remaining garlic bulb in half horizontally and add to the stock. Season and bring to the boil. Cover with foil and braise in a preheated oven at 190°C (375°F) Gas Mark 5 for about 3½ hours until the meat is tender.

When cooked, remove from the oven, cool, then chill well, preferably overnight. When well chilled, remove the string, and cut the lamb into 1.5 cm/¾ inch slices. Defat the stock. Place the meat in a roasting tin and cover with a little of the cooking stock. Cover with foil and place in a preheated oven at 230°C (450°F) Gas Mark 8 to warm through.

Bring the remaining lamb stock to the boil, add the diced tomatoes and chopped fresh herbs.

Remove the lamb from the oven and arrange in the middle of 4 heated dinner plates. Top with the sauce and serve with as many varieties of vegetables as possible, together with potatoes cooked with bacon, herbs and lamb stock.

Serves 6

Fish Cakes

———

500 g/1 lb salmon, skinned and filleted

500 g/1 lb cod, skinned and filleted

500 g/1 lb potatoes

50 g/2 oz butter

2 onions, finely chopped

125 g/4 oz fresh chopped herbs, e.g. basil, parsley and tarragon

about 125 g/4 oz flour

4 eggs, beaten

1 kg/2 lb breadcrumbs

salt and freshly ground black pepper

Poach the fish until just cooked and place in a colander to drain. Boil the potatoes until just cooked (do not boil too rapidly as the outside will fall away before the inside is cooked).

Heat the butter in a small pan and gently fry the onions until softened but not coloured.

Mash the potatoes, flake the fish and mix both together with the onion and chopped herbs. Taste and adjust the seasoning. Mould the mixture into small balls, about the size of an apricot, then roll them first in the flour, then in the eggs and finally the breadcrumbs. Place in the refrigerator for at least 1 hour.

Deep or shallow-fry and serve with a lemon mayonnaise and vegetables.

Serves 10

Baked Egg Custard Tart

with Nutmeg Ice Cream and Blackcurrant Sauce

---

500 ml/17 fl oz whipping cream

6 egg yolks

65 g/2½ oz caster sugar

¼ teaspoon vanilla essence

15 cm/6 inch sweetcrust pastry flan case, baked blind

grated nutmeg, for sprinkling

Nutmeg Ice Cream:

9 egg yolks

150 g/5 oz caster sugar

1.2 litres/2 pints milk

1 whole nutmeg, finely grated

150 ml/¼ pint sugar syrup

300 ml/½ pint double cream

Blackcurrant Sauce:

500 g/1 lb fresh or frozen blackcurrants

125 g/4 oz caster sugar

about 300 ml/½ pint water

2 teaspoons lemon juice

To make the blackcurrant sauce, place the blackcurrants and sugar in a liquidizer or food processor, add half the water and purée until smooth. Add the lemon juice and just enough of the remaining water to produce a smooth consistency. Pass through a fine sieve and chill well.

To make the ice cream, place the egg yolks and caster sugar in a bowl and whisk until thick and creamy. Pour the milk into a heavy-based pan, add the finely grated nutmeg, bring to the boil, then carefully pour on to the egg yolks and sugar and whisk together. Pour into a clean pan and cook gently, stirring constantly, until the mixture coats the back of a spatula. Remove from the heat, pass through a fine sieve, then leave to cool completely.

When cool, add the sugar syrup and cream and freeze in a sorbetière, churning until you have a soft and silky texture.

To make the custard tart, pour the cream into a small pan and bring to the boil. Whisk the egg yolks, caster sugar and vanilla essence together and pour on the boiling cream. Mix thoroughly and pass through a fine sieve.

Pour into the pastry case and sprinkle with a little grated nutmeg. Bake in a preheated oven at 160°C (325°F) Gas Mark 3 for about 40 minutes. (Do not cook the custard too quickly, or it will curdle.) Remove from the oven, cool, then chill overnight.

To serve, place a wedge of tart on a dessert plate, with a spoonful of sauce and the ice cream, which can also be served in a *tuile*.

Serves 8

Stephen Markwick

Towards the end of 1973, an advertisement appeared in the personal columns of *The Times* inviting those who might be interested to apply for the post of general assistant at a small restaurant overlooking the Helford Estuary in Cornwall. The restaurant – called, appropriately, the Riverside – would be reopening in the spring of the following year under new ownership. The advertisement was quite particular about the applicants it sought. They had to be 'fast moving, good looking, clear thinking, artistic, determined and kind'. As an afterthought, the notice also suggested that 'some cooking experience could be useful'.

There was nothing unusual about the construction of these words because their author had been using them over the previous twenty years when he had advertised for staff for his legendary premises at the Hole in the Wall in Bath. He, of course, was George Perry-Smith, patron saint of all British chefs and the begetter of the post-war revival in restaurant cooking.

However, what is remarkable about Perry-Smith's manifesto is that the substance of his words and their realization in practice have touched, inspired and shaped the lives of hundreds of young people who worked with him. The essence of his *modus vivendi* was that, if you were prepared to work hard and devote yourself completely to making others happy, you would also find fulfilment and enjoyment in life. There is no doubt, too, that there was a nobility and a charisma about the man. He was possessed of a quiet but extraordinary aura which is sometimes found in an exceptional teacher. Indeed, he was one. Today his former pupils still look upon him with the same awe and devotion, and the values they share have forged a beneficent fellowship founded on the principles of gentleness, modesty and the preparation of honest food as a way of life rather than as an end in itself. For their guests, the excellence of their cooking is not the message, not the point. The food is purely a medium for courting human contentment and pleasure – an important distinction often overlooked by some of the more egocentrically minded among modern chefs. For the disciples of George Perry-Smith, cooking is a conscious act of giving. They shun self-aggrandizement and all the gastro-gloss of the super-chef circuit. If celebrity comes their way, they do not embrace it. They keep it firmly at arm's length, or even refuse to acknowledge its presence.

Stephen Markwick is the model of this fellowship of alumni. It was he who answered the advertisement in *The Times* in 1973 although his Georgine conversion was to begin on the road to Dartmouth where Joyce Molyneux, Perry-Smith's star graduate at the Hole in the Wall, and Tom Jaine, his stepson, were setting up shop at The Carved Angel on the quayside. Helford would come later. Nevertheless, this was the great watershed in Markwick's life and the six years that followed sealed the character of his cooking in Bristol when he went his own way in 1980. But those years in Devon and Cornwall meant more to him than merely an important influence in his career development. Perry-Smith's way was to create a strong sense of family among his partners and staff.

" The food is purely a medium for courting human contentment and pleasure "

It was this atmosphere, often absent in Markwick's early life, that created the bond and special affection he has for his teacher. Perry-Smith became the father he saw so little of as

" His salmon in pastry . . . is sensational . . . one of those rare masterpieces which have become timeless "

a child. Whereas his upbringing is punctuated by huge gaps, consciously or unconsciously erased from his memory, the descriptions of his years in Helford towards the end of the Seventies verge on the rhapsodic. He was enchanted by the smell of woodsmoke coming from the home fires of the village on a damp winter's evening. He recalls the Riverside's kitchen with its views across the estuary, the restaurant's herb garden which he plundered for thyme, marjoram, rosemary or tarragon, and summer afternoons spent on the terrace talking to 'Uncle George' and Heather, his wife, over a glass of chilled white wine.

Markwick's childhood was neither easy nor carefree. He was a shy and introverted boy who preferred to sublimate his feelings and emotions in a state of permanent activity. At home, at school or on holiday, he was always doing something; playing Rugby and cricket, rock-climbing in Snowdonia, camping or working for pocket money. Born in London in 1947, his family moved to Alderley Edge in Cheshire six years later. His father, a Cambridge law graduate, was chairman of English Sewing Cotton in Manchester and spent much of his business life travelling abroad. So it fell to his mother to rear the family: 'she fed us, clothed us, disciplined us. She was quite good with a hairbrush. We all used to get it!'

Mrs Markwick, like her husband, was a very capable and active person. Towards the end of the Fifties, the family bought a small hotel called the Edge, and she ran it. Stephen took to the hustle and bustle of hotel life with some relish: peeling potatoes before school in the mornings, rushing home to wash up in the evenings, serving afternoon teas at weekends. But much the happiest moments of his childhood were spent in the company of his grandmother at her home in Brompton Square in Knightsbridge. She spoiled her grandchildren and they adored her. She would usher them around the sights of the capital on the top deck of a red bus all day, and at suppertime she cooked and they ate lustily off braised oxtails, liver, kidneys, exquisitely sauced roast pigeons and the best baked custard in England. 'When you visited Gran, she was yours for the week,' Markwick recalls. 'She always helped, always guided.'

In stark contrast to the bosom of Brompton Square, Markwick's education at a public school in North Wales was typically spartan; early morning runs, cold showers, team games and God twice a day. He coped with all that happily, but found the learning side of the system more tiresome. Still, he mustered enough O levels to convince his father that the business career he envisaged for his son should begin with a thorough grounding in accountancy. The experiment was a perfect flop and eventually son persuaded father that, if mother could run an hotel, so could he.

After four years at Ealing College – with practical stints cooking on Escoffier's ancient stoves at the Savoy and waiting upon Aristotle Onassis, Maria Callas and other divinities seated on the 'royal station' in Claridges' restaurant – Markwick was admirably equipped with the credentials for life as a smooth hotel operator. What he had not banked on was that once smart hotel men approach the upper reaches of the pecking order, they are obliged to behave like accountants, not hoteliers.

When he joined British Transport Hotels after leaving college in 1970, life went swimmingly as he progressed smoothly from Aberdeen to Glasgow to Stratford-upon-Avon and Newcastle-upon-Tyne. By 1973, he had married Judy, she had given birth to their first daughter, Clare, and the family was beginning to enjoy the perks that come with seniority in a large hotel company. However, Mr Markwick was not a happy man. Head office's appetite for budgets, business plans and cash flow forecasts bound him to his desk. And number-crunching was not his strong suit.

It was then that he spotted the advertisement – and something about it struck a chord. When he applied, Perry-Smith referred him to his partners in Dartmouth, and Tom Jaine offered him the job immediately. Markwick returned to Newcastle to think. He was attracted to the work and he liked the people enormously, but the move would have cut his salary by half and, with the baby to care for, Judy had left her well-paid job as a secretary. Sense prevailed and he wrote to The Carved Angel turning down the offer. Three weeks later, Jaine telephoned – chasing Markwick for a deci-

sion. He had not received the letter. The call made Stephen think again and he decided to stop being sensible. 'I just wanted to do it,' he says. 'They were my sort of people.'

And so they were. The spirit of his new-found fellowship inspired him and its primary source was Joyce Molyneux who understood and shared the gentle, sensitive nature of her young recruit. Through Joyce, Markwick discovered food like a new stream of consciousness, forsaking the production-line mentality of large hotel kitchens for cooking as a labour of love.

He learned to respect good-quality raw materials and how to treat them. He also learned the backbone of his repertoire in Bristol today, including a number of dishes which were Perry-Smith classics at the Hole in the Wall over thirty years ago. Perhaps the most notable of these is salmon baked in pastry with currants and ginger, which Markwick serves with a fresh, velvety and aromatic sauce of tarragon, chervil, mustard, shallots and cream. The formula may sound over the top in description, but on the palate it is sensational – one of those rare masterpieces which have become timeless. Indeed, the origins of the recipe pre-date Perry-Smith by some three hundred years.

Stephen did well under Joyce's sisterly instruction. But before graduating to the Helford stoves of the don himself, he spent eighteen months running Perry-Smith's coffee shop at the Bristol Guild near the university, cooking pissaladières, moussakas and other simple Mediterranean favourites for lunchtime shoppers and hungry students. When George relinquished the lease on the café, he invited his protégé to join him at the Riverside.

Markwick's two seasons at Perry-Smith's elbow completed his education and it is quite revealing to contrast the perspective each held for the other in the kitchen. The master remembers his pupil being a touch 'heavy handed with garlic, spicing and seasonings'. The pupil recalls that the principal lesson he learned was how to 'develop and balance flavours, and how to season at the right time'. Perry-Smith was a perfectionist, meticulous about the detail of his cooking and now Markwick's menu is impressed with the same degree of care.

On 11th July, 1980, three days after their eighth wedding anniversary, Stephen and Judy Markwick opened Bistro 21 in a parade of shops behind the Bristol Royal Infirmary. The deal was cut within twenty-four hours of seeing the property and the £35,000 purchase price was raised with the help of parents and bank. Even Gran put in £10,000. In no time, the bistro became a lively neighbourhood eaterie where locals and medics could dine splendidly for less than a tenner. The menu featured many of 'the old Riverside originals', such as Provençal fish soup, tarragon chicken, *salade Niçoise*, crab tart, rabbit casserole, *daube* of beef, aubergine fritters and a St Emilion *au chocolat*. 'George Perry-Smith-style food at knock-down prices'

“ In his kitchen, this chef is unmoved by innovation and culinary fad ”

crooned *The Good Food Guide*, which dubbed Markwick's 'Bistro of the Year' in 1983. Publicity of this order now began to win them customers who were happy to spend more on petrol than on dinner. Soon the bank had been paid off – as had Gran, regardless of her vigorous protests.

By 1987, both the chef and hostess felt that they and their customers deserved more elegant premises for the quality of food they wanted to offer. Besides, Clare and their second daughter Zoë were now in their teens. To allow them more time for the children, a new partnership with the Bristolian chef Andy Hunt seemed a felicitous next step. So they sold the business for £60,000 and invested the proceeds, which were all but wiped out by the crash on the stock market in October of the same year.

In spite of this bitter blow, by March 1989 Markwick and Hunt had opened in the civilized and gracious vaulted chambers of the Ocean Safe Deposit beneath the stately Ionic columns of the Commercial Rooms in Corn Street. Ill fate, old wives say, visits the cursed in companies of three. The partnership with Hunt crumbled in acrimony. Stephen and Judy bought him out. They repainted the wrought iron sign over the vaults and faced the future with new hope. But the recession in the early Nineties was the third drubbing – and almost the final straw – in this chronicle of misfortunes, which was mercifully relieved by the support of Markwick's mother and the unsolicited return of Gran's £10,000.

In his kitchen, this chef is unmoved by innovation and culinary fad. He is a traditionalist, a purist of the Perry-Smith and Elizabeth David schools. His buying of tip-top ingredients does not stray out of season and, like the master, he believes in good housekeeping. In summer, red berries are packed into a pudding and all the excess syrup is transformed into a wonderful ice cream of summer fruits.

While the manner of Markwick's cooking betrays an underlying conservatism, his dishes are executed with such care and precision that the effect is to soothe and to comfort rather than to induce a rush of excitement. A breast of Trelough duck (from the Hereford Duck Company) is served with Puy lentils, lardons, shallots and fungi. The gentle sweetness of the Sauternes sauce makes a perfect foil for the pulses and the smoke of the bacon. It is classical, no-nonsense food of the highest order and an example of the equanimity he contrives in all his compositions.

Flavours, colours, smells and textures are wilfully unambiguous but again harmonious: the zip of a tomato pesto in a risotto matches the sweet sprightliness of scallops, while citrus zest and orange alcohol fills the nostrils as three plump soufflé pancakes are set before you. It is this thoughtfulness in Markwick's way with food that has won him such universal praise with the critics. Jonathan Meades talks of his '*douceur* and balance', Matthew Fort of his care and detail, and in 1993, the *Independent* proclaimed Markwick's one of its 'Restaurants of the Year'.

Stephen Markwick has now been cooking seriously for over twenty years. It is a mark of his confidence, as much as the nature of the man, that he has never felt any great urge to develop his cooking beyond the principles and basic style of his mentor. In this sense, he differs from Joyce Molyneux, whose natural creative gifts eventually took flight in Dartmouth. Markwick's cooking is to Bristol in the Nineties what George Perry-Smith's was to Bath in the Fifties and Sixties.

For Judy Markwick, her husband's commitment to the vocation inspired in him by his charismatic teacher created difficulties in the early years. Understandably, she felt alienated from this unique fellowship because she was not part of it. Today she is, and she shares the same selfless spirit of them all: 'We are not in this business for money. Our pleasure is in the glow of people saying thank you and showing their appreciation. That is what keeps us going.'

Rack of Lamb

with Leeks and Sherry Vinegar Sauce

———

75 g/3 oz fine, fresh breadcrumbs

4 tablespoons chopped fresh herbs, e.g. parsley, thyme, tarragon and rosemary

2 racks of lamb, trimmed

1 tablespoon Dijon mustard

50 ml/2 fl oz sherry vinegar

300 ml/½ pint lamb stock

salt and freshly ground black pepper

Leek Sauce:

2-3 leeks, carefully washed

15 g/½ oz butter

2 shallots, finely chopped

50 ml/2 fl oz white wine

50 ml/2 fl oz chicken stock

about 25-50 ml/1-2 fl oz double cream, to finish

25 g/1 oz Cumbrian air-dried ham, cut into thin strips

To make the leek sauce, shred and blanch for a second in boiling water. Drain and refresh in cold water, to halt cooking. Heat the butter in a pan, add the shallots and cook until softened but not coloured. Add the white wine and stock, bring to the boil and reduce to about 50 ml/2 fl oz. Just before serving, reheat, stir in the cream, the leeks and ham.

To make the herb crust, mix the breadcrumbs and chopped herbs together. Roast the racks of lamb in a preheated oven at 200°C (400°F) Gas Mark 6 for about 10–15 minutes, depending on their size. When almost cooked, season with salt and freshly ground black pepper and spread the mustard lightly over the back of the racks. Press on the herb crust, pouring the fat from the roasting pan over the crumbs. Return to the oven or place under the grill to crisp the crumbs.

Add the sherry vinegar to the pan, bring to the boil and reduce to about 1 tablespoon. Add the lamb stock, bring back to the boil and reduce by about half.

To serve, place the leek sauce on heated dinner plates and pour the sherry vinegar sauce around. Carve the racks of lamb and place 3 cutlets on each plate. Baby leeks cooked in red wine make a delicious accompaniment.

Serves 4

Breast of Trelough Duck

with Puy Lentils, Lardons and Sauternes Sauce

---

4 breasts of Trelough or Barbary ducks

75–125 ml/3–4 fl oz Sauternes

300 ml/½ pint duck stock

25 g/1 oz butter, to finish

Puy Lentils:

75 g/3 oz Puy lentils

15 g/½ oz butter

2–3 shallots, finely chopped

50–75 g/2–3 oz smoked streaky bacon or

pancetta, cut into lardons

2 sprigs of thyme

2 bay leaves

To garnish:

12 shallots, roasted

50–75 g/2–3 oz wild mushrooms, lightly sautéed in butter

To prepare the lentils, place them in a saucepan with cold water to cover, bring to the boil, then strain. Cover with fresh water, bring to the boil again and simmer until almost cooked (about 10 minutes, depending on the age of the lentils). Meanwhile, heat the butter in a large pan, add the shallots, lardons, thyme and bay leaves and cook until the shallots are softened but not coloured. Add the lentils and, if necessary, a little of the duck stock to moisten. Continue cooking until tender, then taste and adjust the seasoning.

To prepare the duck, season the breasts and fry, skin side down, in a dry pan at a medium to low heat until the fat runs and the skin is crispy. Pour off the fat as it is produced. Turn the breasts and briefly cook the other side. Remove, season again and set aside to rest in warm place.

To make the sauce, deglaze the pan with a little Sauternes, and reduce to about 1 tablespoon. Add the duck stock and reduce again to about 125 ml/4 fl oz. Beat in the butter to finish.

To serve, carve the duck breasts, place the lentils in the centre of 4 heated dinner plates, arrange the duck on top of the lentils, and pour the sauce around. Add a few roasted shallots and wild mushrooms, to garnish.

Serves 4

Pan-fried Scallops

with Sun-dried Tomato Risotto and Pesto

———

8 large, or 12 small scallops

shavings of Parmesan, to garnish

Pesto:

125 g/4 oz sun-dried tomatoes

50 g/2 oz pine nuts (roasted)

2 garlic cloves

50 g/2 oz Parmesan

olive oil (see method)

Tomato Stock:

2 tablespoons olive oil

1 onion

2 carrots

1 stick celery

2 garlic cloves

1 leek

1/2 head of fennel

6 tomatoes chopped (preferably tinned

whole Italian plum tomatoes)

150 ml/1/4 pint white wine

900 ml/1 1/2 pints water

Risotto:

50 g/2 oz butter

1/2 onion, finely chopped

50 g/2 oz sun-dried tomatoes, finely diced

tomato stock (see above)

250 g/8 oz Arborio rice

about 25 g/1 oz butter

about 25 g/1 oz grated Parmesan cheese,

plus extra, shaved, to serve

To make the pesto, place all the ingredients except the olive oil in a liquidizer or food processor. With the motor running, add the olive oil slowly and carefully, until it reaches the desired consistency.

To make the tomato stock, heat the oil in a pan, add all the vegetables cut into a small dice, and cook briefly until softened but not coloured. Add the wine and water, bring to the boil, then simmer for about 20 minutes. Strain into a jug.

To make the risotto, heat the butter in a heavy-based pan, add the onion and cook until softened but not coloured. Add the sun-dried tomatoes and stir well. Add the rice and stir until well coated with the butter and transparent at the edges. Gradually add the hot tomato stock in small amounts, stirring continually, and cook gently until the rice is tender. Stir in the butter, and a little grated Parmesan.

Cut each scallop into 2 or 3 rounds, depending on size, but leave the roes whole. Quickly fry the rounds in a very hot pan for just a few minutes until slightly caramelized. Prick the corals and add to the pan for about 30 seconds, to cook through.

Serve the risotto in 4 heated deep plates with a spoonful of pesto in the centre. Arrange the scallops in a circle around the pesto, then sprinkle with Parmesan shavings.

Serves 4

Salmon in Pastry

with Currants and Ginger and Sauce Messine

——

750 g/1½ lb salmon, filleted and skinned

3 pieces stem ginger in syrup,

finely chopped

40 g/1½ oz currants

125 g/4 oz butter, softened

250 g/8 oz shortcrust pastry, thinly rolled

egg wash, for brushing

Sauce Messine:

600 ml/1 pint whipping cream

2 shallots, chopped

a good handful of parsley, chervil and tarragon

2 egg yolks

2 teaspoons Dijon mustard

1 tablespoon lemon juice

salt and freshly ground black pepper

To make the Sauce Messine, place all the ingredients in a food processor and blend until smooth. Pour into a double saucepan and cook over gently simmering water – do not cook over direct heat, or the eggs will curdle.

To prepare the fish, add the ginger, currants and seasoning to the softened butter and mix well. Cut the salmon into 2 even, rectangular pieces. Roll the pastry into an oblong shape large enough to wrap the salmon.

Place a piece of salmon near the edge of the pastry. Season, spread half the spiced butter mixture evenly on top, cover with the second piece of salmon, season and spread with butter.

Cover with the pastry and seal the edges well. Keep the pastry as thin as possible, and do not double over when wrapping. Brush with egg wash.

Place the parcel of salmon on greased foil and cook in a preheated oven at 220°C (425°F) Gas Mark 7 for 20 minutes. To serve, remove the foil and carve the fish into portions. Serve with the Sauce Messine spooned around.

Serves 4

Orange and Grand Marnier Soufflé Pancakes

---

3 eggs

15 g/½ oz caster sugar

pinch of salt

seeds from a split vanilla pod

65 g/2½ oz plain flour, sieved

2½ tablespoons double cream

6 tablespoons milk

2 tablespoons melted clarified butter

Pastry Cream Filling:

275 ml/9 fl oz milk

split vanilla pod

50 g/2 oz caster sugar

3 eggs, separated

25 g/1 oz plain flour

50 ml/2 fl oz Grand Marnier

Grand Marnier Sauce:

125 g/4 oz sugar

150 ml/¼ pint water

Grand Marnier, to taste

4 oranges

To make the pancakes, beat the eggs, sugar, salt and vanilla seeds together, then fold in the flour. Mix in the cream, milk and butter, and set aside to rest for 30 minutes.

To make the filling, boil the milk with the vanilla pod. Beat together the sugar and egg yolks, then mix in the flour and Grand Marnier. Pour on the boiling milk and mix until smooth.

Return to the heat, and beat with a wooden spoon until boiling. Remove from the heat and pass through a sieve. Cover with butter paper.

To make the Grand Marnier sauce, place the sugar and water in a saucepan and bring to the boil. Reduce until quite thick, but not burnt. Add the Grand Marnier and the grated zest of all the oranges and boil for 2 minutes. Segment the oranges, and add the segments and juice to the syrup at the last minute.

Cook 2–3 very thin pancakes per person. Cool, then fold into triangles and place on a greased baking tray.

Beat 2 egg yolks into the pastry cream until smooth. Whip 3 egg whites until stiff and fold into the pastry cream. Pipe the filling into the folds of the pancakes. Cook immediately in a preheated oven at 220°C (425°F) Gas Mark 7 for about 10 minutes.

To serve, place the pancakes on heated dessert plates, heat the sauce, and spoon gently beside the pancakes. Dust with icing sugar, garnish with a sprig of fresh mint and serve.

Serves 6

Christopher Chown

Chris Chown is a man of many contradictions. He is a romantic and a dreamer who says he was born two hundred years too late. He claims to be disillusioned with the politics and culture of the late twentieth century but he is at home with new technology and exercises a sharp business mind. He was once a member of the Ecology Party – later the Greens – and talks endlessly about concepts like 'elemental purity'. He hates cities but owns a restaurant in the centre of Bath. He loves modern design and contemporary art, but affirms an equal passion for the classical order and symmetry of Georgian architecture – so perhaps Bath is a forgivable aberration. He is clever with computers but would trade in his car rather than have it go beep at him. Christopher Chown is part-polymath, part-aesthete, permanently in search of harmony in life, and he and his Danish-Færoëse wife, Gunna, have sought it at Plas Bodegroes, their hidden idyll on the Lleyn Peninsula in North Wales. It is a place of great peace and beauty. But now he is talking of selling.

As June turns to July, the erect spears of foxgloves, like an imperial guard of honour, stand sentinel over hedgerows in the narrow lanes criss-crossing this crooked finger of land pressing into the Irish Sea. Above Rhiw – a desolate hillside village with a scatter of primitive dwellings and a chapel, four-square and solid – is a windswept heathland which Chown insisted I see. At its highest

point, looking north-east, is a view of the peninsula, cut on the horizon by a massive grey barrier of low mountains protecting the broad flat plain beneath. Either side is the sea; to the left, Porth Dinllaen where pickled eggs at the Ty Coch Inn on the beach sell for 50p and a pint is £1.60 and, to the right, Porth Neigwl, the wide and angry bay known as Hell's Mouth. These waters provide Chown's kitchen with fish and seafood, and the plain – a patchwork carpet of rich pasture, salt meadows and wood – provides for much of the rest of his abundantly stocked larder. His point was well made. Here at Rhiw was Chris Chown's elemental purity presented on one gigantic visual plate.

It took Chown sixteen months to realize his dream. He began the search in the mid-Eighties to an idealized brief beyond the ken of the local estate agents. The place had to be in North Wales, scene of his late childhood and adolescent years. The house had to be Georgian, perfectly proportioned and able to offer five bedrooms. The location had to be remote, the setting beautiful. Plas Bodegroes fulfilled that vision and today it is the only Michelin-starred restaurant in Wales.

More villa than house, Plas was built for the Sheriff of Cærnarfon in 1780 on low, flat lands near Pwllheli. As there was no view to speak of, landscapers were commissioned to create an aspect for the house which faced the sun at two o'clock GMT, the warmest time of the day. The result was a majestic beech avenue six hundred yards long – a clever ploy in itself because the trees provide a resolute shield against the savage winds which whip the peninsula in winter.

But a warm summer's evening is, perhaps, the moment to enjoy this place at its most blissful. White wicker furniture of the type seen in old sepia prints deck a heather-fringed verandah embracing the house like a floral apron, its cast-iron pillars softened by pale pink roses, wistaria, honeysuckle and dark blue clematis. A glass of chilled wine to hand and the sight of the beeches casting shafts of soft light into the shadows rush to conjure images of a more elegant age. The only sounds to break the evening hush are the squawks of unseen birds in the cherry tree to the left of the terrace or the laughter of diners from within.

In sharp contrast to the period and the pastoral exterior, the dining room strikes a modishly contemporary mood of a style that would not be out of place in central London. Cool grey-green tones set off works by modern Welsh painters, including Kyffin Williams, and a collection of arty photographs by Chown himself show his remarkable gift with a camera. He also designed and installed his own ultra-modern halogen lighting system – a series of tiny, shaded spots, like delicate almond *tuiles*, suspended from thin tram lines carrying the current across the ceiling.

In the wrong hands, this wilful exercise in style-mixing would be discordant, even philistine.

But Chown's gentle, aesthetic eye has turned the apparent cultural contradiction of two disparate centuries into a harmonious blend which is soothing and gracious – with the exterior and interior perfectly united by sets of French windows looking down the beech avenue on one side or opening on to rhododendrons, Japanese maples, tiger lilies and rose beds enclosed by lavender borders on the other.

" His eventual emergence as a chef was circuitous and unorthodox - the result of a confused, even wayward early life "

Chris Chown's approach to his work, his outlook on life and his obvious respect and devotion for Gunna reveal a complex, thinking man who sees his *métier* as chef-proprietor as only part of the answer. Unlike the narrow focus many chefs have for their craft, Chown's two restaurants – at Plas Bodegroes and at the Hole in the Wall in Bath – are created on more universal principles. It makes him no less obsessional than his peers, just that his obsessions embrace details beyond the culinary. Location, setting, design, a sense of partnership with his staff, Gunna's influence and involvement, as much as his recipes and menus, all matter deeply to him. Chown is more the composer-conductor than the virtuoso-soloist. His eventual emergence as a chef was circuitous and unorthodox – the result of a confused, even wayward early life which, more charitably interpreted, means that, in common with many other bright young things from a middle class background, he was struggling for identity and direction.

For a start, the Chown name posed an identity problem. Its origin is Norman – possibly a crude abbreviation of Champenois. But people tended to assume that Dr Chown was Chinese. In 1966, when Chris was just nine years old, the good doctor, his father, presented himself for an interview before a health authority selection panel in Betws-y-coed in North Wales. When he entered the room, the committee were confronted by a six-foot-six Clark Gable look-alike and the ladies on the panel swooned with delight. And so it was that Dr Chown, his wife and young family escaped the creeping suburbanization of Poole in Dorset for the rural peace of Snowdonia.

Chris Chown's adolescent years were shared between a life at home – fishing in the Conwy for eel and salmon or shooting rabbits in the hills – and school in Prestatyn, then Monkton Combe near Bath where he came top in everything, notching up ten O levels by the age of fourteen. He was a precocious youth, encouraged by the academic ambitions of his parents. His mother even made a visit to

the lavatory instructive with a chart of the kings and queens of England pinned behind the door.

At Monkton Combe he reacted against the school establishment, copping out of any serious work and falling in with the wrong crowd. His artistic inclinations had been denied in favour of the more sterile regimes of maths and science. He could not see the point of it all. His parents' high hopes for their brightest child, their thoughts of Cambridge, all evaporated against the sacrifices they had made to educate their three sons. There had been no foreign holidays. Mother had made all her own clothes and Chris had been dressed in hand-me-downs.

In spite of the academic ennui that consumed him at school, Chown won a place at Manchester University to read maths. He hated the place as much as the degree and in 1977 he moved to Buckingham to do accountancy and financial management which at least offered him a more practical outcome. Two years later he graduated respectably with a 2.1.

The years of Chown's late teens and early twenties were also touched by a tragedy at home which, perversely, would ultimately become responsible for illuminating his future. In 1978, his mother died of multiple-myalomatosis, a bone marrow cancer. Chris had always adored her and as the disease gradually gripped her body, he stepped into the kitchen and learned to cook while she sat by and instructed him. He is still racked by memories of her death – a memory tinged by a not-inconsiderable streak of guilt. 'I think my life is spurred by the desire to make up for taking advantage of my mother as a teenager,' he says. 'I was such a lazy sop that I've got to keep assuming that she is somewhere where she can see me being successful.'

By 1980, Chown had joined the herd of two-piece suits who fill the City each weekday: except that his briefcase bore the legend 'Nuclear Power. No Thanks', a statement which was not calculated to impress his employers, Peat Marwick Mitchell. Within a year he had quit, desperate for the sight of a little greenery. Clapham, he found, had trees and it was also a district in a housing action area. He bought a derelict property for £30,000 and with a £21,000 grant he hired a local contractor to rebuild the house on condition that the man employ his employer as an apprentice brickie. After eighteen months, Chown could add designer-builder to his list of credits and in 1984 he sold the property for £102,000, banking a tidy profit which helped him purchase Plas Bodegroes two years later.

The sabbatical in Clapham released Chris's mind to think seriously about his future. He was now twenty-four and the idea of cooking for a career had never occurred to him. Meanwhile, on his visits home, he would often organize dinner parties for his fathers' friends, who were quick to appreciate the doctor's son's skills in the kitchen. An introduction to a higher authority was arranged and Chown met the man who was instrumental in charting his new course. This was Nick Gill, one of the brightest young chefs of the early Eighties, who had just earned a Michelin star for Hambleton Hall, the swish country house hotel on Rutland Water in Leicestershire. Gill insisted on putting the precocious amateur to the test. So Chown organized a lunch party in London and served up a menu of trout mousse and jugged hare. He passed muster and Gill found him a job in the kitchens of a small Kensington restaurant. The experience was short-lived but it finally confirmed Chown's new direction – his determination sealed by a few words of rapturous praise from broadcaster Kenneth Kendall, for an asparagus *feuilleté* with chervil *beurre blanc*. 'I really enjoyed the compliment from someone I didn't know, but who was famous,' he recalls.

Chris Chown's passing success may have primed his adrenalin, but his high ideals were still tethered to pretty flimsy moorings. He needed educating – and fast. Nick Gill introduced him to Lyn Hall who took him on at her cookery school in Richmond in 1983. A year later – and true to his earlier scholastic ratings – he carried away the school's diploma as top student. From Richmond he passed briefly to the Anton Mosimann academy at the Dorchester, and Mosimann then saw to it that Chown was properly finished off in Switzerland – at Rosa Tschudi's starred restaurant, Riesbächli, near Zurich. But the final polish was administered by Frédy Girardet in Crissier, where Chown ate the best lunch of his life and learned that perfection can be achieved without the otiose

❝ *The Good Food Guide* discovered them in 1989 . . . Michelin followed soon after ❞

frills and flounces and the cloche-pulling swank which customarily afflict the grander restaurants of Europe.

Chris and Gunna opened Plas Bodegroes in August, 1986, and by November they came perilously close to throwing in the towel. A silent partner released them from the tyranny of their bank loan but it was not until *The Good Food Guide* discovered them in 1989 that the business took off. Michelin followed soon after and, with Plas secure, in 1994 Chown opened for trade at the Hole in the Wall in Bath – remodelling the place himself with the declared intention of reincarnating the restaurant in the spirit of George Perry-Smith's legendary creation a generation before. The decision to buy the Hole was inspired by the sentiment and nostalgia that are so characteristic of the man. One of the few happy moments of Chown's schooldays at Monkton Combe was a visit to Perry-Smith's restaurant – a memory

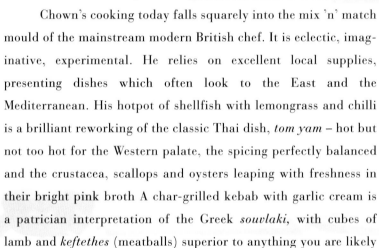

so vivid he recalls every detail of the dishes he ate.

Chown's cooking today falls squarely into the mix 'n' match mould of the mainstream modern British chef. It is eclectic, imaginative, experimental. He relies on excellent local supplies, presenting dishes which often look to the East and the Mediterranean. His hotpot of shellfish with lemongrass and chilli is a brilliant reworking of the classic Thai dish, *tom yam* – hot but not too hot for the Western palate, the spicing perfectly balanced and the crustacea, scallops and oysters leaping with freshness in their bright pink broth A char-grilled kebab with garlic cream is a patrician interpretation of the Greek *souvlaki,* with cubes of lamb and *keftethes* (meatballs) superior to anything you are likely to find in their country of origin.

Chown's globalism is, however, moderated by a streak of culinary political correctness in a show of respect for parochial tradition. Fish with bacon, for example, is very Welsh – a match cleverly illustrated in a delicious warm salad of monkfish, Carmarthen ham and mushrooms, where the salt and texture of the cured meat act as a perfect seasoning agent for the firmness of monkfish. Similarly, Chown uses laverbread essentially as a seasoning for his sea trout baked in puff pastry, with a yogurt and dill sauce. And, just occasionally, he will tease and surprise with a striking display of gastronomic solecism. His crisp parcels of farmhouse cheese wrapped in filo pastry are Greek *tiropiti* no less – but for feta he substitutes Llanboidy, Tyn Grug or Cardigan.

The puddings department is where Chown is more likely to hoist an English ensign. In season, superb local gooseberries are packed between crumbly heart-shaped cinnamon wafers floating on a custard infused with elderflowers gathered from the beech avenue. And a bowl of exotic fruits mulled in port with white chocolate ice cream fills the palate with contrasting sensations of taste and temperature: hot and cold, bitter and sweet – a fresh, clean, fruity finale to a magnificent five-course event and evidence again of Chown's purity and invention.

The restaurants at Plas and the Hole are, stylistically, quite distinct – reflecting the catholicity of Chris Chown's mind. The one is smart, the other more populist. Although some dishes feature on both menus, the Hole's lean towards the hearty. 'The dishes at Plas,' he explains, 'have to be elegant, because the house is elegant and because an elegant woman runs it. We can't put braised lamb shank or cassoulet on here, but we can in Bath.'

Chown insists that he has no further ambitions to expand. And, meanwhile, he has put Plas Bodegroes up for sale. But the

" Chown's cooking today falls squarely into the mix 'n' match mould of the mainstream British chef. It is eclectic, imaginative, experimental "

contradictions in his nature make one wonder in which direction he is going. He is an extraordinarily energetic man with an immensely fertile brain and he tends to get bored easily. At the same time, he yearns for peace and tranquillity, for books, art and music – and he wants more time to enjoy these things with his wife. I suspect that, in the end, it is Gunna who will be the guiding influence. She is eleven years his senior and she is the anchor that holds a driven personality from spinning out of control. Indeed, perhaps there is an element in the relationship where she fills the maternal void he felt so deeply after his mother's death.

Whether he extends his enterprise or contracts it, Chown is an enigmatic individual who has made it to the top of his profession – even if he still has diffi-culty defining his own identity within it. Friends and colleagues admire him greatly. Paul Heathcote puts it neatly when he eats at Plas – 'Not bad for a builder!'

Warm Salad of Monkfish, Carmarthen Ham and Mushrooms

—

1 monkfish tail, about 750 g/1½ lb

125-175 g/4-6 oz Carmarthen ham, sliced

50 g/2 oz button mushrooms

1 tablespoon olive oil

½ onion, chopped

1 garlic clove, chopped

75 ml/3 fl oz vinaigrette

mixed salad leaves such as lollo rosso,

radicchio, curly endive and rocket

freshly ground black pepper

Remove the monkfish from the bone, and trim off the skin. Cut into 2.5 cm/1 inch cubes. Cut the ham into thin strips, and break the mushrooms into large pieces.

Heat the olive oil in a 25 cm/10 inch non-aluminium frying pan. Add the monkfish, chopped onion, garlic, mushrooms and ham, and sauté gently for about 1–2 minutes until the fish is just firm.

Remove from heat and add the vinaigrette.

Arrange the salad leaves on 6 plates. Add the monkfish mixture, then trickle the warm vinaigrette over. Season with freshly ground black pepper and serve immediately.

Serves 6

Crisp Pastry Parcel of Welsh Farmhouse Cheeses

—

250 g/8 oz hard cheese, grated

(e.g. Tyn Grug or Cardigan)

½ Bramley apple, chopped

a few sultanas

a few walnut halves

1 tablespoon mustard

1 tablespoon chopped chives

2 eggs

freshly ground black pepper

250-300 g/8-10 oz filo, strudel or

spring roll pastry

50 g/2 oz melted butter

Place the cheese, chopped apple, sultanas, walnuts, mustard, chives, eggs and salt in a bowl and mix well. Place in the refrigerator and chill until firm.

Cut the sheets of pastry into 15 cm/6 inch squares. Cover with a damp cloth and uncover only as you work with each square.

Place a tablespoon of the cheese mixture in the middle of each square, wrap loosely to form a parcel and brush with melted butter. Bake in a preheated oven at 200°C (400°F) Gas Mark 6 for 10 minutes.

Serve with a green leafy salad, tossed in plain vinaigrette.

Makes 12 parcels

Serves 12 as cheese, 6 as starter

Hotpot of Shellfish

with Lemongrass and Chilli

—

400 g/13 oz shells from prawns, lobsters or langoustines

375 ml/12 fl oz fish stock

375 ml/12 fl oz white wine

25 ml/1 oz tomato juice

peel from 15 g/½ oz ginger

outer husks and root end of 2 stalks of lemongrass

5 bay leaves

2 dried red chillies, crushed

10 coriander stalks

2 star anise

¼ teaspoon fennel seeds

125 g/4 oz cooked meat from lobster, langoustines or king prawns

250 g/8 oz scallops

6 oysters

1 large green chilli, chopped

2 stalks lemongrass, finely chopped

15 g/½ oz ginger, finely grated

1 onion, chopped

zest and juice 1 lime

chopped fresh coriander, to serve

Place the prawn shells in a pan with the fish stock, white wine, tomato juice, ginger peel, lemongrass trimmings, bay leaves, red chillies, coriander stalks, star anise and fennel seeds. Simmer gently for 15 minutes, then strain.

Reheat, adding the chopped chilli, lemongrass, ginger, onion and lime.

Add the scallops and oysters, then the cooked meat from the prawns, lobster or langoustines and reheat for another 30 seconds without boiling.

Using a slotted spoon, lift the seafood out of the broth, divide between 6 heated bowls, then sprinkle over the coriander.

Reboil the broth, pour over the seafood, and serve immediately.

Serves 6

Figs and Kumquats

Mulled in Port with White Chocolate Ice Cream

—

275 g/9 oz white chocolate, broken into pieces

200 ml/7 fl oz milk

300 ml/½ pint double cream

4 egg yolks

65 g/2½ oz caster sugar

50 ml/2 fl oz Bacardi

12 kumquats

250 ml/8 fl oz water

50 g/2 oz sugar

125 ml/4 fl oz red wine

1 cinnamon stick

1 vanilla pod

4 cloves

6 peppercorns

6 figs

125 ml/4 fl oz port

Gently melt the white chocolate in a bowl over a pan of gently simmering water. Place the milk in a saucepan and scald with one-third of the cream.

Beat the yolks and sugar together, then pour on the hot milk and cream, whisking all the time. Cook gently until the custard thickens, then beat into the chocolate. Leave the mixture to cool. Whip the remaining cream and fold into the custard. Carefully stir in the Bacardi, then freeze in a sorbetière or in the freezer.

Cut the kumquats in half and scoop out the flesh into a small pan. Cover with the measured water and boil for 20 minutes, covering the pan with a lid to prevent evaporation.

Strain the liquid over the kumquat shells, cover and bring back to the boil for 30 minutes.

Add the sugar, and continue cooking until the kumquats start to become translucent. Add the red wine and spices, and bring back to the boil for 2–3 minutes.

Slice the figs into quarters vertically and add to the kumquats. Add the port, remove from the heat and steep for 10 minutes. Serve warm around the ice cream.

Serves 6

Carole Evans

———

Whenever I visit friends in Broxwood, a tiny place near Leominster, I always sleep soundly. The locals say it's the trees, but it is also the soothing beauty of the Welsh Marches – that stretch of green and pleasantness embracing Shropshire and Herefordshire. A hundred years ago a melancholic A.E. Housman called it 'the land of lost content'. Today's Shropshire Lad, Julian Critchley, described it as 'a land to be enjoyed' in his book *Borderlands*. For me, the gentle rolling hills, the valleys with their church spires rising above the morning mists, pretty timber-framed villages, stately oaks and screens of tall birch, the hop-yards and cider orchards, evoke a suitably English alternative to the mediæval towers, the pines and cypresses, and the vineyards of Tuscany. The Marches are a landscape that invites rapture and sentimental thoughts of another England.

Mr Critchley, of course, is no melancholic and rarely sentimental. In Ludlow, he says, most people still think a jacuzzi to be a breed of dog and the countryside's pubs are 'devoid of slot machines, plastic seats and juke boxes'. His favourite is the Roebuck Inn at Brimfield, a somnolent backwater off the A49 straddling the Shropshire-Herefordshire boundary. In the opinion of the veteran parliamentarian and bon viveur, a review of Carole Evans's pub for *Shropshire Magazine* noted that her kitchen 'shines like a good deed in a wicked world'.

A drive through Brimfield warns the stranger that the inhabitants of the village like their privacy and fiercely resist the wicked world. Thick *leylandii* and high stone walls hide black-and-white cottages with rose-arched doorways and red brick houses set in perfectly tended gardens. For evidence of life, the Roebuck is the place to be. It is an inn for all-comers, like a suit of many colours, and attracts an eccentric mix of English society who, for once, seem utterly at home in each other's company. At times, the dark panelled lounge bars and Poppies, the inn's bright and lively restaurant, buzz with the cerebral chatter of men of letters, politicians and the art establishment. Anthony Howard, John Biffen and Lord Gowrie – like Julian Critchley – are regulars at the Roebuck and one might almost mistake the place for some rural outpost of the Garrick Club.

Raising pints of Tetley's Bitter or Dunkerton's Cider or, indeed, a glass of very good claret, the highbrow jostle merrily with Ferrari-driving builders, Ludlow burghers and tourists clutching *The Good Food Guide*. Brimfield folk love their local too and they have fitted out their inglenooked 'snug' with a hotchpotch of RAF artefacts from the last war. Their mascot is Charlie Fox, who peers down at them beneath his blue serge cap above the settle in a corner of the room. A short while ago, Carole Evans nearly had a mutiny on her hands when the Roebuck ground crew were denied their usual issue of crisps and peanuts at the bar. In protest, they requisitioned a ration box which now sits defiantly on the counter.

> **❝ It is an inn for all-comers, like a suit of many colours, and attracts an eccentric mix of English society ❞**

Around the inn, inside and out, there are signs which hint at the nature of the woman behind this remarkable place. Hives in the garden produce honey from bees prone to swarm in the magnolia tree by the kitchen door – an event that causes a moment of consternation with the young staff, a fresh-faced and comely bevy of local girls, mostly, with reassuring names like Becky, Louise and Sally. The honey, Mrs Evans's pickles, chutneys, jams and mustards are displayed for sale in cloth-capped jars with floral and check designs and stacked on small shelves and window ledges in the bars.

The immediate impression is that the Roebuck's estimable reputation for its table is unlikely to have sprung from any technical foundation. The mood is more comforting and suggests an enterprise that is rooted in the best traditions of the British domestic household. Eliza Acton and Mrs Beeton instantly come to mind. This impression is not denied in fact, because Carole Evans has never stepped inside a catering college, nor has she cooked in any kitchen other than her own. She was once the wife of a farmer and as such became an industrious and able

cook who took good care to see that her large family and her many visitors were wholesomely fed.

The Roebuck's kitchen is administered as a sophisticated extension of the farmhouse with a refreshing absence of training. Orders arrive on chits with no table numbers. Carole Evans cooks for people, not numbers, and besides many of her regulars have their peculiarities about how they like their vegetables cooked or their meat done. So customers' names are printed at the head of each bill and orders are matched to a pictorial plan posted at the exit to the kitchen. It would never occur to a professionally-trained restaurateur to adopt this marvellously homespun system. But it works a treat for an ex-professional housewife and mother.

Mrs Evans is a feisty lady who belongs to the mother-knows-best school of domestic management. She is super-charged and, in the heat of a busy service, she can look fierce – round dimpled cheeks glistening pink, as her keen eyes inspect a finished dish over the half-moon spectacles perched on the tip of her nose. And then, when she breaks into a smile, you just want to hug her.

Carole, née Bowchier, was born in 1943 and, until her first marriage nineteen years later, home was a substantial country house in Llandewi Skirrid near Abergavenny, a short stroll away from the famous Walnut Tree Inn owned by Franco and Ann Taruschio. The families are related by marriage. Carole's brother Simon was married to Ann's sister Gay and they share nephews and nieces. The Bowchiers, senior figures at the glamorous end of the motor trade, lived well. The house's four acres of land kept the family larder amply provisioned with fruits, vegetables and herbs. Poultry chased the children round the grounds until the fowl met their fate at the hands of Ernie the gardener. They even kept a pig once, 'but it was never eaten because mother became too fond of it'. In time, the much-loved porker was given a ceremonial burial, but in every other respect Mrs Bowchier was a fastidious housekeeper who preserved and bottled the bounty of her garden, stored apples from the orchard and even made cough mixture to a recipe of crushed egg shells, yolks and brandy. These little domestic rituals extended to the gathering of each season's new crop of fresh produce. Mrs B was particularly keen on her asparagus beds and, as the heads appeared out of the ground, there would be a rush of anticipation in the household for the moment she would instruct Ernie to make the first cuttings.

For Carole it was an idyllic upbringing. It also defines the spirit and approach of her cooking today in a context which is outside the experience of most other British chefs. Here we have a culinary education inspired almost entirely by the effect of food on the senses rather than by any formal instruction or example. The mutuality between raw produce and cooked food during her formative years touched those sensuous instincts critical in any gifted cook. Some of her most vivid recollections are of smells; chutneys, tomato and marrow coming from the Aga, the warm aroma of baking permeating the entire house, smoked bacon and fried bread in the mornings, parsley sauce and the smell of cloves in boiled ham at lunchtime.

❝ Mrs Evans is a feisty lady who belongs to the mother-knows-best school of domestic management ❞

She remembers running her hand along the thyme bushes in the garden, the smell of fresh strawberries and mint rubbed gently between finger and thumb.

So it was inevitable that young Carole Bowchier was cooking from the moment her tiny head could see over the top of the kitchen stove. And if she was not driving her poor mother to despair making fudge and toffee, she would be playing truant from school to ride her pony or hunt with Harry Llewellyn's foxhounds. It was a blissful existence and one set to continue into an adulthood with no greater ambition than to settle down and raise a family in the manner and style of her parents before her.

By 1963 she had married into a prosperous farming family but it was a turbulent and unhappy match which ended in divorce ten years later. In that time, she bore four children, managed a busy household and developed her kitchen repertoire with the help of a subscription to a set of Cordon Bleu part-works. As a farmer's wife, she also learned to cope with the bloodier side of the food chain. While at home Ernie would take care to slaughter the poultry away from the gaze of impressionable young eyes, on the farm Carole was expected to grip the flailing wings of manic turkeys as her husband slit the birds' throats – their feathers sticking to the tears rolling down her cheeks.

In 1974 she married John Evans, a manager with Ansells the brewers. By now she was living in Herefordshire and, very gradually, she began to forge the transition from suppliant Welsh housewife to thrusting professional restaurateur. Her earlier blooding had left its scar and with it came a growing determination to make good the humiliations of the past. Carole Evans's final apprenticeship in the ways of the trade revolved around her new husband's business life, his captaincy of Bromyard Cricket Club and his passion for the shooting season. She managed the catering for Ansells' box at Ludlow races, she made the teas in the cricket pavilion and she cooked magnificently for his shooting parties. As the compliments grew, so did her confidence.

But the break that was to make her future name came disguised in an unexpected twist of misfortune. In 1982, Ansells closed their Aston brewery and Mr Evans became a casualty in a round of management redundancies. The blow to their lives was mitigated by an offer to take on the tenancy of the Roebuck Inn and shortly after midday on 1st March, 1983, Mrs Evans dished up her first lasagnes, home-made faggots and cottage pies.

For the forty-year-old ex-housewife from Llandewi Skirrid, this was a brave, if modest, beginning to a new career. Her sceptical husband gave her twelve months, but within that time she had transformed the pub's children's room into a pukka restaurant – naming it Poppies after the Remembrance Day eve of its opening. Carole Evans, chef-proprietor, was on her way. Before long they bought the freehold and in 1986, Richard Binns, the distinguished restaurant-eye, spotted her talent and has been fostering it enthusiastically ever since. By 1987 she had won her first entry in *The Good Food Guide* which noted her 'honest home cooking' – spiced with a dash of Franco Taruschio, her senior family mentor and close ally.

Throughout these years, and until his untimely death from cancer, John Evans remained the reluctant partner, who preferred his country pursuits over his wife's gastronomic ambition. Nevertheless, he played mine-host with great good humour. In spite of the strains in their marriage, Carole by now was unstoppable and she was not going to let go: 'It's very sad and it's very calculating in a way – but having lost out once, I was succeeding now, and come hell or high water, I was going to stick it out.' When the Roebuck won its greatest prize, the Egon Ronay Pub of the Year Award in January, 1992, John's death weeks later almost seemed like a cruel Nemesis.

Carole Evans's cooking is intriguing in that it has slowly evolved along two parallel tracks which are at once complementary and conflicting. The cultural forces at play divide between her domestic culinary inheritance, which is instinctive, flowing deep in her veins, making her eligible for the title of a modern Mrs Beeton. The newer adopted influences betray her desire to compete on what she perhaps perceives as a loftier culinary playing field. Practically, in the presentation of her dishes, the bar menu tends to address the former, and Poppies Restaurant the latter, with puddings becoming common territory to both sides.

❝ Carole Evans's cooking is intriguing in that it has slowly evolved along two parallel tracks which are at once complementary and conflicting ❞

In a perverse way, the dilemma here is her prodigious talent as a cook. While she does not desert her solidly British roots, her extraordinary mastery of technique sometimes propels her into areas more usually the preserve of the European masters.

The pudding menu graphically illustrates this collision of cultures. Listed with old-fashioned favourites like strawberry shortbread and bread and butter pudding is a caramel pyramid – a brilliant feat of trigonometry – inspired by a visit to Puymirol in south-west France, the seat of the great modern culinary-architect Michel Trama. It took Carole months to perfect this brittle, pale and translucent construction which would comfortably score a three on the Michelin stellar scale. Shimmering beneath the stained glass caramel is the British connection – and the real prize – a spiced brown bread ice cream.

Carole had never visited France in her life – a fact which shocked Richard Binns, whose opinionated guides, *French Leave*, have been an indispensable gastronomic pathfinder to thousands of British tourists. In 1990, Binns drew up an itinerary and faxed half-a-dozen top toques with instructions to give Mrs Evans the benefit of their method. The fax ended with the injunction '*Allez mes amis!!*' so that there could be no doubt about the seriousness of the mission. The trip left its mark – the Trama pyramid being one such outcome.

For my part, I am not sure whether Binns is to be cursed or praised for momentarily luring his protégé away from the kitchen she knows best. Her technique is equally manifest in all that she does on the home front and for me this is where she has the edge – a unique gift, touched by integrity and its own natural invention, which can stand proud without recourse to foreign embellishments. A stunning example of her originality and invention is her ice bowl – an idea redolent of nineteenth century still rooms in English country houses. Fresh flowers and leaves are frozen into moulds – cherry blossom in spring, roses in summer, chrysanthemums in autumn, holly at Christmas – the ice cavities then filled with fruit sorbets according to season. It is a memorable finale to a meal at the Roebuck.

66 Of the new generation of pub-restaurants now proliferating in the wake of the early pioneers . . . Carole Evans is at the top of the league and an outstanding example of the values . . . beginning to democratize eating out in this country 99

At heart, Carole Evans's kitchen bears the hallmarks of Britain's culinary tradition in its purest form and it is very exciting (because it is so rare) to find a cook who seems, apparently quite spontaneously, to have adapted for today the themes and accents which gave British food such an enviable reputation in the eighteenth and early nineteenth centuries.

Spices, pickles, pies, crisp herb toppings and the matching of fruits with meat are just some of the principles she applies with zeal and immense finesse. Nutmeg is a favourite seasoning as it was two hundred years ago when silversmiths fashioned pocket graters as an essential accessory for gentlemen. Carole uses the spice in her mashed potatoes, on spinach and cabbage, in a ragout of asparagus and as one of a mix of seasonings in her home-made pork sausages.

Walnuts, from a tree nearby, are harvested on St Swithin's day – 15th July – and pickled to provide a tart counterpoint to a well-hung fillet of Hereford beef. And chicken livers come plump and pink with peeled grapes and a sherry sauce to foil any lingering fattiness in the offal. There's more. Mrs Evans's pie-making demonstrates the brilliance of those defamed old classics when they are done to perfection. The Roebuck's updated version of the old-fashioned steak and kidney pie is succulent, melting and gently perfumed with ground cloves and oregano, bay and parsley. A chicken pie is moistened with cider, Bramleys and sweet onion – ambrosial provender to seduce and satisfy an Englishman's tum on a cold winter's day.

Right: One of Carole Evans's most popular dishes – Chicken Livers with Peeled Grapes and a Sherry Sauce (recipe page 178)

Of the new generation of pub-restaurants now proliferating in the wake of early pioneers like Franco Taruschio at the Walnut Tree and Richard Smith at the Beetle and Wedge in Moulsford, Carole Evans is at the top of the league and an outstanding example of the values which are beginning to democratize eating out in this country. In spite of the tests and tribulations which have beset her life, it was the good fortune and influence of her early years which laid the foundations of her success today. Her father used to tell his daughter that if a job was worth doing, it should be done well. The Roebuck is a convivial monument to Mr Bowchier's worthy advice.

Chicken Livers

500–750 g/1–1½ lb fresh chicken livers

(hand drawn – must be firm and shiny)

50 g/2 oz clarified butter or olive oil

2 shallots, roughly chopped

4 tablespoons dry amontillado sherry

2 tablespoons tomato purée

150 ml/¼ pint reduced chicken stock

1 teaspoon lemon juice

125 g/4 oz seedless grapes, skinned

1 teaspoon chopped fresh tarragon

4 half rounds of brioche or toast

salt and freshly ground black pepper

chopped fresh flat leaf parsley, to garnish

Trim the chicken livers, removing any veins or tubes. Pat dry on kitchen paper. Heat half the butter or oil in a heavy, non-stick sauté pan until smoking hot. Add half the livers and fry for 2 minutes on each side, until still pink in the middle. Remove and keep warm. Fry the remaining livers in the same way.

To make the sauce, heat the remaining oil or butter in the pan, add the shallots, and cook until softened but not coloured. Add the sherry, tomato purée and stock. Bring to the boil and reduce by half. Taste and adjust the seasoning. add the lemon juice, grapes and tarragon, then heat through.

To serve, place the brioche or toast on 4 heated plates, place the livers on top, pour over the sauce and sprinkle with parsley.

Serves 4

Chicken in Dunkerton's Cider

1 organically raised, free-range chicken,

about 1.75–2 kg/3½–4 lb, jointed

2 bay leaves

6–8 black peppercorns

parsley stalks

1 celery stick

600 ml/1 pint Dunkerton's organic cider,

or other good, dry cider

150 ml/¼ pint water

50 g/2 oz butter

3 onions, chopped

2 Bramley apples, chopped

4 teaspoons flour

150 ml/¼ pint double cream

2 teaspoons dried thyme

puff pastry or pastry of your choice, for lid

egg wash, for brushing

salt and freshly ground black pepper

Place the chicken in a large pan with the bay leaves, peppercorns, parsley stalks, celery, cider and water. Bring to the boil, cover and simmer gently for 1¼ hours. Remove from heat and allow the chicken to cool in its own stock.

When cool, remove the meat from the bone and leave in a cool place, if possible overnight. Strain the stock and spoon off the fat.

Heat the butter in a pan, add the onions and cook gently. Add the apples and flour, and stir gently until the flour is well cooked. Add the stock and bring to the boil.

Add the chicken pieces, then add the cream, thyme, salt and pepper. Brush the edge of the pie dish with egg wash. Cut a narrow strip of pastry, and press around to form a collar. Brush with egg wash. Roll out a pastry lid, place on top, then roll with a rolling pin. Set aside to rest for 10 minutes. Do not make a hole in the top. Decorate the lid with pastry leaves, trim off any overlapping pastry with a sharp knife, keeping the knife upright to get a good edge. Brush with egg wash. Sea salt can also be placed on the leaves for a decorative effect.

Place in preheated oven at 200°C (400°F) Gas Mark 6, for about 20–30 minutes, until the top is well browned.

Serves 4-6

Old-fashioned Steak and Kidney Pie

500 g/1 lb ox kidney, halved and cored

1 kg/2 lb chuck steak, cut in 2.5 cm/1 inch dice

125 g/4 oz plain flour, well seasoned with

salt and freshly ground black pepper

groundnut oil, for frying

3 large onions, sliced

about 600 ml/1 pint home-made beef stock

½ teaspoon ground cloves

1 bay leaf

1 tablespoon chopped fresh parsley

1 tablespoon chopped fresh marjoram

puff pastry or pastry of your choice, for lid

egg wash, for brushing

Cut the kidney into 1 cm/½ inch pieces and soak in cold water for 1 hour or overnight, changing the water once. Drain and pat dry.

Roll the steak in seasoned flour and shake off any excess. Heat the oil in a frying pan, add the steak and fry in batches, stirring constantly until well browned, then place in a casserole. Fry the onions until golden, then add to the casserole. Add extra oil to the pan, seal the kidneys, then add to the casserole.

Moisten with beef stock, add the ground cloves and herbs and stir. Cook in a preheated oven at 190°C (375°F) Gas Mark 5 for 1 hour, then stir. Continue cooking for another hour, until the meat is tender. Skim off any excess fat, then cool and skim again. Place in a pie dish or individual dishes.

Roll out the pastry and cut strips about 2.5 cm/1 inch wide to go around the top of the pie dish or dishes. Brush egg wash around the rim, press a strip of pastry around the edge and brush again. Place an egg cup or pie funnel in the middle of the dish, then place on the lid of pastry. Press the edges to seal. Decorate with pastry leaves, and brush with egg wash again. (If using shortcrust or flaky pastry, make a slit in the lid to allow steam to escape. Do not make a slit if using puff.) Cook in a preheated oven at 200°C (400°F) Gas Mark 6 for 20 minutes, or until the pastry is well browned.

Serves 4

Ice Bowls filled with Sorbet and Ice Cream

---

4 plastic 150 ml/¼ pint basins

4 plastic 300 ml/½ pint basins

sellotape (sticky tape)

flowers, holly, herbs or fruit

To serve:

lime sorbet and raspberry ice cream

cat's tongue biscuits

Place the smaller basin inside the larger one, and stick sellotape over the top and down the side to form a cross.

Gently push the flowers between the two basins, using a pointed instrument. Arrange them in a pattern, but do not use too many.

Half-fill the cavity with water and place in a deep freeze. When frozen, fill the water to the top of the ice bowl and the flowers will remain in place (otherwise the flowers float to the top of the cavity and leave the bottom bare). Return to the freezer and store until required.

Ice bowls are practical in summer, as they keep the sorbets from melting too quickly. At Christmas, they look wonderful made with holly and filled with redcurrant and raspberry sorbet.

When ready to serve, remove from the freezer and run cold water into the small basin and the two will part, leaving an ice bowl. Place the bowl on a plate with a small doily, to stop it sliding, and place sorbets or ice creams in the middle. Serve with cat's tongue biscuits.

Serves 4

Caramel Pyramid

with a Spiced Brown Bread Ice Cream

——

200 g/7 oz sugar

75 ml/3 fl oz water

Spiced Brown Bread Ice Cream:

250 g/8 oz brown breadcrumbs

250 g/8 oz demerara sugar

ground cinnamon, to taste

malted wheat grains (optional)

600 ml/1 pint whipping cream

2 tablespoons brandy

Caramel Sauce:

250 g/8 oz caster sugar

3 tablespoons water

125 g/4 oz butter

150 ml/¼ pint double cream

To serve:

12 slices of banana, 1 cm/½ inch thick

icing sugar, for dusting

150 ml/¼ pint raspberry coulis

150 ml/¼ pint crème anglaise

To make the 16 templates for the 4-sided pyramids, draw 16 triangles, with 20 cm/8 inch bases and 38 cm/15 inch sides, on grease-proof paper with a black marker pen. Turn over and place on a non-stick baking sheet.

To make the caramel, dissolve the sugar in the water over low heat. Increase the heat and boil until the sugar is dark golden brown. Lift off the heat and spread in a thin layer on the baking sheet, using a palette knife. Score along the lines with a sharp knife as the sugar cools and sets. When set, break along the marked lines very carefully. Store between greaseproof paper in an airtight container for up to 12 hours.

To make the ice cream, spread the crumbs on a roasting tin, add the sugar, cinnamon and wheat grains, if using. Toast in the oven until brown and crunchy, turning every 10 minutes. Remove and set aside to cool.

Break up the bread and sugar, add to the whipping cream and churn in a sorbetière until thick. Add the brandy and churn for 2 minutes. Do not overchurn, or the ice cream will curdle. Remove and freeze. Place in the refrigerator for 10 minutes before serving.

To make the caramel sauce, place the sugar in a dry, heavy-based pan, dissolve slowly and cook to a golden caramel. Remove from the heat, cool for a few minutes, then add the water, but be careful of the hissing steam.

Return to the heat, add the butter, and cook over a low heat until thoroughly mixed. Cool, then stir in the double cream. Store for up to 5 days in an airtight container in the refrigerator.

To prepare the banana, place the slices on a metal tray and dust liberally with icing sugar. Flame with a blowtorch until golden.

To assemble, place 2 walnut-sized balls of ice cream, one on top of the other, on each plate. Place 1 teaspoon of caramel sauce on top and encase in 4 triangles of caramel to form a pyramid. Decorate with 3 slices of banana, a spoonful of raspberry coulis and a drizzle of thin *crème anglaise*.

Serves 4

Tessa Bramley

Tessa Bramley is the picture of everyone's favourite country aunt. She is cuddly and plump; her cheeks glisten like a pair of ripe peaches and when she laughs her eyes close and crinkle merrily. But Mrs Bramley's bosomy warmth and kindliness disguise a grittier side to her nature – and if she had not rebelled as a teenager, England might have lost one of the most indigenously inspired cooks of her generation and possibly one of the last to draw directly from a tradition rooted in the principles of Cobbett's *Cottage Economy* and the practices of the landed classes of the Victorian and Edwardian eras.

At school, Tessa Hardwick was marked as a potential scholar, but to the consternation of her headmistress and her father, she refused to go to university. Tessa had other ideas. She wanted to cook for a living. If she had behaved like any other obedient daughter of that time, one can only speculate as to what might have become of her. Articulate and unequivocal in her opinions about life, she would have made a formidable politician in the Thatcherite mould. She might even have taught Norman Tebbit a thing or two about riding bicycles. 'I have always believed that people did not get things by right but had things because they got off their backsides and worked for them,' she explains, pouring scorn on airy liberals who confuse duty with their 'rights'. In 1960, as a

twenty-one-year-old domestic science teacher in Sheffield and the youngest member of staff, she objected angrily to the teachers' strike. 'If any of you had to make a living in the real world, you'd starve,' she told a packed meeting. This is the measure of Tessa Bramley's backbone.

Self-reliance is more than a central nostrum in this remarkable woman's personal outlook on life, it is embedded in her family background and it underpins the direction of her kitchen. Tessa Bramley is not just a good cook, she is in a state of complete union with her garden, and with the farms, fields and woodland which surround her home and provision her restaurant at the Old Vicarage in Ridgeway, a mid-Victorian manse overlooking the Moss Valley, some ten minutes' drive south-east of Sheffield. With the exception of fish, one is left with the impression that it is only out of desperation that she resorts to specialist suppliers like Vin Sullivan in Abergavenny. Tessa was born in Gleadless, two miles from Ridgeway, and she grew up here. She is a child of this parish and she has never been entirely comfortable away from home. 'I only felt I was with real people and that the air was clean when I got to Chesterfield,' she says of a year spent at college in London.

The wellspring for this communion with home and rural neighbourhood, and the seminal force which laid the foundations for Tessa Bramley's kitchen came from her grandmother, Sarah Hardwick. Widowed young and left with a three-year-old lad to raise (Tessa's father), Sarah went into service as a parlourmaid in some of Sheffield's grandest houses. In the Forties and Fifties, Sarah – now long retired – lived in a cottage in Hollins End, a short walk across the fields from Gleadless, where the Hardwicks kept a drapery store and lived over the shop with their three children; Tessa, and her younger brother and sister.

At weekends the children would love visiting their grandmother. 'These marvellous smells would come from the cottage as we walked up the hill,' Tessa recalls, 'and inside the aromas would hang in the atmosphere. I knew then that I wanted to have something to do with cooking.'

In spite of the exigencies of war and the austerity that followed, the Hardwick family, like most country folk, lived and ate well on the strength of their native resourcefulness as hunters, trappers, foragers and growers, and by the simple expedient of barter and exchange. No one knew better how to use the fruits of the land than Sarah, and she had a willing pupil in her granddaughter. She cooked on an old-fashioned open range and Tessa learned how to prepare chickens, rabbits and pigeons for casseroles and pies.

The traditional ritual of killing a pig in the village before Christmas would have been applauded by William Cobbett, and Tessa Bramley's vivid recollection of her grandmother's cellar where she cured the bacon – 'well lit, airy, cool' – uncannily echoes Cobbett's instructions: 'The place for salting should, like a dairy, always be cool, but always admit a free circulation of air . . .' Pickling was another essential part of Sarah's pre-Christmas preparations, and her cellar would be lined with dozens of jars of pickled red cabbage, onions and cauliflower.

In the warmer months, rosehip, elderflowers and berries gathered from the hedgerows and fields for syrups, cordials, jams and jellies all contributed to Tessa's education. In Sarah's cottage garden, she picked a profusion of herbs, and learned to appreciate their uses. So too for spices. Tessa would be dispatched to the chemist to buy whole nutmegs for rice puddings and egg custards, and her grandmother would tick her off for chewing the ends of the cinnamon sticks she used for baking and in casseroles.

> **" Tessa Bramley is not just a good cook, she is in a state of complete union with her garden, and with the farms, fields and woodlands which surround her home and provision her restaurant "**

Meal times were always an event which observed its own particular ceremonial. Sarah had been well schooled as a young parlourmaid and, on Saturday and Sunday afternoons, she assumed some of the fancy ways she had seen in the big houses of her former employers. Tea was held in the parlour where Sarah lit a fire in winter. Everything would be spick and span. In the morning Tessa would trim the wicks for the gas lights and polish all the ruby glass. A beautiful Chinese screen stood in a corner of the room and treasured ornaments rested on hand-crocheted doilies. Sarah's special china and silver Apostle spoons would be laid out before her and, as she poured the tea, the eyes of her three grandchildren would gaze in wonder at the tiered cake-stand by her side. On it there would be a Dundee cake, a spice loaf and the little maids of honour which Tessa helped to make.

Half a century on, the Old Vicarage at Ridgeway is a Proustian tribute to Sarah Hardwick. 'In many ways, I suppose I am recapturing my youth,' admits Tessa Bramley. 'It was a very fulfilling and exciting time in my life.'

The sense of times past is pervasive from the moment you turn into the drive and set eyes on the Gothic revivalist features of the house. When you park, there can be no illusion where the heart of the kitchen lies. The car park is bordered by a kitchen garden, greenhouses and a small orchard. An ancient pear tree, its

espalier long forsaken, reaches up the wall of an outbuilding, arms flailing like a crooked man, and a huge bushy bay stands symbolically by the vaulted porch.

When I visited this pocket of rural Derbyshire on a dank and misty November afternoon, the sound of guns reverberated across the valley. Peter Ward, a local landowner, and his friends were shooting partridge. As I wandered round the gardens of the Old Vicarage, its grounds strewn with fallen leaves, I suddenly became aware that I had company. A platoon of partridges had taken cover on the croquet lawn. These birds are nimble creatures and within seconds they had scurried through a hedge, disappearing like manic midges into the fields beyond. The delicious irony of this little episode is that at dinner a few hours later I sat down to eat one of Mr Ward's excellent birds.

Inside the house the atmosphere is warm and homely – the smell of woodsmoke coming from a crackling fire in the drawing room. Again, the feeling of that other time is palpable; a Victorian *chaise longue* against the bay window, an ornate bell-pull hanging beside the fireplace, lace cloths and crocheted mats. In the dining room, the walls are hung with gilt-framed pictures, and silver candlesticks sparkle on the tables. And, on the staircase, a teddy bear sits glumly in a beautifully crafted nursery chair – a gift to Sarah from a grateful employer.

The spirit of the Old Vicarage, its ethos of self-sufficiency and its alliance with the natural rhythms of land and season differ little from life in a country house a hundred years ago. The only incongruity lies in the modern reality of such places, where your hosts and the senior servants happen to be the same people. While Tessa Bramley minds the kitchen, the role of butler falls to Andrew, her son, a tall, elegant and earnest young man with a striking resemblance to Jeremy Irons. The Old Vicarage is very much a family enterprise. But the pause between the formative experiences of Tessa's youth and the realization of her dreams in 1987 was long and eventful.

After the famous show-down with her headmistress, Tessa Hardwick agreed to submit to three years of teacher training in home economics – thereby appeasing the father she adored, without denying her own desire to cook. But, as we have seen, Tessa's early excursion into the world of teaching was not entirely harmonious. Her next adventure – with Findus Frozen Foods – also brought her into conflict with her superiors. Her brief was to demonstrate the virtues of the company's products in supermarkets, but this independently-minded young woman preferred to extemporize on her portable stove. The idea of cooking fish fingers did not appeal. Instead, she demonstrated the art of making exotic risottos and – as an afterthought – she incorporated the occasional frozen briquette.

By 1963 Tessa had had enough. Besides, the age of Carnaby Street and Swinging London had spread north, and our sassy heroine was looking for a bit of fun. She joined a new all-female sales force set up by Sutherlands, manufacturers of potted meats and fish spreads, fitted herself out with bright red boots and a mini-skirt, and dashed around the country in a smart company car fluttering her long false eyelashes at unsuspecting store managers. Not only did she have 'a good laff', she also ended up as Sutherlands' top salesperson. But no sooner had Tessa's peripatetic life begun than a chance encounter with another high-flying rep on Grimsby pier led to romance and, in 1965, she was married to Peter Bramley, the sales manager for a drugs company.

The couple settled near Dronfield – barely a three-mile crow's flight from Ridgeway – and a year later Andrew was born. For the next fifteen years Tessa took care of home and family. But she

" The spirit of the Old Vicarage . . . the natural rhythms of land and season differ little from life in a country house a hundred years ago "

was never idle and there were moments when the Bramley nest was transformed into a minia ture industrial estate for the manufacture of trendy novelties – all the product of Tessa's fertile imagination and artistic energy. She started with stuffed pigs for children to use as pouffes. Then she began to import materials from Hong Kong to make silk flowers – either in individual stems or as decorative arrangements.

The key to the extraordinary success of these cottage ventures lay with Peter who, by now, was in the business of selling hairdressing products for Wella, and later Clairol. He and his motor car were the sales force and means of distribution to the salons in the north of England – and they all fell for Tessa's wily crafts with a passion. Peter's employers were equally seduced and on one occasion Clairol commissioned an order for five thousand silk flower arrangements as an incentive offer to their customers.

In 1981, an unhappy career move for Peter forced the family to rethink the future. 'Something in cooking' had always been an option simmering quietly at the back of their minds, and Tessa's talent for throwing dinner parties, combined with Peter's marketing nous, persuaded them to have a go at running their own coffee-shop-cum-bistro in Sheffield. In August the same year, the Bramleys opened Toffs just off one of the city's principal shopping centres and close by a con-centration of office buildings. Their formula was simple but clever. Toffs was to be a daytime café which exuded an image of freshness and light – its sharp white decor softened by a forest of greenery – and the food would be wholesome and homemade. To prove the point, Tessa moved into the shop window in the early morning, decorating her cakes in full view of the shoppers and

commuters who streamed past. Crowds gathered to watch and by lunch time the same people were queuing up to get in. When *The Good Food Guide* eventually discovered Toffs, its enthusiastic notice began with a sigh of relief: 'At last,' wrote the editor, 'some Real Food in Sheffield.'

Tessa's menus were a mixture of ancient and modern, from soused herrings and casseroles *à la grandmère* to voguish salads with exotic fruits and vegetarian items. But the big sellers were her quiches and, by 1985, she was getting bored with the grinding labour and monotony of a production line which could barely keep pace with the voracious demand. By now, Andrew had also joined their burgeoning enterprise and the family decided to begin the search for a serious restaurant, a place they could call home and a quality of life which had become elusive in the city centre.

It took two years to find and restore the Old Vicarage. In the meantime, Peter, Tessa and Andrew went into rehearsal by opening Toffs for dinner on Friday and Saturday evenings – a successful exercise in itself which confirmed their enthusiasm for moving up-market.

In the spring of 1987, with a yellow tide of daffodils lining the approach to the house, the Bramleys received their first guests. Tessa – now in her late forties – had at last fulfilled her childhood dream. Two-and-a-half years later, just before Christmas, the vision she now shared with her family was shattered with Peter's death at the age of fifty-four. While the tragedy affected mother and son deeply, it never diminished their resolve, and the Old Vicarage today has blossomed into one of Britain's most fêted restaurants.

Writing in the *Guardian*, Tom Jaine – editor of *The Good Food Guide* at the time – defined Tessa Bramley's style as 'the British answer to French imperialism . . . the home kitchen facing up to the elegant refinement of the restaurant'. The aura of Sarah Hardwick and her stone cottage in Hollins End continues to glow, and remains the inspiration at the core of Tessa's cooking. There may be fashionable twists and modern conventions in presentation and some executions – but the bedrock is grandmother and menus

“ Her message is as clear as a bell: there is a British way – and it is exciting, versatile and as noble as the rest ”

are dictated by the seasons, the garden and the land. Her recipes are a fascinating conspiracy between her intellect, an acute culinary sensibility and timing. She talks about her own 'vocabulary of flavours': how it germinates in the mind and evolves with the passage of the year. As the seasons change, so do her feelings and gustatory senses. As autumn turns to winter, so she thinks of stronger flavours – of spice and of woodsmoke. She also knows that the Old Vicarage is in the 'special occasion' trade. Her visitors have high expectations and Tessa's natural invention is capable of being wilfully contemporary in its old-fashioned ways.

A simple pork fillet smoked over the woody stems of sage and served with spiced plums scored with an Italianate theme. The meat rests on a rich dollop of creamed polenta, and an arrangement of broccoli buds and prunes is seasoned with crispy pancetta and toasted pine nuts. This is an ambitious composition delivered with great precision and gusto – the waves of contrasting flavours and textures breaking over the senses, piano and fortissimo like Pavarotti in full flight. By the end of the aria you feel quite exhausted.

Classicism reverts to a purer form in other winter productions. Tessa Bramley's braised oxtails are the business; slow, slow cooked and served on the bone, the succulent meat – touched by a hint of cinnamon and clove – just falls away on your fork. Mr Ward's famous partridges – perfectly hung – are plain-roasted, delicately gamey. Tessa presents them with forcemeat balls (very English, very eighteenth century) and a compote of blueberries and shallots. The base for the compote is a crystal jelly made from the crab apples in her garden and, typically, it is used as a stock item for a variety of herb, flower or fruit preparations to match with meats and game.

In the spring and summer months, the versatility of Tessa Bramley's repertoire is unusual and astonishing. She is self-sufficient in herbs, often using their flowers in her cooking. Lavender is roasted with quail and she scatters the tiny flowers of chives, oregano and borage in her salads. Tessa also gathers an abundance of wild flowers which grow in the surrounding woodland and countryside; sweet woodruff to make ice cream, and wild violets to crystallize for decoration on her chocolate puddings.

From her beguiling and utterly seductive sauces to the crumbling, light and melting sweet-ness of her pastry, there is so much in the detail of Tessa Bramley's kitchen that it is impossible to do her full justice in these pages. The recipes will speak for themselves. Throughout, the ring of her childhood experience is almost deafening and, at last, her work has been properly celebrated in a book – *The Instinctive Cook* – which was published in the spring of 1995. She already writes a column for the *Yorkshire Post* and more books are an inevitability. Tessa Bramley has a lot to say, and the theme at the heart of her message is clear as a bell: there is a British way – and it is excit-ing, versatile and as noble as the rest.

Meanwhile, at the Old Vicarage, there are two Egon Ronay stars and a reputation to guard. Mother and son are here to stay and there is planning permission for the construction of eight bed-rooms. But the big debate between the two is Andrew's future role and whether or not he will hang up his double-breasted suits in favour of a set of kitchen whites.

Roast Fillet of Cod,

with a Garlic and Herb Crust

——

4 thick cod fillets, about 250 g/8 oz, skinned

125 g/4 oz prosciutto, cut into batons

olive oil (see method)

12 whole garlic cloves

a little milk (see method)

1 teaspoon sugar

15 g/½ oz butter

250 g/8 oz spinach leaves

Herb Crust:

50 g/2 oz fresh white breadcrumbs

finely grated zest of 2 lemons

2 large cups chopped, parsley

1 tablespoon chopped fresh chives

2 crushed garlic cloves

3 tablespoons extra-virgin olive oil

salt and freshly ground black pepper

Tomato and Herb Dressing:

150 ml/¼ pint extra virgin olive oil

25 ml/1 fl oz white wine vinegar

2 fresh bay leaves, torn in half

a handful of fresh chives, torn

2–3 parsley stalks

a strip of lemon zest

1 red pepper, skinned, deseeded and

roughly chopped

1 teaspoon salt

1½ teaspoons sugar

freshly ground black pepper

10 tomatoes, deseeded

3 large sprigs of fresh basil

Place the first 10 dressing ingredients into a large bowl with 8 of the tomatoes, roughly chopped. Mash roughly with a wooden spoon. Leave in the refrigerator overnight to infuse.

The next day, using a ladle, press through a coarse sieve to form a thickish dressing. Finely dice the remaining 2 tomatoes. Finely shred the basil leaves.

When ready to use, heat the dressing gently, whisking well to emulsify. Add the diced tomatoes and basil just before serving.

To make the crust, mix the breadcrumbs with the lemon zest, herbs, garlic and seasoning, then stir in the olive oil until the crumb mixture holds together.

Make horizontal slits in the cod with a sharp knife and insert a piece of prosciutto in each slit. Press the crumbs thickly and firmly on to the top of each fillet. Place, crumb-side up, in a roasting tin and drizzle with olive oil.

Roast in a preheated oven at 230°C (450°F) Gas Mark 8 for about 4–5 minutes, depending on the thickness of the cod. The crust should be crisp and golden, and the fish just oozing a milky whiteness.

Blanch the garlic in milk 3 times, discarding the milk each time. Place the garlic in a small roasting pan, sprinkle with sugar and a drizzle of olive oil and roast until golden.

Heat a little butter in a pan, and quickly wilt the washed spinach. Season lightly.

To serve, set the spinach on serving plates and place the cod on top. Pour the hot dressing around and scatter over the roasted garlic.

Serves 4

Sage-smoked Pork Fillet on Polenta

---

2 pork fillets, well trimmed

25 g/1 oz butter

6–7 stems of fresh sage

a little olive oil

Polenta:

1 small onion, finely chopped

1 fat garlic clove, crushed

600 ml/1 pint milk

300 ml/½ pint single cream

2 tablespoons chopped mixed fresh herbs,

including thyme, sage, chives and

a little rosemary

2 tablespoons chopped fresh flat leaf parsley

½ packet of quick-cook polenta

2–3 tablespoons double cream

salt and freshly ground black pepper

Broccoli and Pancetta:

12 strips of pancetta

2 tablespoons extra-virgin olive oil

2 tablespoons pine nuts

12 pitted prunes, roughly chopped

2 heads of broccoli, broken into florets

Make stock with the pork trimmings and reduce until syrupy and well-flavoured. Strain and finish by whisking butter into the stock just before serving.

To cook the polenta, put the onion, garlic, milk and cream in a large pan.. Bring to the boil and cook until the onion is softened. Add the herbs. Stirring briskly, add the polenta in a steady stream. Beat well until smooth. Cook over a low heat, stirring all the time, for about 5 minutes, until the mixture resembles fluffy mashed potato. If the mixture appears too stiff, beat in extra milk. Taste and adjust the seasoning: it should taste herby and slightly sweet. Beat in a little double cream at the last minute and keep warm.

To cook the pork, place the smoker over the gas or electric hob. Strew the rack with sage and heat until a steady stream of smoke is given off. Reduce the heat to keep the smoke constant.

Sit the seasoned fillets on the wire rack and replace the lid. Smoke on one side for 3 minutes. Turn the fillets and smoke on the second side for 3 minutes. Remove from the smoker.

Place the sage in a roasting tin. Brush the fillets with olive oil and place on top of the sage. Roast in a preheated oven at 230°C (450°F) Gas Mark 8 for 5 minutes, then set aside to rest in a warm place for 5–10 minutes.

Cook the pancetta in a dry frying pan until very crisp. Remove from the pan, and add the olive oil. When hot, add the pine nuts and cook until golden. Add the prunes and allow to plump up in the oil. Remove. Add the broccoli and stir-fry until cooked. Stir in the pine nuts and the prunes. Season lightly and sprinkle with the crisp pancetta.

To serve, place the polenta on heated dinner plates. Slice each pork fillet diagonally and arrange overlapping slices over the polenta with a little sauce poured round and the broccoli and pancetta beside.

Serves 4

Roast English Partridge

with Forcemeat Balls and a Cake of Celeriac Purée

—

4 greyleg English partridge, properly hung

4 shallots, diced

1 carrot, diced

1 leek, diced

150 ml/¼ pint brown chicken or game stock

150 ml/¼ pint red wine

1 bouquet garni

1 tablespoon dry (sercial) Madeira

3-4 juniper berries, crushed

8 small sprigs of fresh thyme

50 g/2 oz unsalted butter,

plus extra to finish the sauce

250 g/8 oz spinach, wilted in a little butter

salt and freshly ground black pepper

Forcemeat Balls:

½ pork fillet, about 175 g/6 oz, well trimmed

175 g/6 oz game or chicken livers

25 g/1 oz fresh white breadcrumbs

1 shallot

1 tablespoon fresh thyme leaves

2 tablespoons chopped fresh parsley

1 tablespoon chopped fresh chives

1 dessert apple, peeled, cored and finely diced

2 teaspoons plain flour

2 tablespoons olive oil

salt and freshly ground black pepper

Celeriac Purée:

225 g/8 oz peeled potatoes

500 g/1 lb peeled celeriac

grated nutmeg, to taste

50 g/2 oz unsalted butter

salt and freshly ground white pepper

Blueberry and Shallot Compote:

2 tablespoons olive oil

500 g/1 lb small shallots or pickling onions

1 tablespoon white wine vinegar

1 tablespoon dry sherry

1 teaspoon caster sugar

2.5 cm/1 inch root ginger, peeled and grated

2 tablespoons apple or crab-apple jelly

zest from 1 large orange, blanched

125 g/4 oz fresh blueberries

To make the blueberry compote, heat the oil in pan, add the shallots or onions and cook until lightly coloured. Add the wine vinegar, sherry, sugar and ginger, shaking the pan. Continue cooking for 4–5 minutes, until almost tender. Add the jelly and orange zest and cook through. Add the blueberries at last moment – do not allow to cook – and serve immediately.

To make the forcemeat, chop the pork, livers, breadcrumbs, shallot and seasoning very finely in a food processor. Stir in the herbs and diced apple. Fry a small piece of the forcemeat in a pan, taste and adjust the seasoning. Form into walnut-sized balls and roll in the flour. Just before serving, heat the olive oil in a pan and fry the forcemeat balls until golden.

Remove the partridge legs at the hip joint. Place the legs in a casserole or roasting tin, add the diced vegetables, stock, red wine, bouquet garni, Madeira and juniper berries. Bring to the boil, then place in a preheated oven at 180°C (350°F) Gas Mark 4 for 45 minutes, until the skin is glossy and the legs tender (test with the tip of a knife). Keep warm until ready to serve.

Make an incision each side of the breast-bones and tuck in little sprigs of fresh thyme. Lift the skin away from the breast and smear a little unsalted butter under the skin. Season.

Heat the remaining butter in a heavy-based pan, sear the breasts on both sides, then sit them on their sides in a roasting tin.

Place in a preheated oven at 220°C (425°F) Gas Mark 7 for 5–6 minutes. Turn over and continue roasting for a further 5 minutes. Remove and rest in a warm place for 5 minutes.

Meanwhile, cook the potatoes with two-thirds of the celeriac. Mash, beat in the nutmeg and half the butter, and check the seasoning. Form into small cakes and fry in the remaining butter until crusty and golden. Keep hot.

Cut the remaining celeriac into fine julienne. Stir-fry quickly in butter, until crisp. Season.

Strain the cooking liquid from the leg, reduce by half and whisk in a little butter. Remove the breasts from the carcasses.

Place the legs and forcemeat balls on heated dinner plates. Arrange the celeriac julienne in the centre with the breasts on top, the sauce spooned around, and the celeriac cake to one side. Serve with spinach and blueberry compote.

Serves 4

Caramelized and Glazed Apple Tarts

———

1½ teaspoons lemon juice

2 tablespoons iced water

1 egg

250 g/8 oz plain flour

1 teaspoon icing sugar

½ teaspoon salt

75 g/3 oz cooking fat, chilled

75 g/3 oz butter, chilled

Apple Purée:

2 Bramley apples,
peeled, cored and sliced

1 tablespoon water

1½ tablespoons caster sugar

1 twist of lemon zest

1 tablespoon Calvados

Pastry Cream:

½ split vanilla pod

300 ml/½ pint single cream

2 egg yolks

1 tablespoon plain flour

⅓ teaspoon cornflour

1 tablespoon caster sugar

Apple Topping:

1 tablespoon water

1 tablespoon caster sugar

40 g/1½ oz butter

4 Cox's apples,
peeled, cored and thinly sliced

To make the pastry, beat the lemon juice, water and egg and chill until thickened.

Sieve the dry ingredients, then rub in the fat and butter. Add all the liquid and stir until the mixture binds into a loose dough. Turn out and knead lightly until smooth. Wrap and chill for 30 minutes.

Line 4 individual fluted tart tins with one-third of the pastry. Bake blind in a preheated oven at 180°C (350°F) Gas Mark 5 for about 20 minutes. Cool.

To make the apple purée, stew the Bramleys gently in a heavy-based pan with the water, sugar and lemon zest until the apples fall to a froth. Continue cooking to a dry, thick purée. Add the Calvados, then taste for sweetness.

To make the pastry cream, scrape the vanilla seeds into the cream, add the pod, then bring the cream to the boil. Blend the yolks, flour, cornflour and sugar in a bowl. Gradually whisk the hot cream on to the yolks, return to the rinsed pan and cook gently, stirring, until thickened. Place buttered greaseproof paper or clingfilm on top to prevent a skin forming.

To cook the apple topping, heat the water, sugar and butter in a pan until dissolved. Bring to the boil. Add the apple slices and cook for 2–3 minutes until soft and coated with syrup.

Fill the tart bases with pastry cream and add 1 tablespoon of apple purée. Overlap the apple slices on top. Bake in a preheated oven at 220°C (425°F) Gas Mark 7 for 7–8 minutes until the edges are a deep golden caramel.

Top with a tiny bay leaf, dredge gently with sieved icing sugar, and serve with a scoop of cinnamon ice cream and a hot caramel sauce.

Serves 4

Paul Heathcote

'Nothing has been achieved in Lancashire without a fight against climate and circumstance: with all its graciousness it is not an easy county in which to work and live. Perhaps it is because of this we are known for our hard heads . . . We love a fight and admire a fighter. "He's a good plucked 'un" is the highest compliment we can pay a man.'

These words, written by Sylvia Lovat Corbridge in her book *It's an Old Lancashire Custom*, could not be more true of the life of Paul Heathcote. Lancashire honours its heroes and Heathcote is rapidly becoming something of a local legend. It is rare for a week to pass without his bright, genial features beaming off the pages of the *Lancashire Evening Post*. Mrs Nelson, who keeps a B&B in Knowle Green, has filled a scrapbook with his press cuttings and her house is like a shrine to the great chef with displays of his arty brochures and publicity hand-outs in her bedrooms and hall. 'He puts a lot back in, does our Paul,' says Mrs N, talking proudly of Heathcote's charity work, his visits to schools and his cookery classes.

Paul Heathcote opened his eponymous restaurant in Longridge near Preston on Friday, 13th July, 1990. He is not a superstitious man but the date could hardly have been less propitious. The national economy was nosediving, he had sunk all his assets and savings into the business, interest rates were running at eighteen per cent and he had taken on borrowings of over £200,000. Not least, the location he chose for his brand of supergrade cooking was about as promising as an oil strike in the Ribble Valley. Twelve days later, in the early hours of 25th July, Heathcote sat on the bonnet of his car watching incredulously as his place went up in flames. Mercifully, the fire brigade made quick work of the blaze, which had been caused by a gas leak in the kitchen and, within forty-eight hours, an adrenaline-fuelled chef, aided by all his staff and an electrician, succeeded in reopening the restaurant. But it took Heathcote another four weeks to recover from the shock. For the first time in his life he started walking in his sleep, stalking his stoves every night, occasionally waking up on the kitchen floor.

In January 1994, just three-and-a-half years on, Michelin awarded Heathcote's two stars, pitching the restaurant among the top ten in Britain and installing its chef on a pedestal as lofty as his teacher, Raymond Blanc. Paul Heathcote is 'a good plucked 'un' by any standard. He is a man who comes from an extraordinary family – and one which might explain the nature of his phenomenal drive and energy.

Like many of his kind, great-grandfather Heathcote settled in Lancashire from Ireland bringing 'a certain reputation' in his wake. Joe, his son, was a miner who supplemented his income as a prize-fighter until he broke his back in a tragic pit accident from which he emerged the sole survivor. In his late fifties, Joe also survived two strokes and, at the age of sixty-three, he started to run marathons before going on to compete in a number of European veterans' races. He is now in his eighties and still works out every day in his son's health studio in Bolton. Ken Heathcote, Paul's father, is no less of a star. Junior Mr North-West 1965 and a brickie by trade, he turned body-building into a business with the health studio and regularly hit the headlines with his spectacular feats of endurance on the steps of Bolton Town Hall. In his mid-forties, he even attempted to run the nine hundred miles from Land's End to John o' Groats in ten days. After six hundred and seventy miles he was forced to retire injured, but he succeeded in collecting £25,000 for charity and forty minutes of national television coverage for his pains.

The male line in this family history reeks of machismo to the point of fanaticism. Some four generations on, Paul Heathcote is no less robust and driven but the manic streak seems to have worked itself out of the system. His restaurant walls are smothered with the trophies, engraved china and certificates of his success, but the only other visible symbol of his ego is parked outside on the forecourt, a white-upholstered blue BMW coupé which appears to bear the legend M1 CHEF on the registration plate. In fact the C is an 0 with a stud carefully bolted

ʕʕ Lancashire honours its heroes – and Heathcote is rapidly becoming something of a local legend ʔʔ

midway down the right-hand perpendicular of the letter. It is a harmless affecta-
tion. When you meet Heathcote, what impresses is the genuine niceness of the
man, his warmth and boyish enthusiasm, and an easy modesty which at once is
not shy of acknowledging his achievements. He is a brilliant self-publicist and his
friend Terry Laybourne teasingly calls him 'the other Paul' – a reference to Bocuse
in Lyon. But, in character, Heathcote's model
(and great hero) is Richard Branson. It is an
intriguing and strikingly apt comparison, in
spite of the very different social backgrounds of
the two men.

" His debt to Blanc is enormous . . . he has deep affection for him "

Paul Heathcote was born in October, 1960, and for most of his childhood
he and his sister Karen lived in the family's two-up-two-down terrace on Kildare
Street, New Bury, a seamy district south of Bolton. Like the rest in the street, the
house came with a small backyard and an outside lavatory. 'New Bury's a place
you don't walk through at night,' says Heathcote. 'Even a dog's no use because
it'll get killed. My aunty's got through five. It's that rough.'

By the time Paul had reached his teens, and with the growing success of the
Bolton Health Studio, his mother applied a little feminine pressure on her husband
to move the family into the more gentrified surroundings of Bromley Cross to the
north of the town. 'My mum wanted better for us,' he says, adding mischievously
that if his mother had the choice, she would like to have seen his sister married to
a solicitor.

Heathcote's earliest experiments at a stove began in the home. Both parents
worked extremely hard and it was not unusual for their son to cook for his father
at night if his mother was hosting a ladies' evening at the health club. At school
– where he earned a notorious reputation as a fighter – Paul pleaded with his
headmaster to allow him to take domestic science but the option was denied in
favour of chemistry, which he loathed.

At sixteen, Heathcote left school with one decision firmly fixed in his mind.
By now his father had become a local celebrity and it was assumed that Paul would
follow him in the business. 'Much as I admired him,' he says, 'I did not want to
be known as Ken Heathcote's son.' From the outset, Heathcote junior's attitude to
his future was going to be independent and
utterly singleminded. He knew what he wanted
and he set himself personal goals which he was

determined to achieve. But for all his youthful zeal, he was also headstrong and naïve. After a three-year catering course at Bolton Tech., Heathcote took a dud job in Lockerbie which at least taught him the sort of place where he should not be working. He called home and the shout for help led to a lunch meeting between father and son at a point midway between Bolton and Lockerbie – at Sharrow Bay on Lake Ullswater.

'That day changed my life,' Paul Heathcote muses, recalling every detail of his first visit to Francis Coulson and Brian Sack's famous Cumbrian retreat. The young man was spellbound by the warmth of his greeting from the staff, by the exquisiteness of the food and by the ornamentation of the house (and even its loos) with its antiques and artefacts, which glittered like Aladdin's cave.

Over the next two years, Heathcote posted eight letters to Francis Coulson asking for a job and he received eight more by return politely refusing his requests. In the autumn of 1981, while he was working in Switzerland, his mother called to tell him that his latest appeal to Sharrow had met with success. Mr Coulson was inviting him for an interview. Heathcote's elation put him into marathon-mode. At six o'clock on a dark October morning, he leaped into his car – a rusty Ford Capri in those days – and drove from Berne to Bolton in twenty-six hours, stopping only for Mars Bars and plastic cups of coffee from vending machines at refuelling stations.

When Sharrow Bay reopened in March, 1982, Heathcote joined Francis Coulson's kitchen, where he stayed for two blissfully happy seasons. 'Brian and Francis spoil their staff as much as their guests,' he says. 'They are a rarity.' But the seeds of Heathcote's searing ambition had long taken root. By the end of the following year, he felt it was time to move on – vowing that, like Sharrow, one day he would win panegyrics from Egon Ronay in his own right.

In the winter of 1983, Paul Heathcote exchanged the Wordsworthian ideal of the English Lakes for the Orwellian tyranny of a big London kitchen. The sheer hostility of the regime at the Connaught came as a rude shock after the cosy bliss of Ullswater. On his first morning, Heathcote reported for duty half-an-hour early. When he was introduced to his section head, the chef gripped his right hand, crushing his fingers, then jerked Heathcote's face forwards so that their noses touched. 'You're fuckin' well late,' hissed the kitchen bully. It was a cruel induction and it took Heathcote a while to come to terms with a system which, at one point, even reduced this tenacious Lancastrian to tears. But for all its ungodliness below stairs, the Connaught's reputation was superb and, as well as learning to look after his own, he swiftly acquired the culinary disciplines Michel Bourdin demanded of his fifty-strong brigade.

When he moved to Le Manoir aux Quat' Saisons near Oxford in 1985, Paul Heathcote was

subjected to another turbulent change of gear – although this time the rigours of the regime were inflicted in the elusive pursuit of aesthetic perfectionism. The doctrine of fixed methods and rigid procedures – essential to a kitchen like the Connaught's – was anathema to the mercurial genius of Raymond Blanc's artistic mind-set. From one day to the next, nothing stood still. 'I thought he were a bloody nutcase!' says Heathcote, describing Blanc's restless experiments and constant changes to aspects of his dishes. If a fillet of sea bass was right one day, that did not make it perfect the next. To make the point, Blanc's teaching methods often lapsed into a perverse and graphic theatricality. Masking the sides of Heathcote's eyes with his hands, Blanc would tell him not to be blinkered about food: to think and always to keep an open mind.

Flavours and textures were all and Blanc would constantly entreat his cooks to 'taste, taste, taste' – a principle Heathcote now insists on in his own kitchen. Again, lessons would be administered with dramatic force. On one occasion, Heathcote had not properly descaled a fish. A furious Blanc scraped another clean and put a spoonful of scales into his terrified pupil's mouth.

His debt to Blanc is enormous and, in spite of the trials he suffered at his master's hand, he has deep affection for the man. 'Raymond changed my attitude and approach to food,' he says. 'My time at the Manoir was the greatest influence on the way I cook today. I just wish he could have found as much happiness in his personal life as he has in his food and the place he has created.'

By 1987 Paul Heathcote wanted to come home. For some time now, his goal had been to open his own place before his thirtieth birthday and he was adamant that he should do it in his native Lancashire. Heathcote's appointment as head chef of the Broughton Park Hotel near Preston was the perfect stepping-stone and a very clever move. The next three years gave him the vital time he needed to learn how to manage a business and to begin the difficult task of sourcing local growers and suppliers who might be willing to submit to his demanding specifications for top-quality raw materials. Broughton Park was also an ideal warm-up act before the big show opened in 1990. It was at this notable hotel that Heathcote began to rehearse his talent for impressing the local media by initiating his own gastronomic promotions.

So, when the moment arrived to unveil his pukka restaurant in the old quarrymen's cottages on the fringes of Longridge and, regardless of the challenges of place and timing, there was already a fair wind of enthusiasm blowing behind Heathcote's stretched sails. Eighteen months later and exactly ten years after he first set eyes on an *Egon Ronay Guide*, the private vow he made at Sharrow Bay was fulfilled when the 1992 edition awarded Heathcote's one star. Greater honours and a second star were to follow, but this was the first. 'I was jumping for joy,' he says. 'It was like walking out on to Wembley for the first time.'

Although his menus were susceptible to European influence, like most other chefs of his background, they have now become less Europhile and more obviously focused on British tradition. His nearest soulmate is probably Phil Vickery. Heathcote's style is branded by an inspired patriotism, cultivating a more purist line defined by the home stable. Like Vickery, he is making a conscious effort to explore the gastronomic potential of dishes with a declared English – even regional – orientation. There the comparison ends for, while Vickery's sophisticated but essentially simple, modern style is framed in the historical context of English classicism, Heathcote marshals the detailed intricacy of the techniques he learned under Blanc and reworks them on his own quintessentially British ideas.

> **❝ Much of his cooking relies on long-standing relationships forged with his local suppliers of fish, meat, poultry and herbs ❞**

The results are quite extraordinary because Heathcote's repertoire, for all its native provenance, bears the unmistakable lustre of his French master. The result is a sort of British definition of modern *haute cuisine*.

Given this premise, one wonders what this chef can make of a menu which offers tomato juice as a starter and bread and butter pudding to finish – items so banal they ring with the echoes of dreary provincial dining in the Fifties. The tomato juice turns out to be an exquisite elixir served *en tasse* – a chilled, crystalline liquid tinged with the palest lemon-pink hue. It is the pure essence of the fruit – strained through muslin – with colour, texture and aroma provided by floating cubes of tomato flesh and thin green ribbons of basil.

The famous nursery pudding is similarly elevated. Here, Paul Heathcote re-choreographs music hall into grand opera. The setting is an ornate china plate dusted with icing sugar, dressed with redcurrants and dried apricots cooked in stock syrup with vanilla. The pudding, centre stage, is so delicate, so unctuous, so perfectly fashioned, it wobbles gently like a bosom in bathwater.

Heathcote's loyalty to home is not skin-deep. He is a true believer and much of his cooking relies on the long-standing relationships he has forged with his local suppliers of fish (from Fleetwood), meat, poultry, vegetables and herbs. In the beginning – at Broughton Park – he had to cajole and re-educate. Those who responded have flourished and now supply many of the best hotels and restaurants in the North West. In Goosnargh, three miles west of

Longridge, Reg Johnson used to rear broilers in his World War II Nissen huts. He had never heard of corn-fed chicken. Now he is a bespoke poulterer and, at Heathcote's, his ducklings are the centrepiece for a symphonic dish which comes dressed with little dumplings made from the leg meat, caramelized apples and a sublime gravy perfumed with cider.

Predictably, Lancashire's more obvious contributions to the anthology of the English kitchen do not escape Heathcote's poetic mind. The sour-sweet flavour of sultanas gently poached in wine vinegar and added to a black pudding of sweetbreads remodels this northern staple into a less fatty and quite brilliant confection. Again, it is typical of his class and brio. Hotpot potatoes, with rack of lamb, are redolent of the traditional casserole and make an equally distinguished and melting Lancastrian riposte to the ubiquitous *gratin dauphinois*.

Ultimately, it is all these dishes which define Paul Heathcote as a chef and set him apart from the rest. He is one of the few who is demonstrating the gastronomic credibility of British food

" He is one of the few who is demonstrating the gastronomic credibility of British food "

which too many others are quick to dismiss or simply lack the imagination to consider.

While the Bransonian tendencies in his character are driving him on to expand his business into the popular brasserie market, it is also clear that Heathcote's goal posts are moving. Having achieved so much so young, he is now in search of a greater quality of life. He would like to marry one day and he admits that his ambition has been responsible for the break up of some of his per-

sonal relationships. He has also seen how the pressure of a high-powered kitchen has affected the health of one close colleague. 'I do not want to have a stroke like Blanc,' he says bluntly. 'And I'm not going to kill myself to get three Michelin stars. There are other things in life.'

Among the many awards displayed in Heathcote's restaurant, there are also portraits of Raymond Blanc and Francis Coulson. They are a touching gesture of gratitude to the two men who have inspired him. But, while Blanc taught him his craft, the gentleness and ethos of Coulson have probably had the most profound influence on his outlook today.

In the end, the one certainty is that Paul Heathcote will remain true to his beloved Lancashire and I have no doubt that one day the admiring burghers of Bolton will place a blue plaque outside that modest terrace in Kildare Street.

Clear Tomato Juice
with Chervil and Vegetables

——

1.25 kg/2½ lb ripe tomatoes

50 g/2 oz basil, chopped

125 g/4 oz chervil, chopped

1 bunch of flat leaf parsley, chopped

3 sprigs of thyme, roughly chopped

1 shallot, chopped

1 garlic clove, roughly chopped

125 ml/4 fl oz dry white wine

salt and freshly ground black pepper

To garnish:

1 large tomato, skinned, deseeded
and finely diced

1 tablespoon cooked, diced carrot

1 tablespoon cooked, diced courgette

1 tablespoon cooked, diced celeriac

2 tablespoons cooked, skinned broad beans

2 tablespoons cooked green peas

6 sprigs of fresh chervil

Place the washed tomatoes in a bowl. Add the chopped herbs, shallot, garlic, white wine, salt and pepper.

Crush the tomatoes with your hands, tie in muslin and hang overnight with a container underneath to catch the juices.

Serve a small amount of the strained juice in 6 consommé cups. Mix all the garnish ingredients together and divide between the cups. Alternatively, serve in soup bowls, as shown in the photograph.

Serves 6

Black Pudding of Sweetbreads

on a Bed of Crushed Potatoes, with Baked Beans and Bay Leaf Sauce

———

50 g/2 oz sultanas

3 bay leaves, crushed

125 ml/4 fl oz white wine vinegar

500 g/1 lb veal or lambs' sweetbreads

olive oil (see method)

500 ml/1 lb pigs' blood

¼ onion, chopped and boiled until soft

50 g/2 oz rolled oats

leaves from 1 sprig of rosemary

leaves from 1 sprig of thyme

1 black pudding skin 45 cm/18 inch stick size,
making 20 slices of black pudding

2 large potatoes

200 g/7 oz unsalted butter, diced

300 ml/½ pint veal stock

8 button onions, cooked

50 g/2 oz cooked white haricot beans

50 g/2 oz carrot, diced and cooked

salt and freshly ground black pepper

Place the sultanas in a bowl with 1 bay leaf, add the vinegar and soak until it has been thoroughly absorbed.

Transfer to a pan, bring to the boil and simmer gently over a low heat until most of the vinegar has evaporated (do not allow to caramelize). Remove the bay leaf.

Blanch the sweetbreads in boiling water for 1 minute, then lift out and peel off the outside membrane. Cut into large dice. Heat the olive oil in a pan, add the sweetbreads and fry until golden brown. Set aside.

Place the blood in a warm *bain-marie* and stir occasionally until it starts to thicken. Pass through a sieve to remove any membrane.

Gently mix the blood with the sweetbreads, sultanas, cooked chopped onion and rolled oats. Add the rosemary, thyme and seasoning, then carefully fill the pudding skin.

Poach in a *bain-marie* at just below boiling point – about 82°C (180°F) – until the pudding has reached 75°C (165°F) in the middle when tested with a thermometer.

Cool, slice 4 portions of the pudding, brush with olive oil and place under a hot grill for about 4–5 minutes, until hot.

To make the crushed potatoes, boil them in their skins until cooked but still firm, then peel while still hot. Mash the diced butter with a fork and crush with the potatoes. Taste and adjust the seasoning.

To make the sauce, bring the veal stock to the boil with 2 bay leaves and simmer gently until reduced to a coating consistency. Remove the bay leaves.

To serve, place a mound of crushed potatoes on 4 heated dinner plates and arrange the slices of black pudding on top. Add the cooked button onions, haricot beans and diced carrot to the sauce, reheat, then pour over and around the black pudding.

Serves 4

Roast Rack of Spring Lamb

with Hotpot Potatoes, Braised Lentils, Roast Shallots, Rosemary and Thyme-scented Juices

———

1 kg/2 lb potatoes, sliced

2 carrots, sliced

250 g/8 oz butter, clarified

1 onion, sliced

4 racks of lamb, 200–300 g/7–10 oz each

9 shallots, 1 finely diced

1 tablespoon olive oil

1 litre/1¾ pints lamb stock

50 g/2 oz Puy lentils

50 g/2 oz smoked streaky bacon, diced

1 tablespoon chopped fresh rosemary leaves

1 tablespoon chopped fresh thyme leaves

salt and freshly ground black pepper

a selection of baby vegetables, to garnish

To make the hotpot potatoes, place the sliced potatoes and carrots in a bowl and pour over the clarified butter. Arrange 3 layers of potatoes in the bottom of a mould, then add a layer of carrots, then of onion, followed by another layer of potatoes. Season each layer. Cook in a pre-heated oven at 200°C (400°F) Gas Mark 6 until crisp (about 1–1¼ hours). Remove and set aside.

Place the racks of lamb in the oven and roast at 200°C (400°F) Gas Mark 6 for 20 minutes. Remove and set aside to rest. Place the 8 whole shallots in an ovenproof dish, drizzle with the olive oil and roast until brown and tender.

Place half the lamb stock in a pan, add the lentils, bacon and diced shallot, bring to the boil and simmer until tender. Add water if necessary to prevent drying out. Set aside. Pour the remaining lamb stock into another pan, add the rosemary and thyme, bring to the boil and reduce to a coating consistency (about 150 ml/¼ pint).

To serve, place a wedge of the hotpot potatoes at the top of each plate, cut the racks of lamb in half and place 2 cutlets on either side. Garnish with the braised lentils, baby vegetables and roasted shallots, and pour over the herb-scented lamb stock.

Serves 4

Roast Breast of Goosnargh Duckling

with Cider Potatoes, Peas, Caramelized Apples, Dumplings, Cashew Nuts and Cider-scented Juices

———

2 ducks, about 1.75 kg/3½ lb each

1 Savoy cabbage, shredded

12 button onions

125 g/4 oz peas

500 ml/17 fl oz duck stock

Dumplings:

1 shallot, finely shredded

125 g/4 oz butter

125 ml/4 fl oz water

150 g/5 oz flour

4 eggs

50 g/2 oz roasted cashew nuts, chopped

50 g/2 oz fresh flat leaf parsley, chopped

2 tablespoons olive oil, for frying

salt and freshly ground white pepper

Cider Potatoes:

4 potatoes

125 ml/4 fl oz cider

275 g/9 oz clarified unsalted butter

salt and freshly ground white pepper

Caramelized Apples:

2 Cox's apples

1 tablespoon olive oil

125 g/4 oz icing sugar

Remove the legs from the ducks and roast the legs and breasts on the bone in a preheated oven at 200°C (400°F) Gas Mark 6 for about 12–15 minutes, until pink. Remove the breasts from the oven and keep them warm. Continue cooking the legs until well cooked, then chop up the leg meat and reserve for the dumplings. Cook the Savoy cabbage, button onions and peas in separate pans of lightly salted water and set aside.

To make the dumplings, place the shallot, butter and water in a pan and bring to the boil. Remove from the heat and add the flour. Beat well until the paste falls from the side of the pan. Allow to cool for 5 minutes.

Add the eggs, one at a time, beating well, then add the cashew nuts, the leg meat from the duck, the parsley and seasoning.

Pipe the dumpling mixture into strips 5 x 1 cm/2 x ½ inches, drop into boiling water and simmer for about 5 minutes. Drain through a colander, then pat dry with a cloth.

Heat the olive oil in a heavy-based pan and fry the dumplings until golden. Set aside.

Slice the potatoes into 6 cm/2½ inch circles, about 1.5 cm/¾ inch thick. Pour the cider into a pan (reserving a little for the sauce), add the clarified butter and simmer gently until cooked and golden, then season well.

To make the caramelized apples, peel the fruit and make apple balls, using a melon baller. Place the rest of the apple in a pan with the duck stock and bring to the boil. Add the reserved cider, then strain and set aside.

Pour the olive oil into a hot pan, add the icing sugar and apple balls and cook until golden brown. Set aside.

Remove the breasts from the bone and place under a hot grill until the skin is crisp.

Place the cider potatoes and cabbage in the centre of 4 heated dinner plates. Slice the duck breasts and place in a fan over the top. Scatter with the peas, apples, onions and dumplings, then pour over the cider-scented stock.

Serves 4

Bread and Butter Pudding

5 slices of white bread, buttered

3 eggs

50 g/2 oz sugar

225 ml/7½ fl oz milk

225 ml/7½ fl oz whipping cream

1 vanilla pod

50 g/2 oz sultanas

50 g/2 oz apricot jam,

melted with a little water

Cut the slices of bread in half diagonally and remove the crusts.

Place the eggs and sugar together in a bowl and whisk, then add the milk and cream. Split a vanilla pod and scrape the seeds into the bowl. Mix well.

Place the slices of bread and the sultanas in layers in an ovenproof dish, then pour over the vanilla custard.

Place the dish in a *bain-marie* and cook in a preheated oven at 150–180°C (300–350°F) Gas Mark 2–4, for about 25–30 minutes.

Remove from the oven and allow to cool. When cool, place under a hot grill to brown, if necessary, and glaze with melted apricot jam.

Serves 6

Terence Laybourne

On 8th October, 1994, a bold headline on the food pages of the *Independent* read: 'The Newcastle stotty bounces back'. According to Terence Laybourne, who wrote the article, a 'stotty' is a kind of local cake which takes its name from the habit of bouncing, or 'stotting', the freshly baked dough on the kitchen floor to test its quality. The better the bounce, the tastier the stotty. Laybourne goes on to describe the origins of this flat, discus-shaped speciality, explaining that it used to be a staple of the 'poverty cuisine' which sustained the miners and shipyard workers in the Twenties and Thirties. The recipe, one notes, includes a pinch of white pepper and several pinches of salt. Laybourne is being perfectly serious about all this – for the record, Greggs of Gosforth bake 70,000 stotties a week – but he is a Geordie, and Geordies love to take the mickey.

They are also a fiercely proud people who cling to their roots with an ethnic fervour. While they enjoy a gag at their own expense, they are equally quick to raise two fingers at the rest of the world. 'Coals to Newcastle' is a redundant metaphor, but we still use it, harking back as it might to cultural associations and implying social nuances about a place which sometimes make smoothie southerners prone to poke fun, even sneer. Patronize a Geordie and he'll smack you with a one-liner.

Novocastrians are like their city – noble, strong and defiant. If you stand on the battlements of the mediæval castle keep, its heart and history are spread below in one 360° turn; the broad sweep of the Tyne, the engineering brilliance of its bridges, the legacy of the age of rail and steel, the monument to Earl Grey at the head of Grey Street, a Corinthian-columned thoroughfare as handsome as Regent Street, and the rising thrust of technology with the BT building dominating

the central motorway. It is a mighty architectural collage of ancient and modern. It may not be all beautiful, but it is breathtakingly impressive.

Terry Laybourne's skills and professional pedigree as a chef are such that he could have set up shop anywhere and succeeded. But to do so would have been unthinkable – and close to an act of treachery against his native city. That headline in the *Independent* serves as an allegorical tattoo of the man's life. Like a stotty, Laybourne bounced out of a council estate in an old mining village, rising up to embrace all the middle-class garniture of cosmopolitan dining, finally landing with his own place on Newcastle's Quayside. His mother used to make stotties at home – now she bakes brioche at 21 Queen Street. His wife and partner Susan – Tyneside's answer to Cilla Black – injects zest and fun into the place. And Laybourne's most celebrated invention – a terrine of ham knuckle and *foie gras* served with pease pudding – is a character reference rather than a signature dish, telling us bluntly that, as a cook he has arrived, but as a bloke he will never let go of his wry Geordie humour and working-class background.

When Sir Kingsley Amis ate at 21 Queen Street, he came away having had 'jolly good fun'. 'If much more of this kind of thing turns up so far away,' concluded our senior man of letters, 'London will find its pretensions dented.' A rare snook cocked at the capital: Laybourne must have revelled in it. There is nothing he enjoys more than a little competitive needle and he likes to win.

1955 was a great year on Tyneside. Newcastle United won the FA Cup and, in August, Terence Laybourne was born. Thirty-nine years later, when he took me on a tour of Lemington – the village five miles west of the city centre where he grew up – his car radio was tuned into a match. Kevin Keegan's boys were playing Aston Villa. Oblivious of my own ignorance, I casually asked him how his team was doing in the league. 'Where've you been, man?' he snapped. Next to cooking, soccer is Laybourne's religion – Newcastle was top of the Premiership and unbeaten in the season so far. Mercifully, they notched up another victory (2-0) and the tension in the car eased.

Lemington lies on a south-facing slope close to the Tyne where Terry used to fish for perch and dace as a boy. His roots in the village go back through several generations of miners, although his father worked for the Caterpillar Tractor Company and was a staunch member of the Boilermakers' Union. There have been a few changes since his childhood. The playing fields at the top of his street have been levelled out and the slag heap has disappeared. 'It was a monster,' he says, 'and we used to hot rod our bikes all over it.' He loved action and excitement, forever dreaming of playing centre-forward for Newcastle United or being an ace racing driver. A cousin built him a bogie out of metal piping and pram wheels which was his greatest pride, and 'the fastest on the block'.

School was less exciting, although he excelled in practical subjects like woodwork, metalwork and technical drawing. 'Did you play truant?' I asked. 'No never,' he replied. 'My mother was very good at writing sick notes.' When Laybourne came to leave in 1970, he fancied something in motor engi-

> **❝ His most celebrated invention – a terrine of ham knuckle and foie gras . . . is a character reference rather than a signature dish ❞**

neering, but with the three-day week and industry in a state of gloom, prospects looked bleak. His mother and sister suggested cooking as a career – an idea he dismissed instantly as a trade 'for poofs'. But when a friend showed him a book filled with photographs of butter sculptures, ice carvings, decorated fishes buried in aspic and a host of other extravagant buffet displays, he changed his mind. The pictures were a revelation. For what the young Laybourne saw were fantastic feats of engineering rather than anything remotely connected with cooking. This was the business. Kitchens were where it all happened. And he was going for it.

Terry's first move was to get a haircut – a major sacrifice, this, as for months he had been cultivating a rich mane in the style of Rod Stewart. He attended interviews and, just turned fifteen, he started work as a trainee in the larder section of Newcastle's Swallow Hotel. The moment he set foot in the kitchen, his heart sank. The larder chef, wearing baseball boots and a ripped jacket branded 'condemned' by the laundry, had a head of hair hanging half-way down his back. 'He was a dead ringer for Alice Cooper,' groaned Laybourne. 'I was gutted.'

The blow to his tonsorial pride soon passed. Laybourne threw himself at the job and loved every moment; the buzz of a busy service, the pressure and the camaraderie. For him this was better than rock 'n' roll. But eighteen months later his confident beginning was brought to an abrupt stop. An horrific accident on his motor bike put him in hospital for three months and out of action for another four. When he returned to the Swallow, the old gang had moved on and somehow the *esprit* that had meant so much to him was lost. But the disaster triggered a new direction

and one which would propel him off his home turf and into Europe.

While there was no sense of ambition at this stage of his life – he was still only seventeen – Laybourne's canniness and native instincts kept him on track. He had never eaten in a restaurant and he was completely unaware of the meaning of good food. At home, corned beef with pickled onions and chips was his great favourite – a dish, he says, he still loves: 'It's one of the all-time great marriages, for God's sake!' But if he made a duff career move – and he made a few – he knew it, and moved on. Laybourne never minded hard graft, in fact he thrived on it, but he did want to learn and learn well. He was easy-going, a bit of a likely lad – but even as a teenager, he had strong views about what he sensed to be good or bad. 'It had to feel right,' he says. 'I needed to do it right and be seen to be doing it right.'

In March, 1973, Terry Laybourne took a call from an old colleague from his days at the Swallow offering him a job on Guernsey. The good times were back. On the Friday evening he threw a grand farewell party in Newcastle. On the Saturday he packed his best summer gear. And on the Sunday he flew into the island. 'I thought Guernsey was Bermuda,' he says sheepishly. 'When I got off the plane in my T-shirt, jeans and platform shoes, I expected to be hit by the sun, but it was pissing with rain.' His miscalculation was compounded by the hotel, which was shambolic, and by the following Thursday he had quit. Having left Newcastle like a conquering hero, Laybourne could not face the disgrace of returning home. So he took the hydrofoil to Jersey and it was here that he met the man who became his inspiration, counsellor and referee.

Claus Mollin, head chef of Jersey's Mermaid Hotel, was a walking parody of his own nationality. Six feet three inches tall, blond cropped hair, a disciplinarian, Herr Mollin believed in *deutsche Ordnung*. If you stepped out of line, he fined you – the money deposited in the kitchen 'pig' for a party at the end of the season. It was a regime Laybourne could respond to and he began to learn the basics of good kitchen practice in an environment that was tough, competitive, but highly motivated. He also started to appreciate the taste of good food, properly prepared. Staff meals were a formal ritual punctually observed and Herr Mollin insisted that his brigade was fed as well as his customers. Suddenly, Laybourne discovered the pleasures of supping on *entrecôte* Café de Paris and delicious risottos with fresh langoustines.

In 1975 Claus Mollin packed his protégé off to Baden-Württemberg and for the next two years Laybourne's education took shape in a

“ Staff meals were a formal ritual punctually observed and Herr Mollin insisted that his brigade was fed as well as his customers ”

round of seasonal tours in some of the top resort hotels in Germany and Switzerland. He began at the Bellevue in Baden-Baden where he mastered the language with typical Geordie guile, forever jotting words and phrases on the inside of his toque. 'It was a bit of a bastard when your hat went to the laundry,' he cracks. But the

> **" He mastered German with typical Geordie guile . . . jotting words inside his toque. 'A bit of a bastard when your hat went to the laundry' "**

experience that made the deepest impression was a winter season at the Schloss Hotel in Pontresina under Heinz Winkler, a rising star who went on to make his name at Tantris in Munich. 'Winkler was a wonderfully talented chef,' he says, 'but a lousy communicator.' It didn't matter. The brigade at the Schloss was a blue chip squad who had worked in Europe's best, and Laybourne, realizing how much he had to learn, absorbed their methods swiftly, careful never to betray his own ignorance. 'There was this guy fumbling with what looked like a lump of clay,' he said. 'So I asked him what it was.' It's *foie gras* replied the chef incredulously. 'Oh yes,' retorted the Englishman thinking *foie gras* was a substance that only came in tins. 'So it is!'

By the summer of 1977, Terry Laybourne was on his way home. He spent one last season with his old mentor on Jersey, and the following year took a job at the Fisherman's Wharf in Newcastle – a restaurant that was popularly regarded as the city's finest in spite of a menu based exclusively on frozen fish products delivered by the box-load. After his years of strict tutelage, Laybourne was horrified, though he didn't care much, as his well-padded wage packets helped finance his passion for fast cars and nightclubs. He was home again and it was time for a bit of fun.

When Laybourne was promoted to head chef, his professional pride resumed control and he began to transform the place, delighting his boss, Franco Cetoloni, who had never seen gastronomic action quite like it. In 1980, when Cetoloni set up the Fisherman's Lodge in Jesmond Dene Park, he immediately installed his young 'super chef', giving Laybourne *carte blanche* in the kitchen.

A year later, Terry and Susan were married. They honeymooned in the South of France and ate at Vergé's Moulin de Mougins. 'We flipped,' he says, 'and it got Susan hooked on the business.' By now, Laybourne was reading avidly, drawing inspiration particularly from Quentin Crewe's famous book *The Great Chefs of France*. These giants became his heroes. He worshipped them and he began to dream of his own place.

The encouragement he needed to break loose came from Alain Coutourier, a young French restaurateur from Tours, who had trained under Charles Barrier. Coutourier, married to a girl from Newcastle, had been impressed by Laybourne's cooking at the Fisherman's Lodge and the two men became firm friends, visiting each other

every year. But there was still a lingering doubt – an odd psychological wire that prevented Laybourne from making the final move too soon. Then, in 1983, when Michelin announced the award of a third star to Tantris in Munich, the spell broke. 'Once I saw that Heinz Winkler had three stars, I knew I could do it,' he says. 'I thought these people were gods. But I'd worked for Winkler. I'd seen him make mistakes.'

21 Queen Street opened in September, 1988, and three years later Terry Laybourne won his first Michelin star. While his food is branded by the rigour of his education and a palate tuned by a great deal of eating in France, I have never seen cooking that so accurately celebrates the personality of its chef. On a sure platform of culinary intelligence, Laybourne has created a gastronomic stage set effervescing with his wit and prone to exploding with special effects. He is something of a pyrotechnician. He loves the fun and excitement of his craft, but still prefers to describe himself unglamorously, and unfairly, as a 'food engineer' in much the same spirit when, as a teenager, he first set eyes on the picture book of buffet displays.

The terrine of ham knuckle and *foie gras* with pease pudding (bound with walnut oil to give it a rich moussey body) is a classic example of this culinary personification that is central to Terry Laybourne's themes. Colour, shape, texture and flavour are delivered on a grand scale and the magnitude of his technical conceits seem boundless. If he were not a cook, he could have become Ascot's darling of the millinery trade. A filo disc, supporting the bright red and green of

❝ Terry Laybourne has created a gastronomic stage set, effervescing with his wit and prone to exploding with special effects ❞

a tomato and *pistou* base, is planted with an arrangement of deep-fried herbs – a miniature garden of sage, rosemary, thyme, basil, mint, tarragon and flat leaf parsley. A similar creation is constructed on a thin puff pastry roundel spread with raspberry Chantilly and slivers of strawberry. The garden plantation consists of a variety of other soft fruits dusted with icing sugar and crowned with a jaunty little sprig of mint.

Laybourne has this extraordinary ability for mixing gastronomic gravitas with flashes of levity. A roast turbot with an onion compote has you howling with laughter because the fish is hidden beneath an enormous potato crisp, artfully assembled to look like a sunflower. In fact, the recipe is serious stuff, demanding a sound understanding of the interaction of its different elements. The saucing is meat, not fish, based. In the wrong hands this can be a dangerous culinary ploy. Here a light veal *jus* is tempered with herbs and lemon juice and, if the balance is right, the result gloriously points up the natural meatiness of the turbot.

A minestrone of fruits with a mascarpone sorbet is another clever and playful invention (the only ingredient missing is the pasta!) This warm soup-cum-fruit salad is wonderfully fresh and honeyed, and a sprinkling of pepper on the sorbet adds an edge to the sweetness of the confection. Laybourne is 'big on crunch', so texture is provided by a fine dice of courgettes, carrots and tomatoes. Food, he says, should be fun and the minestrone, like pease pudding and *foie gras*, confirms his inclination to shuffle the simple with the sophisticated, bistro ideas with luxury ingredients. A superb potato salad with lobster, French beans and truffle oil is Laybourne's up-market make-over of the brasserie favourite of warm potato salad and herrings. Indeed, his latest adventure is a neighbourhood bistro which opened in November, 1994, in the Newcastle suburb of Darras Hall. A second outlet, perhaps, but Laybourne remains the craftsman through and through, leaving the business details largely to his brother Laurance.

Back in his car, as we drove through Lemington and down the streets where he used to race his bogie as a boy, I asked Terry Laybourne how he saw himself as a chef. A note of diffidence crept into his voice and he confessed to having something of a chip on his shoulder. 'Raymond Blanc,' he says, 'claims to be self-taught, but I don't accept that. He had the advantage of growing up with good food. I did not. I had to learn for myself and, in that sense, I am self-taught because good cooking starts with the palate. With taste. It is a matter of culture and background. If you're brought up to eat well, you can learn to cook in no time.'

He is dead right and it is a lesson too few British cooks understand. But what is equally true is that Laybourne came home. With rare exceptions (Rankin in Belfast, Heathcote in Lancashire), our most talented and enterprising chefs drift away to seek glory in London or elsewhere. If more of them returned home, our provincial cities would not be such gastronomic wildernesses.

If Peter Beardsley is Newcastle's local hero, then Terry Laybourne is one of his city's most favoured sons.

Terrine of Ham Knuckle and Foie Gras,

with Pease Pudding

———

4 ham knuckles

65 ml/2½ fl oz white wine vinegar

2 large onions

6 carrots

3 celery sticks

1 bunch thyme

2 bay leaves

8 parsley stalks

½ head garlic

2 cloves

10 peppercorns, sea salt and coarsely ground black pepper

Foie Gras:

1 foie gras, about 625 g/1¼ lb

1½ teaspoons salt

¼ teaspoon freshly ground white pepper

½ teaspoon sugar

a pinch of mace

2 tablespoons Armagnac

2 tablespoons tawny port

Pease Pudding:

275 g/9 oz yellow split peas

65 ml/2½ fl oz walnut oil

2 tablespoons white wine vinegar

1 pinch chopped blanched tarragon

salt and freshly ground white pepper

To prepare the pease pudding, cover the peas with plenty of cold water and allow to steep overnight. When ready to cook, drain the peas, cover with fresh cold water, bring to the boil and simmer gently for 40 minutes, or until tender. Drain, allow to cool and, when cold, place in a liquidizer or food processor, add the walnut oil, vinegar, blanched tarragon and seasoning, then purée until smooth.

To make the terrine, begin 3 days before. Soak the ham knuckles overnight in cold water to cover. Place the *foie gras* in tepid water for 15 minutes to soften. Drain, remove the fine outer skin and any veins, plunge into heavily-iced water and chill for 4 hours. Dry well on a clean cloth, place on a tray and season with the salt, pepper, sugar and mace. Sprinkle with Armagnac and port. Cover with clingfilm and marinate overnight.

Next day, allow the *foie gras* to return to room temperature, then roll in clingfilm into a sausage 30 cm/12 inches long, and about 5 cm/2 inches in diameter. Rewrap in foil and twist the ends tightly.

Bring a pan of water to the boil, reduce the heat, add the wrapped *foie gras* and poach at 70°C (160°F) for 20 minutes – the water should be barely shivering – then plunge immediately into iced water. When cool, but not cold, twist the ends of foil over again, to create a neat sausage. Chill overnight.

Place the knuckles in a large pot, add cold water to cover, bring to the boil, skim and add the vinegar, vegetables, herbs, cloves and peppercorns. Return to the boil, then simmer very gently for 4 hours. Remove the ham knuckles and carrots, and discard everything else.

Line a 1.5 litre/2½ pint cast-iron terrine with clingfilm. When the ham is cool enough to handle, strip off the skin and set aside. Strip off the meat in large chunks, and cut the carrots into 5 mm/¼ inch slices.

Scrape and discard any excess fat from the ham and skin. Line the base of the terrine with

a layer of skin, then fill to one-third with ham, and scatter with carrot. Season to taste.

Unwrap the *foie gras*, discard any excess fat and lay the *foie gras* in the terrine. Pack the remaining ham and carrots around and over the *foie gras*, seasoning well.

Finish with another layer of ham skin. Cover with clingfilm, place a wooden board on top, then add a very heavy weight. Chill, weighted, overnight.

Turn out the terrine, cut into thick slices and brush with a little walnut oil. Season with sea salt and coarsely ground black pepper.

Serve, accompanied by pease pudding and a leafy green salad, dressed in walnut oil.

Serves 12

Thin Tomato Tart

with Pistou and a Friture of Herbs

———

1 tablespoon olive oil

½ onion, finely chopped

1 garlic clove, finely chopped

500 g/1 lb ripe plum tomatoes, skinned,

deseeded and coarsely chopped, and

6 very red, very ripe plum tomatoes,

skinned and cut in 5 mm/¼ inch slices

1 bouquet garni

6 sheets filo pastry

125 g/4 oz unsalted butter, melted

olive oil (see method)

6 tablespoons pistou

salt and freshly ground black pepper

Friture of Herbs:

vegetable oil for deep-frying

1 egg, size 1

450 ml/¾ pint iced water

125 g/4 oz plain flour

50 g/2 oz cornflour

⅓ teaspoon bicarbonate of soda

½ teaspoon salt

1 large bunch assorted herbs, e.g. leaves of

basil, flat leaf parsley, tarragon and sage and

young tender shoots of thyme and rosemary

Heat the olive oil in a pan, add the onion and garlic and cook until softened but not coloured. Add the chopped tomatoes, bouquet garni and seasoning, and simmer very gently until the tomatoes melt into a thick, dry purée.

Remove the bouquet garni and sieve the mixture.

Brush the filo with melted butter and stack 1 sheet on top of another, 4 sheets thick. Cut 4 discs of pastry, 12 cm/5 inches in diameter.

Place on a buttered baking sheet, with another sheet on top. Cook in a preheated oven at 200°C (400°F) Gas Mark 6 for 10 minutes or until golden. Remove, then cool on a wire rack.

Spread each filo base with 2 tablespoons of tomato mixture, and arrange the tomato slices on top. Season well, drizzle with olive oil and return to the oven for 7 minutes.

Meanwhile, heat 5 cm/2 inches of vegetable oil in a deep pan to 190°C (375°F).

Beat the egg with the iced water in a bowl. Mix the flour, cornflour, bicarbonate of soda and salt. Stir carefully into the egg.

Working in batches, dip the herbs in the batter, fry until golden brown (about 1 minute), drain on kitchen paper and season with salt.

Spread the tarts with a little pistou and arrange the herbs on top. Serve very hot.

Serves 4

Roast Turbot

with Onion Confit, Wild Mushrooms, Crisp Potatoes and Meat Juices

—

4 turbot fillets, about 175 g/6 oz each

4 tablespoons hazelnut oil

1 garlic clove, crushed

1 sprig of rosemary and ½ teaspoon
chopped fresh rosemary leaves

juice and blanched zest of 1 lemon

blanched zest of 1 lime

200 ml/7 fl oz clarified butter

2 large onions, finely sliced

500 ml/17 fl oz brown chicken stock
or veal stock

4 large baking potatoes, finely sliced

2 shallots, finely chopped

1 sprig of tarragon, blanched and chopped

2 tomatoes, skinned, deseeded and diced

200 g/7 oz wild mushrooms

salt and freshly ground black pepper

Marinate the fillets overnight with the hazelnut oil, garlic, sprig of rosemary and the blanched lemon and lime zests.

Heat half the clarified butter, and sauté the onions until golden. Season, add 125 ml/4 fl oz of the chicken stock and simmer slowly until the onions are very soft.

Sprinkle the potato slices with a pinch of salt, allow to stand for 2–3 minutes, then dry on a clean cloth. Brush a 12 cm/5 inch non-stick frying pan with clarified butter. Place 1 potato slice in the centre and arrange others, overlapping, around it. Fry over a gentle heat until crisp and golden on both sides. Repeat to make 4 potato discs.

Bring the remaining stock to the boil, reduce by one-third, add 1 chopped shallot, the chopped rosemary, tarragon and diced tomato. Taste and adjust the seasoning with salt, pepper and a little lemon juice. Keep warm.

Sauté the wild mushrooms in the remaining clarified butter, season, add the remaining chopped shallot and cook for 2 minutes more. Keep warm.

Remove the turbot from the marinade and sear in a hot, cast-iron frying pan. Place in a preheated oven at 200°C (400°F) Gas Mark 6 for 3–5 minutes until just cooked, depending on the thickness of the fish. Season with a squeeze of lemon juice.

To serve, divide the onion confit between 4 heated plates. Place the turbot fillets on top, scatter the mushrooms around and spoon the sauce over. Place the crispy potatoes on top of the fish and serve with buttered spinach.

Serves 4

'Minestrone' of Fruits

with Mascarpone Sorbet

———

500 g/1 lb ripe strawberries,

plus 4 large ones

250 g/8 oz caster sugar

150 ml/¼ pint water

1 vanilla pod

2 small, new-season carrots, cut

into 5 mm/¼ inch dice

1 small courgette, cut

into 5 mm/¼ inch dice

12 raspberries

12 redcurrants

12 blackcurrants

1 small, ripe mango

½ banana

coarsely ground black pepper

lemon juice, to taste

4 large, fresh basil leaves,

coarsely shredded

Mascarpone Sorbet:

200 g/7 oz caster sugar

350 ml/12 fl oz water

½ tablespoon lemon juice

½ tablespoon orange juice

250 g/8 oz mascarpone

To make the mascarpone sorbet, mix the caster sugar with the measured cold water in a saucepan, bring to the boil and allow to cool. When cold, whisk in the lemon juice, orange juice and mascarpone.

Churn in a sorbetière, then transfer to a container, cover, and place in the freezer until ready to use. When ready to serve, form the sorbet into into 4 quenelles, using a tablespoon.

Wash the 500 g/1 lb of ripe strawberries, then carefully pat them dry. Hull them, then cut into quarters. Place in a bowl and sprinkle with 200 g/7 oz of the caster sugar. Cover the bowl tightly with clingfilm, place on top of a pan of gently simmering water and cook gently for about 1½ hours.

Remove the strawberries from the heat and tip the contents of the bowl into a fine muslin or jelly bag and allow to drip though for 3–4 hours. Do not force or squeeze – the juice must be very clear and limpid.

Bring the measured cold water to the boil, add the remaining caster sugar and the vanilla pod. Add the carrots and courgettes to the pan and poach gently in the vanilla syrup.

Pick over the raspberries, redcurrants, blackcurrants and the 4 extra strawberries, wash and dry. Cut the mango, strawberries and banana into neat 3 mm/⅛ inch dice.

Pour the strawberry juice into a stainless steel pan and combine with the fruits. Warm very carefully – do not overheat. Add the diced carrots and courgettes, season to taste with the coarsely ground black pepper and add lemon juice to taste.

Divide the strawberry minestrone and shredded basil leaves between 4 small soup plates. Drop a quenelle of mascarpone sorbet into the soup at the last moment and top with a grind of pepper.

Serves 4

Tartlet of Soft Fruits

————

200 g/7 oz puff pastry

about 2 tablespoons icing sugar

4 tablespoons whipping cream, chilled

12 large, ripe strawberries

a selection of soft fruits, e.g. raspberries, wild strawberries,

redcurrants, blackcurrants and cape gooseberries (physalis)

4 sprigs of mint

crème anglaise, to serve (optional)

Raspberry Coulis:

200 g/7 oz raspberries

65 g/2½ oz icing sugar

lemon juice, to taste

To make the raspberry coulis, place the raspberries, icing sugar and lemon juice in a food processor or liquidizer, blend until smooth, then press through a fine sieve. Chill.

To make the tarts, place the puff pastry on a flat work surface, dredge with icing sugar and roll out to about 3 mm/⅛ inch thick. Roll up like a Swiss roll, then chill.

Slice off 4 rounds, 1 cm/½ inch thick, and roll out on icing sugar as thinly as possible. Chill and rest for 15 minutes. Place on non-stick paper on a baking sheet and place another sheet on top (to prevent the pastry rising). Cook in a preheated oven at 190°C (375°F) Gas Mark 5 until golden. While still warm, trim into neat rounds, using a 10 cm/4 inch pastry cutter. Cool.

Whip the cream until firm, fold in 4 tablespoons of the raspberry coulis very gently, using a rubber spatula, then chill.

Wash and hull the strawberries, dry carefully and slice into vertical slices 3 mm/⅛ inch thick. Pick over the other fruits and wash if necessary.

Cut four 12 cm/5 inch squares of non-stick paper. Place a 10 cm/4 inch diameter pastry cutter on each piece. Arrange the sliced strawberries neatly inside the rings and put 1½ tablespoons of raspberry cream into the centre. Place a puff pastry disc on top of each and press down gently.

Invert the tarts (still in their rings) on to dessert places. Arrange the other fruits decoratively on top, remove the rings, then top with a sprig of mint. Sprinkle with icing sugar and spoon the remaining raspberry coulis around, together with a little *crème anglaise* (optional).

Serves 4

Paul Rankin

O n the morning of 27th November, 1983, Paul Rankin and Jeanne Lebrun woke up in a cheap
hotel in Lanzhou, central China. It had been an uncomfortable night and Paul was in bad
shape. He had eaten dog on the long train journey from Xining on the Tibetan border and, if that
was not enough to deny him his sleep, in the early hours, a rat had burrowed into a large stuffed
chair in the corner of their room. The only way Jeanne could think of getting rid of the beast was
to shove the chair into the corridor outside their door.

But their spirits were high. They were on their way home – Paul to Belfast, Jeanne to
Winnipeg, after almost two years travelling together through the Indian subcontinent, Australia
and the Far East, their minds now firmly set on the future. Paul was already drafting a letter in
his head, which he planned to send to Albert Roux when he reached London. Their experiences,
recorded in Jeanne's diaries, read like the writings of a gastronomic Marco Polo. The foods they
had eaten, the places they had worked in, had ignited a passion to cook seriously for a living, but
they needed to learn their craft and they were now twenty-four years old.

The story of the Rankins is a tale of love, adventure and self-discovery – one of those boy-
meets-girl scripts which Hollywood film-makers kill for and one of those screenplays where you

" The foods they had eaten, the places they had worked in, had ignited a passion to cook seriously for a living "

just know there has to be a happy ending. The casting is pretty perfect too. Jeanne is meltingly beautiful – a modern woman without the hard edges. Her exuberance and *joie de vivre* are infectious: her energy exhausting, a charismatic personality with a warm and friendly disposition, not laid on like greasepaint, but as genuine as the blood in her veins. Paul is tall, slender, gentle – a Renaissance figure with the Christ-like features of a Florentine fresco. But behind the long hair, the beard, the high forehead and the soft crinkly eyes lies the quiet fervour of a gifted teacher whose inspiration is touching a new generation of Irish cooks.

Roscoff, the restaurant they opened in Belfast in 1989, is more than just another Michelin star and the first in Northern Ireland. This place eschews the assumptions, expectations and clichés of top-drawer dining in Britain because, like no other, it speaks for the outlook, passions and ideas of its owners. To understand Roscoff, we must first tell the tale.

Paul Rankin spent the first ten years of his life in Ballywalter – a seaside village on the Strangford peninsula in County Down. He and his two elder brothers attended the local primary school and spent much of their free time outdoors: building huts in the woods and baking potatoes in camp fires, catching crabs on the beaches and fishing in the rock pools. In 1969, the family moved to Belfast and Paul entered the Royal Belfast Academical Institution, the city's principal boys' public school. By his early teens, he had become deeply religious – the result of an evangelical Protestant upbringing – and in his lunch breaks he would go to prayer meetings believing that he was destined to become a missionary or a preacher. At seventeen, he won a place at Queen's University to read biochemistry where he spent more time reflecting on the meaning of his own life than on the chemistry of other living organisms. For a sensitive and independently minded young man, he found the uncompromising nature of his religion too much to accept. Disillusioned, he gave it up, dropped out of university and set off to hitch-hike round Europe. On his return, and more out of a desire to appease his parents, he enrolled at the British School of Osteopathy in London. After four months, he dropped out again, re-packed his rucksack and headed for the Eastern Mediterranean. He was twenty and free.

By the time he got to Greece, Paul was broke. He found himself a job as a boat painter in a marina just ouside Athens. And it was here that he met Jeanne – an American national raised and

" In Sri Lanka . . . they feasted on tropical fruits, grilled shark and crabs so sweet they could not stop eating "

living in Winnipeg – who was taken on as a ship's cook. 'I liked her immediately but I was too shy to talk to her,' he recalls. 'In the end, she seduced me.' They took off and skipped haphazardly around the fabled islands of the Aegean – 'a lovely place to fall in love.' When the drachmae ran out, Jeanne persuaded Paul to return with her to Canada where she worked as a lifeguard on the white sand beaches of Lake Winnipeg. She had a cottage to live in, he could play frisbee all summer and the two of them would plan their next adventure.

For the following eighteen months they lived and worked in Canada – their only aim to save enough money to satisfy their yen to travel the world. When the season drew to a close on the Lake, Jeanne introduced Paul to the restaurant scene in Vancouver and Edmonton where the tips were good waiting at table. He was struck by the buzz and energy of these places and he loved the North American mentality of running restaurants where fun, excitement and a sense of theatre were the essential ingredients of a successful show.

By the end of 1981 they had earned the wherewithal to fly to the East and after a stop-over in Ulster to celebrate Christmas with the Rankin family, Paul and Jeanne set off for India to begin the remarkable journey that would ultimately lead them to their vocation.

In Sri Lanka they marvelled at the foods in the markets and feasted on tropical fruits, grilled shark and crabs so sweet they could not stop eating. They went

on to Goa, up to Delhi and on to Nepal, Himachal Pradesh and Kashmir. In Kathmandu, they traded in their paperbacks to buy Katie Stewart's *Sunday Times Cook Book*. And in Srinagar, Paul fell upon Elizabeth David's *Italian Food*. He had never even heard of Mrs David but he was touched by the way she wrote about food. 'To have stumbled across this book in India,' he says, 'is almost like there's someone looking after you.' Later, trekking in the Himalayas, they used their small gas stove to cook vegetable soups, rice and other dishes inspired by their modest library, even though they could not find the right ingredients for the recipes.

If India was their culinary awakening, in Australia Paul and Jeanne found the advice which was to harness their future. In

early 1983, having already served in some of the best restaurants in Melbourne and Sydney, they met Daniel Luttringer, the chef at Simpson's in Sydney, who had worked under Haeberlin and Vergé in France. Luttringer urged them to return to Europe as soon as possible. They were getting old, he said. They needed to train in a serious kitchen and, through mutual friends, they were given an introduction to Albert Roux in London. But their wanderlust was not sated. By the middle of the year, they were forging a course through Malaysia, Thailand and China.

It was in China where the experiences of our two gastronomic nomads made the deepest impression. Spicings, flavourings and undiscovered textures of marvellous foods leapt out of woks and street-side cooking vessels in all the towns and cities they passed through. They also encountered ingredients and notions of fresh produce quite alien to western menus. In Guilin, house specialities were advertised live – in cages offering owls, black snakes and even monkeys whose brains were a rare and expensive delicacy. But with the exception of Paul's unfortunate sampling of dog on the train from Xining, their eating habits were altogether more conservative and an affirmation that at last the moment had arrived to start cooking themselves.

In January 1984, Paul Rankin started washing dishes in the staff canteen of Le Gavroche in London. Within a year he was in the thick of the kitchen and cooking for his life. M. Roux, accustomed to sackloads of mail from eager novices, had been struck by the passion of the Ulsterman's appeal and he was not disappointed. 'I saw talent,' he says. 'Paul was living for food and he made a lasting impression on me.'

Jeanne joined Paul two months after his arrival in London and, on 22nd March, they were married. If Albert Roux had been impressed by Paul, he was enchanted by his wife. 'She was so charming,' he sighs, recalling their first meeting. 'She could sell central heating to the Arabs and fridges to the Eskimos.' Roux offered her a job on the spot.

After two-and-a-half years, the Rankins had served their apprenticeship with distinction – Paul under a chef demanding the rigorous disciplines of a three-star restaurant and Jeanne in the pastry of Le Poulbot, Roux's City outlet. In 1986, they returned to Canada and in August, Claire, their first daughter was born. The following year, the young family moved to California where Paul was appointed executive chef at the Mount View Hotel in Calistoga in the Napa Valley. He hired Jeanne as his pastry cook – a job she gladly shared with motherhood by arriving at work in the middle of the night to bake the breads and prepare the desserts before returning home at ten in the morning to take over from Paul.

But California was a mixed blessing. While the new chef's Franco-Oriental menus soon attracted the curiosity of the region's zealous food scene, his shadowy employer failed to pay their wages. In December, 1988, they quit – $6,000 the poorer and Jeanne six months pregnant with Emily.

In Belfast, Paul's brothers – both businessmen and both well connected –

" Candlelight and Michelin ritual are for stuffed shirts. Roscoff is restaurant-Americana cloaked in Versace chic "

persuaded him to return home, promising to help him set up shop in the city. And, in July 1989, the Rankins opened on the site of a bankrupt Indian restaurant in Shaftesbury Square. Eighteen months later, in the pit of the recession, Roscoff looked like going the way of its predecessor. In the middle of a sombre meeting with his brothers to discuss a new, and distinctly down-market, direction for the business, Paul took a call from his restaurant. The local papers had telephoned to break the news of their Michelin star – a unique award for Ulster and the springboard to the Rankins' solvency and success.

Television images have a shameless knack of twisting the mind, and none more so than the mere flicker of the latest news pictures from Belfast. To borrow from Trollope: 'The Irish people did not murder me, nor did they even break my

head. I soon found them to be good humoured, clever . . . and hospitable.' Belfast is not a city under siege, it is a vibrant commercial centre akin to, say, Birmingham or Newcastle. You sense a prosperity in a people determined to get on with life. Roscoff has become part of the cultural establishment and they go there to eat, to laugh and to enjoy. The place is permanently packed and the atmosphere is as animated as the bubbles in Champagne.

Behind the frosted glass exterior, the room is long like a modern gallery, the lights are dazzlingly bright, and music, tuned low, beats with a throbbing undercurrent of jazz and soul, sax and trumpet. Even the waiters look like models, wearing ties and waistcoats bearing zany designs of galactic storms and the *aurora borealis*. Candlelight and Michelin ritual are for stuffed shirts. Roscoff is restaurant-Americana cloaked in Versace chic: the action on the floor brilliantly choreographed to the leitmotiv of the Rankins' experience.

In the Roscoff kitchen, the uniform also deviates from European convention – the brigade wear baseball caps – and the atmosphere on the stoves is deceptively laid-back, given the high-performance output of the menu. Rankin loves using words like funky, freaky and wacky to express the diversity, excitement and energy of his cooking. This is nothing more than the self-effacing language of the man's modesty because his food, regardless of its natural invention, transcends the basics of skill and technique. There is a very acute palate at work here – someone with a highly developed understanding of the complexities of taste, balance and seasoning.

'Albert Roux,' he claims, 'is the father of my food.' Roscoff's passionfruit tart is the Rankins' dedication to the man because it is modelled on the Gavroche's legendary *tarte au citron*. The Roux factor is, of course, the critical underpinning of Rankin's stock as a chef. It endowed him with his classical foundations. But, unlike so many Roux graduates, Paul Rankin is no clone. The intelligence of his palate, honed by the extraordinary breadth of his experiences in the East, California and Europe, has given him the ability to explore a marvellously protean repertoire. Indeed, he has no repertoire to speak of because his menu is so restless. And, unusually for a chef, he will not identify any particular dish as his 'signature'. In this sense, Rankin likes to live dangerously, but then he is an unusual and exceptional performer who has both the courage and the confidence to tread his high-wire without a safety net.

A crispy pork confit with a tomatillo salsa and a spiced sole tempura with a lobster and coriander aïoli are typical displays of Rankin's 'wacky' experimentation, total gastronomic control and feverish desire to plunder the globe for inspiration. He still has to keep travelling, sublimating the wanderlust of his youth in his Belfast kitchen. The pork is a spin on the duck confit with Chinese spices featured in Paul and Jeanne's book and immensely engaging TV series *Gourmet Ireland*. It also echoes California where they enjoyed eating Mexican food (tomatillos are small, green, tomato-like fruit grown in Mexico). The sole tempura is an exotic arrangement which breaks over the taste buds like rolling waves – the crunch of crisp batter freckled with sesame, the firm moist fish, the silk and spice of the saucing.

Rankin may be unwilling to brand his dishes with a personal trademark but he does possess one signal gift which, I think, sets him above his peers. He is a master at transforming the simple into the exceptional; gathering ingredients in their natural state, preparing them with the minimum of fuss and finally dressing the plate to create compositions of real brilliance.

For a summer salad, he mixes rocket, tatsoi, mizuna, Chinese red mustard and other leaves he first discovered in the Napa Valley and which are now grown for him by John Hoey, a local organic smallholder. To these he adds red and yellow cherry tomatoes, peeled broad beans, a boiled egg, cucumber, slivers of radish, a few herbs and some lobster meat. But it is the two dressings which activate this marvellous mosaic; a light balsamic vinaigrette on the leaves and a basil mayonnaise, touched with a hint of garlic and cream, on the rest. The effect is fragrant and seductive, consuming the senses like a roll in a hay meadow.

Seared beef – a carpaccio charred at the edges – with rocket, Parmesan and celery is elevated from the familiar to the extraordinary by the union of these simple ingredients with a lubricant made from the celery's braising liquid and a white truffle essence mellowed by the addition of a little olive oil. The banality of a smoked salmon sandwich is overhauled and reconstructed into a wheaten bread triple-decker enlivened with marinated red onions and a cream cheese-crème fraîche mix. The only other chef I know who made a big deal out of smoked salmon sandwiches was the famous three-star Frenchman, Louis Outhier at the Oasis in La Napoule.

" Summer salad . . . the effect is fragrant and seductive, consuming the senses like a roll in a hay meadow "

For Paul Rankin there are no boundaries to his culinary landscape and it has made him one of Britain's most exciting chefs. His scope and fertile imagination have resulted in a style which is refreshingly liberated but – like freedom itself – he knows how to regulate his prodigious output against the well-defined principles he learned under Roux.

In recent years, the Rankins' success has led them into television and writing, new challenges which bring the inevitable problems of balancing the conflicting demands of these outside interests with the restaurant and the needs of two growing daughters. They are problems which preoccupy them deeply but which are eased by their natural ability to instil their values into the team at Roscoff. Where Jeanne is the inspirational tornado (she still gets up at 4.00 a.m. to do the baking), Paul has trained a brigade which has already produced a number of rising new chefs. Most of all, theirs is still a love affair as fresh as the breezes which carried them across the Aegean Sea.

Spiced Sole Tempura

with a Lobster and Coriander Aïoli

——

3 Dover sole, about 625 g/1¼ lb each,

skinned, filleted, and trimmed

1 egg white

2 tablespoons whipping cream

oil for deep-frying

Spiced Flour:

150 g/5 oz plain flour

1½ teaspoons salt

3 tablespoons sesame seeds

(black and white mixed, if possible)

2 teaspoons white pepper

2 teaspoons chilli powder

2 teaspoons curry powder

Aïoli:

2 egg yolks

1 tablespoon tomato purée

1 tablespoon chopped garlic

1 teaspoon white wine vinegar

75 ml/3 fl oz reduced lobster stock (optional)

1 teaspoon Dijon mustard

2 anchovies, finely chopped

200 ml/7 fl oz sunflower or vegetable oil

lemon juice, to taste

3 tablespoons chopped fresh coriander

salt and white pepper

To make the aïoli, combine the egg yolks, tomato purée, garlic, vinegar, lobster stock (if using), Dijon mustard and anchovies in a liquidizer or food processor. With the machine still running, slowly pour in the oil, and process until smooth. Season with salt and pepper, and add lemon juice to taste. Add the fresh coriander, and reserve in a small bowl.

To cook the sole, first heat the oil in a deep-fat fryer or large saucepan to 190°C (375°F). Check the sole fillets are completely dry, then cut each in half on a slight diagonal.

Combine the egg white and cream in a bowl, then rub the sole fillets in this mixture so each piece has a sticky coating. Combine all the ingredients for the spiced flour. Cover the fish thickly with the spiced flour, pressing it in firmly so it coats thoroughly and evenly. Fry in two batches until golden brown (about 2 minutes), and drain on kitchen paper. Serve immediately on warmed plates, with the aïoli.

Serves 4

Summer Salad Roscoff

with Lobster and Basil Mayonnaise

—

2 eggs

1 live lobster, about 750 g/1½ lb

mixed salad leaves

6 red cherry tomatoes, halved

6 yellow cherry tomatoes, halved

½ avocado, sliced

**50 g/2 oz fresh broad beans,
blanched and peeled**

¼ cucumber, peeled, deseeded, and sliced

Vinaigrette:

3 tablespoons white wine vinegar

3 tablespoons balsamic vinegar

½ teaspoon salt

½ teaspoon freshly ground black pepper

2 teaspoons Dijon mustard

250 ml/8 fl oz olive and/or vegetable oil

Basil Mayonnaise:

1 tablespoon wine vinegar

1 tablespoon Dijon mustard

3 egg yolks

500 ml/17 fl oz vegetable oil (or light olive oil)

6 tablespoons chopped fresh basil leaves

salt and freshly ground white pepper

Boil the eggs for 9 minutes, drain and cool in a bowl of cold water. When ready to assemble the salad, shell the eggs and cut lengthways into quarters.

To make the mayonnaise, whisk the vinegar, mustard, salt and pepper in a bowl until the salt is dissolved. Beat in the egg yolks, then whisk in the oil slowly, drop by drop. As the mayonnaise starts to thicken, you can add the oil slightly faster, but incorporate each addition fully before adding more.

Just before serving, add the chopped basil, taste and adjust the seasoning.

To make the vinaigrette, place the vinegars in a small bowl or blender, add the salt, pepper, and mustard, and stir or blend until dissolved. Whisk in the oil slowly, a tablespoon at a time at first, to allow it to be incorporated, then a little faster. Taste and adjust the seasoning. This can be made in advance and stored in the refrigerator for up to 2 days.

To cook the lobster, heat a big pot of water to a vigorous boil. Put the lobster in and let it cook for about 14 minutes. To stop the cooking process, plunge the lobster into a pot of ice-cold water. Shell and clean the lobster, and slice the meat neatly.

To serve, toss the mixed salad leaves in the vinaigrette, and pile in the centre of each plate. Surround with the red and yellow cherry tomatoes, the sliced avocado, broad beans, cucumber slices, quartered hard-boiled eggs and lobster meat. Spoon over the basil mayonnaise, either in one generous dollop, or drizzled over the dish. Serve immediately.

Serves 4

Seared Beef Salad

with Celery and Truffle Oil

——

500 g/1 lb beef fillet, trimmed and

free from fat and sinew

½ teaspoon salt

½ teaspoon cracked black peppercorns

1 tablespoon light olive oil

Celery:

6 celery sticks, lightly

peeled, and sliced

150 ml/¼ pint water

2 garlic cloves, crushed

½ teaspoon salt

2 tablespoons virgin olive oil

pinch of cracked black peppercorns

Dressing:

50 ml/2 fl oz virgin olive oil

50 ml/2 fl oz white truffle oil

50 ml/2 fl oz balsamic vinegar

50 ml/2 fl oz beef gravy

salt and freshly ground black pepper

To garnish:

125 g/4 oz rocket leaves

4 tablespoons fresh Parmesan shavings

Heat a heavy cast-iron pan over high heat, until very hot. Cut the beef fillet in half lengthways, and season with the salt, pepper, and oil. Sear in the very hot pan for 1 minute on each side, until charred on the outside but very rare in the middle. Allow to cool.

Place the celery, water, garlic and salt in a small pan. Bring to the boil, cover and simmer for about 5 minutes, or until the celery is cooked. Remove from the heat, add the olive oil and cracked black pepper, and allow to infuse for at least 1 hour.

Place all the ingredients for the dressing in a small bowl and stir gently with a spoon.

To serve, slice the cooled beef into slices 5 mm/¼ inch thick. Place a layer of sliced beef on 6 cool plates, then add the cooked celery, rocket, and Parmesan shavings, repeating until you have used up all the ingredients. Drizzle the truffle oil dressing generously over each plate, and serve at once.

Serves 6

Peppered Duck Breast

with Spinach, Chanterelles and Cream

—

4 large duck breasts, Aylesbury or Barbary

4 tablespoons cracked black peppercorns

15 g/½ oz butter

2 tablespoons light olive oil

1 tablespoon finely chopped shallots

125 ml/4 fl oz Cognac

1 tablespoon sherry vinegar

200 ml/7 fl oz reduced duck stock

200 ml/7 fl oz double cream

1 tablespoon finely chopped dried cèpes, soaked in 1 cup boiling water

salt

To garnish:

6 tablespoons butter

200 g/7 oz fresh spinach

6 tablespoons vegetable oil

200 g/7 oz chanterelles

Remove the skin from the duck breasts. Spread the cracked black peppercorns over the breasts, pressing down to form a thick crust. Season with salt.

Heat the butter and oil in a frying pan, and sauté the duck breasts for 3 minutes on each side for medium rare, or 6 minutes on each side for well done. Remove the duck breasts and set aside to keep warm. Slice just before serving.

Add the chopped shallots to the pan and cook over a low heat for 30 seconds. Do not allow the shallots to colour at all. Deglaze the pan with the Cognac and sherry vinegar, stirring well to scrape up the meat juices. Add the duck stock and cream, bring to the boil and reduce until the sauce coats the back of a spoon.

To make the garnish, heat half the butter in a pan and sauté the spinach until wilted. Heat the oil and remaining butter in another pan, sauté the mushrooms gently and mix with the spinach.

To serve, spoon the spinach and mushroom mixture on to plates. Arrange the sliced duck breasts on top and spoon the sauce around. Serve with potato skins on the side.

Serves 4

White Chocolate and Raspberry Trifle

―――

6 eggs, separated

2 teaspoons vanilla essence

275 g/9 oz white chocolate, melted,

then cooled slightly

125 g/4 oz caster sugar

375 ml/13 fl oz raspberry coulis

275 g/9 oz fresh raspberries

White Chocolate Mousse:

2 eggs

125 ml/4 fl oz crème anglaise,

at room temperature

375 g/12 oz white chocolate, melted,

then cooled slightly

400 ml/14 fl oz whipping cream,

whipped to soft peaks

To serve:

75 g/3 oz white chocolate

75 g/3 oz dark chocolate

a few mint leaves

Line a baking sheet with greased grease-proof paper. Mix the egg yolks and vanilla into the melted chocolate. Whisk the egg whites and sugar to firm and glossy peaks. Fold the whites into the chocolate mixture, making sure it is well mixed and homogenous. Spread thinly and evenly over the prepared baking sheet – it should be about 1 cm/½ inch thick.

Bake in a preheated oven at 180°C (350°F) Gas Mark 4 for about 15 minutes, or until the mixture is firm and coming away at the edges.

Place the biscuit on a wire rack to cool – it will sink slightly as it cools.

When cool, cut out pieces in suitable shapes to line the trifle dish or sundae glass.

To make the mousse, place the eggs in a mixing bowl over a pan of simmering water. Whisk over gentle heat until slightly warmer than body temperature. They will have doubled in volume, and lightened in colour. Place the mixing bowl on a mixer with a whisk attachment and continue to whisk, at medium speed, until cool. Slowly add the *crème anglaise*, followed by the chocolate. Take off the machine at this point, and whisk in the cream by hand. This mousse will remain quite soft.

To assemble the trifles, put a layer of the chocolate biscuit into the bottom of a trifle or sundae dish, and soak with the raspberry coulis. Add a few raspberries, then ladle in white chocolate mousse until the dish is one-third full. Add more chocolate biscuit, then more coulis, and a generous layer of berries. Add another layer of the white chocolate mousse. Refrigerate until ready to serve.

Make curls of plain and white chocolate by shaving them off the block with a vegetable peeler. To serve, decorate the edges of the trifle with a few more berries, pile the chocolate curls high in the centre, then add mint leaves.

Serves 6-8

Hilary Brown

As you drive east of the City Bypass, leaving endless columns of articulated transports to thunder on down the A1, the coast road to North Berwick opens on to a bleak landscape of black boulders, sluiced by a grey sea – Cockenzie Power Station, like a mindless cosh, bruising this southerly shore of the Firth of Forth. At Aberlady, there is an abrupt change of scene. The road twists through the village and past a green where old men walk their dogs in the early morning. Gullane is two miles further on and you are now in serious golfing country. Undulating hillocks and broad plains, a jigsaw of long grasses and greens shaved smooth, are dotted with figures hauling buggies and squat trees flattened by the winds sweeping off the North Sea.

Gullane was created for golf, or so it seems. As you approach the village, the first building you see is the clubhouse, a low-slung cream and orange construction at the head of Main Street. In less than a minute you will be through and out the other side. There is a bank and a filling station, a butcher, a baker, a grocer and all the other unremarkable shop fronts you might expect to see in an unremarkable village high street. To the impatient motorist, the only noteworthy feature might be an enormous willow tree reaching high over the roof-tops, its loose-limbed boughs spreading half-way across the road.

The willow bears a symbolic charm. Like a lovers' tryst, it admits the few who have come to know and share its secret but it gently excludes the rest of the universe. Pass under the tree and you enter a different world. It is as if you were Alice passing through her looking-glass into Looking-Glass House, except that the tiny cottage hidden behind the hanging foliage is La Potinière. This dream is real and its two inhabitants certainly bear no resemblance to Tweedledum and Tweedledee. Still, there is a sense of fantasy about the place fulfilling, as it does, a romantic illusion conceived by its owners, David and Hilary Brown. La Potinière is a restaurant like no other. To enjoy it and to understand it, the uninitiated have to suspend all the preconceived notions of how restaurants usually behave. In Gullane, I would not wonder if most of the local people did not know it existed – or if they do, they may think it is still a tea room, as it was many years ago before it disappeared from view.

The last word in the title of David and Hilary Brown's book *La Potinière and Friends* (Century, 1990) neatly suggests the spirit of this unique gastronomic hideaway. In its introduction, one brief sentence bluntly states their *raison d'être*: 'We really only want to be found by those who want to find us.' These are not the arrogant words of a haughty, pretentious restaurateur. The Browns are modest and warm-hearted, demure, but also terrific fun. La Potinière exudes a civilized homeliness which cuts through money, class, chic and all the other social sensibilities that consume posh eateries. These words, then, are a simple statement of the way Hilary and David prefer to conduct their lives – lives which happen to coincide with an occupation to which they are completely devoted. As such, the joy of living is the greater if they are able to relate to their visitors in a genuine spirit of friendship rather than as customers. It is the ultimate expression of hospitality – an act of giving and receiving which only becomes a sham if they and their visitors are unable to enjoy each other's company.

Eating at La Potinière is like visiting friends at home. If you are coming to lunch, you are asked for one o'clock. Dinner is served at eight and latecomers apologize politely to their host.

" La Potinière is a restaurant like no other. To enjoy it and to understand it, the uninitiated have to suspend all the preconceived notions of how restaurants usually behave "

There is no staff – except for a washer-up at weekends. There is no menu because you eat what Hilary has cooked that day. There are no 'ladies' and 'gents' – just the guest loo.

These two remarkable people serve one meal a day for up to thirty people – dinners are on Fridays and Saturdays. They declare Wednesday as their day off but it is taken up with a shopping expedition to Edinburgh and, in the evening, their dining room is usually booked for a private party. This has been their routine since 1975. By any measure, it is an heroic achievement – and one which has demanded a regime that is almost saintly in its fidelity and self-discipline. To survive, they keep themselves spanking fit. In twenty years, they have never been ill – they daren't – and the only day they have closed was when David's mother died. But, like some psychosomatic pressure gauge, David invariably goes down with a stinking cold at the beginning of October – the month of their annual holiday – and Hilary then dutifully follows suit.

The first time I passed under the willow and into the cottage, I had arrived unconscionably early. The room was empty but it embraces you immediately with an indefinable glow of old-fashioned welcome. Nothing startles, everything soothes – pristine, pretty, cosy and comforting all at once. An arrangement of white and yellow lilies set in September flower exploded out of a copper wine cooler on a lace-draped table in the centre. A fine oak dresser heaved with dozens of bottles. The low-beamed ceiling was hung with baskets and bunches of dried flowers. The tables, immaculately set, were laid in pink, and the chairs – simple, wicker-backed – were perfectly in place. As I stepped into the room, I nearly tripped over a Hoover and a head appeared from under a table. This is how I met David Brown. He was busy with his final chore – on hands and knees – meticulously combing out the tassels at the end of the carpet.

In the kitchen at the back of the house, music played quietly from a CD, sharing space on a shelf with jars, tubs and stacks of loose paper. Hilary Brown – in striped apron and yellow rubber gloves, her shock of frizzy hair held back by a pert black bow – was also busy. It was nearly one o'clock, nearly time. It was a moment no different in mood from any other domestic scene just before the arrival of guests.

Hilary Stanley and David Brown were teenage sweethearts who met at school in 1967. She was fifteen, he sixteen. They have been inseparable ever since and Hilary's brilliance as a cook owes everything to their devotion for each another. They treasure their close friends but the rare bond between these two people still blushes with an intimacy and a mystery which is their own.

They both grew up in Glasgow in neighbouring middle-class districts south of the city centre. She came from Newlands which was considered slightly smarter than Shawlands where David lived. 'But we were at the Newlands end of Shawlands,' he cracks wryly. Both were the youngest members of their families and both were educated at Hutcheson's Grammar.

Shy and a little coy, Hilary did not mix easily with other children, preferring her home comforts, spending hours watching her mother in the kitchen. She always enjoyed her food and ate sweets constantly, exercising her curiosity by sucking Fry's Chocolate Creams, Crunchies and Walnut Whips, layer by layer, until they made her tongue sore.

> **" Her food may betray the occasional touch or idea of some stellar Frenchman, but the style is unmistakably her own – uniquely Potinière "**

At school she came top in needlework and designed and made her own dresses. She was also junior athletics champion but she failed to make the senior grade because by then she had met David who was captain of the boys' team. 'Meeting ruined our sporting careers,' he smiles. 'It took the legs from us!'

When they left Hutcheson's, David went to Glasgow School of Art and Hilary enrolled on a three-year course at the city's College of Domestic Science. From her first day at a stove she was hooked. 'College did not teach me anything elaborate,' she says 'but it did teach me to have standards.' At home, she read her way through the family's small collection of cookery books and, eventually, a compliant mother gave way to her in the kitchen after she complained that the gravy for Sunday's roast and the cheese sauce to go with the cauliflower were not being properly made.

That David Brown and Hilary Stanley would eventually marry seems to have been written from the moment of their first encounter. She had to wait until the last dance. He claims he was nervous. One heady turn around the floor. One sweet kiss. And the match was made. So, as Hilary advanced through college, her growing confidence as a cook was resolutely harnessed to provide for the future. She and a friend devised an up-market 'meals-on-wheels' service, she sold her own shortbreads and home-made mince pies, she ran buffet parties for her family and friends, and she took a summer job in British Steel's staff canteen.

These extra-curricular activities were valuable experiences but they do little to illuminate the path that would finally lead to Gullane. Hilary and David were a young, sensitive, artistic couple who became utterly absorbed in one another and they found that restaurants provided the most agreeable setting to be alone together. At first they ate in local steak bars and Italian bistros, and gradually a keener interest took root. It was their courtship and the way it was pursued which laid the foundation for what eventually ripened into a unique personal and professional partnership. 'It wasn't for the gammon steak and pineapple,' says Hilary. 'Restaurants were romantic places.'

By the early Seventies they had discovered Houstoun

House, Keith and Penny Knight's celebrated sixteenth century pile at Uphall near Livingston. The Knights offered no choice on their menus and, unwittingly, Houstoun became the seminal spell which set the formula at La Potinière five years later. Meanwhile, David and Hilary's enthusiasm for eating out became an eccentric addiction. To celebrate her twenty-first birthday, Hilary prepared a grand buffet at home and then left her family to enjoy the party while she and David ate in splendour at Malmaison, Glasgow's plushest restaurant.

In December that year, 1973, Hilary and David were married. They honeymooned in Paris and returned twelve months later to celebrate their anniversary at Le Grand Vefour – their first taste of a three-star restaurant, and one which was followed over the years by visits to every single three-star palace in France – a feat of gastronomic endurance unmatched by any other restaurateur I know.

By now, Hilary was teaching home economics at a Catholic school in Pollock – a job she hated – and David had put himself through a post-graduate degree before accepting a design consultancy with an architectural practice. He had also become a serious amateur wine buff. At home they began to throw dazzlingly recherché dinner parties at weekends. Hilary's five-course menus would be served by David with a succession of exceptional wines and they kept a card index system noting all the details. A dinner in September 1974, for example, featured *oeuf en gelée*, onion soup, *gigot d'agneau farci* (a stuffing of mushrooms, kidneys and thyme) with Dauphinois potatoes, cheese and a fresh fruit *brûlée*. The wines included Château Léoville Poyferré 1923 and the port was Fonseca. They still have these reference cards – dozens and dozens of them – all carefully annotated with observations which read like a comic guide to the connoisseurship (or lack of it) of their family and friends; 'Barbara and Elspeth left the jelly' . . . 'Dad finds skin indigestible' . . . 'John had second helpings of cheesecake. Faith left an onion' . . . 'David particularly likes fish in sauce but Susan not a jelly person' . . . A similar index is maintained religiously at La Potinière today.

‟ There is an elusive serenity about this food which corresponds perfectly with the timeless simplicity of La Potinière itself ”

The Browns believe that such meticulous record-keeping is essential to assist her in planning her daily menus, as it avoids serving the faithful with dishes they may have eaten in the past. Sometimes the selection process can be as complex as a game of chess, but this degree of care for their guests is central to their philosophy.

'It is important,' she says, 'to keep in touch with the people I am cooking for and to remember that they are all special.'

David and Hilary's passion for dining out and the pleasure of entertaining at home made the decision to open their own restaurant inevitable. But there was another reason – more personal, more fundamental. Hilary was unhappy in her work and the demands of David's design studio kept them apart. 'I've always been quite possessive,' she confesses, 'and I really didn't like the fact that we weren't together during the day. After all, David's my best friend – we missed one another.'

On 1st October, 1975, David and Hilary Brown woke up in their new premises. La Potinière's previous owner had been a French Algerian lady. They had eaten there from time to time in the past, and the size and feel of the place suited them perfectly. But on that first morning, Hilary was in a daze, still overcome by the excitement of the move and completely unprepared for the ten lunch bookings in the diary. Stepping out into Main Street, she visited the butcher and the grocer, and her first menu consisted of celery soup, chicken legs in a Provençal sauce and ice-cream from the French Algerian lady's deep-freeze. Two decades on, this tiny unassuming restaurant in Gullane ranks with the best in Britain.

While Hilary Brown's cooking has evolved over the years, menus remain true to the principles established in 1975. The same may be said of the buying. With the exception of a few specialist foods, nothing is delivered to the kitchen door. The Browns shop at Sainsbury's and Marks & Spencer in Edinburgh, and items like olive oil, Parmesan and Puy lentils are bought from Valvona & Crolla, a delicatessen in Elm Row which makes Fortnum & Mason look like a corner shop.

Evolution, however, should not be confused with elaboration. Certainly, much of the cooking has been informed by the Browns' annual tours of France – and indeed elsewhere. But Hilary's way is not derivative. She is no mimic. Her food may betray the occasional touch or idea of some stellar Frenchman, but the style is unmistakably her own – uniquely Potinière. At heart, this is dinner party cooking of the highest order presented in the same spirit as her gastronomic soirées in Glasgow. It is the unembellished cooking of the gifted amateur. The intention is not to impress by invention or display. Instead, she beguiles you with the clarity of her flavours, the precision of her seasonings and the purity of her sauces. There is an elusive serenity about this food which corresponds perfectly with the timeless simplicity of La Potinière itself. When you leave Gullane, you leave happy and content.

To begin, there is soup – usually of vegetable and always served with a herb leaf floating on a pool of lightly whipped

cream, a Hilary Brown trademark. This bright, comforting potage may be tomato and basil or pea with mint. If it is her pea soup, a long-running classic, its secret lies in the choice of vegetable. The peas must be Birdseye Frozen – nothing less will do. She has tested the recipe with fresh peas and all the other frozen brands. But for a perfect purée and a sweeter flavour, Birdseye is best.

Fish courses, and the principal dishes which follow, demonstrate Hilary Brown's range – the depth of her learning and the breadth of her skills. They also illustrate the detail and thought she applies to produce the exact balances of flavour and texture she wants out of each composition. A muscular wedge of salmon – seared on its surface, pink and juicy within – is pitched against a pile of spiced lentils: these two elements beautifully modulated by a sauce of morels and chanterelles. In contrast, a lemon sole with pesto is gentler and more feminine, its olive oil lubricant marbled with the concentrated essence of spinach – a trick she spotted on a visit to Michel Trama in Puymirol. Similarly, a honeyed leg of guinea fowl stuffed with dried apricots and mint strikes a North African note while a breast of mallard with pearl barley has echoes closer to home.

These main courses are accompanied by Hilary's Dauphinois potatoes – a famous Potinière standard, but one in which she occasionally substitutes lemon zest for garlic. The same single-mindedness comes with the cheese. It is always a beautiful unpasteurized brie in peak condition. Why, one wonders, are the Browns so uncompromising in their choice? 'Keep it simple and do it right,' they cry. If Pyramide in Vienne always served Saint-Marcellin, Potinière in Gullane can serve brie: a whopping slice of gastronomic casuistry, perhaps (there are good cheeses in Lothian), but the principle is sound.

To finish, Hilary's puddings are as versatile as everything that has gone before – from a melting lemon surprise based on her grandmother's recipe to a sublime raspberry gratin inspired by Robuchon in Paris. Both are different, both are exquisite – but each shines with that simplicity and comfort that you immediately associate with home.

For all the pleasure of eating at La Potinière, the exhilaration of Hilary's remarkable gift matched equally by David Brown's extraordinary knowledge of wines might suggest a question about the limitations they have imposed on their ambition. The answer returns to where this story began. It lies deep within the personal life force which binds these two rare people. 'It is not so much a question of recognizing our limitations as recognizing a balance between peace of mind, enjoying life and yet doing something worthwhile,' says David. 'If we were to get on the treadmill of something grander, Hilary and I would suffer.' And so would the pleasure of their many friends.

Tomato and Basil Soup

—

50 g/2 oz unsalted butter

250 g/8 oz onions, finely sliced

1 kg/2 lb tomatoes, the redder the better

75 ml/3 fl oz dry sherry

1 tablespoon caster sugar

20 g/³/₄ oz fresh basil

salt and freshly ground black pepper

To garnish:

a little lightly whipped cream

6 sprigs of basil

Melt the butter in a saucepan. Add the onions and cook gently until softened but not coloured. Stir from time to time with a wooden spoon.

Add the tomatoes whole, with skins and stalks, then add the sherry and sugar. No water is required at this stage. Stir well, cover, then simmer for 45–60 minutes. Stir occasionally.

Ladle the mixture into a liquidizer or food processor, and blend until smooth. Add the fresh basil and process for 15 seconds.

Pour the soup through a *mouli* into the rinsed-out pan. Stir, then add enough water to correct the consistency. It should have plenty of body, so do not add too much water – the tomatoes should have created enough liquid. Season to taste with 1–2 teaspoons salt.

Just before serving, reheat and ladle into 6 warmed soup bowls or a large tureen. Garnish with lightly whipped cream and a sprig of basil.

Serves 6

Lemon Sole

with Pesto, Sauce Vierge, and Crispy Courgettes

———

3 tablespoons olive oil

25 g/1 oz finely chopped red pepper

1 small garlic clove, finely chopped

6 fillets of lemon sole, about 125 g/4 oz each

3 tablespoons pesto

750 g/1½ lb dark green courgettes

vegetable oil, e.g. sunflower, for deep-frying

375 g/12 oz fresh spinach, washed and dried

about 23 leaves of fresh basil

15 g/½ oz unsalted butter

salt and freshly ground black pepper

To make the *sauce vierge*, gently heat the olive oil, add the red pepper, 3 of the basil leaves, the garlic and salt. Keep warm.

If necessary, skin the sole. If it has been skinned already, the membrane may still be intact and cause the fish to curl during cooking. If so, cut a few slashes along the membrane, without actually going right through the fish. Cover and refrigerate until needed.

Wash and dry the courgettes. Remove the ends. Preferably using a mandoline, cut into long matchsticks, 2 mm/¹⁄₁₆ inch thick. Using your fingertips, lift and separate the strips.

Pour the oil into a heavy pan to about 2.5 cm/1 inch deep. Heat to 190°C (375°F) and, wearing rubber gloves to stop you being splattered with oil, drop in the strips of courgette. Stir around, then leave to fry until golden.

Using a slotted spoon, transfer the crispy strips on to an ovenproof tray, lined with a double layer of kitchen paper. Tease them so that they are light and airy, then sprinkle with salt.

If you have a juice extractor, press in the basil and 90 g/3½ oz of the spinach, and place a jam jar under the hole. Switch on. A small amount of highly concentrated spinach and basil juice will pour into the jam jar. Cover and refrigerate until needed.

Lay the sole on a chopping board, skin-side up. Season lightly, then spread with a teaspoon of pesto. Fold over, with the thicker end over the tail end. Arrange the sole on a buttered ovenproof tray, leaving a little space between each one. Sprinkle with cold water and season lightly.

Place the remaining spinach in a large pan, add the butter, salt and 1 tablespoon of cold water. Cover and place on a high heat until wilted, then drain through a colander, shaking to remove excess liquid.

At the same time, cook the sole in a preheated oven at 240°C (475°F) Gas Mark 9 for 5–6 minutes, depending on the thickness of the fish. Don't overcook it!

To serve, place the spinach on 6 heated dinner plates. Using a pointed spoon, drizzle some *sauce vierge* around it, then, using a teaspoon, drop little blobs of the spinach and basil juice through the oil. Top with a piece of sole (use a fish slice), then balance a mound of courgette strips on top. (Reheat for 1 minute in the oven when you remove the sole.) Serve immediately.

Serves 6

Mallard with Barley,

Wild Mushrooms and a Red Wine Sauce

——

3 mallards

2 teaspoons hazelnut oil

2 teaspoons olive oil

2 teaspoons Chinese five-spice powder

6–12 dried morels

15 g/½ oz dried trompettes de la mort

90 g/3½ oz unsalted butter

2 leeks, white part only, finely chopped

1 garlic clove, crushed

200 g/7 oz pearl barley

300 ml/½ pint red wine

2 teaspoons redcurrant jelly

300 ml/½ pint defatted home-made duck or chicken stock

salt and freshly ground black pepper

The day before cooking, remove the mallard breasts with a small, sharp knife. Place them, skin-side down, on a chopping board and remove the layer of fat, as if skinning a piece of fish. Place the breasts in a bowl, add the oils and spice, mix well, cover with clingfilm and refrigerate until required. Remove from the refrigerator at least an hour before cooking. (Use the chopped-up carcasses to make stock.)

Soak the morels in a little hot water, and the trompettes in 300 ml/½ pint hot water.

Melt 75 g/3 oz of the butter in a saucepan, add the leeks and garlic, cook gently until softened, then add the barley. Stir, add most of the trompettes and the strained soaking liquid. Stir, bring to the boil and simmer for 5 minutes until slightly thickened. Place in an ovenproof dish and cover with foil (and clingfilm under the foil if it touches the barley). Cook in a preheated oven at 150°C (300°F) Gas Mark 2 for 1 hour.

Remove from the oven, discard the foil and loosen the barley and mushroom mixture with a fork. Taste and adjust the seasoning. Increase the temperature to 240°C (475°F) Gas Mark 9.

Place the wine and jelly in a pan, bring to the boil and reduce by three-quarters. Add the stock and the remaining butter and reduce by fast boiling to a slightly syrupy consistency. Whisk with a balloon whisk occasionally. Lift the morels out of the soaking liquid and add to the sauce, along with the remaining trompettes.

Meanwhile, heat a dry frying pan until very hot. Add the pieces of duck and cook, skin-side down, for 30 seconds. Turn and cook for another 30 seconds – just enough to brown.

Place on an ovenproof tray, sprinkle with salt, and place on the middle shelf of the oven for 9 minutes. Deglaze the pan with a little water and add to the sauce. Remove the duck and allow to rest for a few minutes. Reheat the sauce if necessary, taste and adjust the seasoning. Whisk with a balloon whisk until smooth.

To serve, reheat the barley mixture and place a spoonful on 6 warmed serving plates. Place the breasts on a chopping board and slice at an angle into 5–6 slices, and arrange on top of the bed of barley. Spoon a little sauce over or around them and serve immediately.

Serves 6

Raspberry Gratin

350 g/12 oz caster sugar

1 packet powdered gelatine

150 ml/¼ pint double cream

150 ml/¼ pint lemon juice

25 g/1 oz cornflour

10 egg yolks, and 7 egg whites, size 2

275 g/9 oz fresh raspberries

icing sugar, for dusting

Place 300 g/10 oz of the caster sugar with 175 ml/6 fl oz cold water in a saucepan. Bring to the boil, stirring gently until the sugar dissolves. Boil rapidly until reduced to 150 ml/¼ pint of sugar syrup.

Measure 75 ml/3 fl oz of cold water into a cup, sprinkle the packet of gelatine over and stir. Place in a pan, containing enough water to come halfway up the sides of the cup, and simmer, stirring gently until the gelatine has dissolved. Remove from the heat but leave the cup in the water.

Pour the cream into a pan. Use a little of the lemon juice to slake the cornflour, then add to the cream. Add the remaining lemon juice and bring to the boil, whisking with a balloon whisk until thickened. Cook for a further 2 minutes, then add the yolks, all at once, and whisk together over a medium heat until thickened further. (It will look curdled at this point, but will right itself.)

Sieve the lemony mixture into a bowl, pressing it through with a spatula. Add the dissolved gelatine and mix gently. (The gelatine should still feel hot to the touch.)

Whisk the whites in a spotlessly clean bowl, using a hand-held or free-standing mixer, until lightly whipped.

Gradually whisk in the remaining sugar, until the mixture forms soft peaks. Pour in the hot sugar syrup in a slow stream, continuing to whisk to a dense, stiff consistency. (Take care not to over-beat, or the whites will become dry and lumpy.)

Whisk one-quarter of the beaten whites into the lemony mixture, then fold in the remainder.

Place ten 10 cm/4 inch non-stick muffin rings on a tray lined with waxed paper. Using a ladle or a large spoon, half-fill each ring mould with lemon mixture. Place 8 raspberries in each mould, then fill them up completely with the mixture. Smooth level with the top of the rings, using a palette knife. Refrigerate until needed, for up to 24 hours, or freeze. (If using frozen mixtures, allow to defrost for at least 2 hours before grilling.)

Thirty minutes before serving, preheat the grill to very hot. Slide a fish slice under each ring, transfer to heatproof serving plates, run a knife round the inside edge of the rings and lift off. Dust thickly with icing sugar, place on a heatproof tray and slide under the grill, close to the heat source. Watch them like a hawk, as they burn quickly: the sugar should just turn an even, golden, crisp caramel.

Remove, place on an underplate and serve immediately – they don't like waiting around!

Serves 10

Citron Surprise

50 g/2 oz unsalted butter, softened

2 eggs, size 2, separated

90 g/3½ oz caster sugar,

plus extra for sprinkling

15 g/½ oz plain flour

finely grated rind and juice of 1 lemon

250 ml/8 fl oz milk

Place the butter, egg yolks, sugar, flour and grated lemon rind in a food processor and blend until smooth. Add the milk and lemon juice, and blend. Pour into a bowl and leave for at least 1 hour.

Place the egg whites in a spotlessly clean bowl and, using an electric beater or balloon whisk, beat until stiff. With a large metal spoon, gently fold into the lemon mixture.

Place six 150 ml/¼ pint ramekins in a *bain-marie*, ladle the mixture into the ramekins and pour enough boiling water into the *bain-marie* to come half-way up the sides of the ramekins. Carefully place on the front of the middle shelf in a preheated oven and cook, undisturbed, at 180°C (350°F) Gas Mark 4 for 35–40 minutes. By this time they will be slightly risen, rounded on top and golden brown.

Sprinkle with extra caster sugar, place on plates or saucers and serve immediately.

Serves 6

John Webber

In the days when the taxidermist's art was admired, the billiard rooms of our great country houses traditionally doubled as galleries for their estates' noblest trophies. There is good shooting at Kinnaird, pheasant mostly, and some roe-stalking too. But the true passion of the Ward family – since 1927 owners of these 9,000 acres of Perthshire by Dunkeld – was salmon fishing. For this magnificent estate also comes with three miles of the River Tay.

On the walls above the cedar panelling in Kinnaird's billiard room, seven glass cases display the evidence of this family's sporting prowess. It is not without drama. On the morning of 12th October, 1928, Major the Hon. Sir John Ward caught a whopper. It weighed forty-four pounds (about 20 kg) and, in euphoric mood, his feat was properly celebrated at luncheon. That afternoon, his eighteen-year-old cousin, Miss Lettice Ward – a strapping muscular young lady by all accounts – landed a fish which out-weighed her host's by a clear six pounds. Dinner that evening was altogether more subdued with Sir John barely able to disguise his irritation at being out-classed by his teenage junior – and a female to boot.

Some seventy years on, the lure of the Tay is as irresistible as ever. The Wards' family and friends may have been replaced by escapees from city boardrooms, but the peace and the pleasure is the same. One early September morning, as I sat rodless by the banks of the river on Kinnaird's lower beat, it was pleasure enough for me to watch, unseen, a lonely figure waist-deep in the water – absorbed, whipping his line in figures of eight across the shimmering surface. At last, the mists were lifting off the hill behind the house and the sun was on my back.

The sight and sound of the river is mesmerizing – a noisy kaleidoscope of light and shade, rush and rumble. As the river swings through ninety degrees around an apron of white boulders, the deep-throated bass notes mid-stream are mixed with a lighter chorus of gurgling eddies which fade into breathless murmurs by the water's edge. Suddenly, from somewhere beneath this bubbling swirl, there was an inexplicable commotion and finally my patience was rewarded. To my astonishment, a salmon leaped out of a ballooning pool – a beautiful silvery plume, seen and then gone like a comet in the sky.

John Webber's arrival at Kinnaird in 1988 may have been ordained. Fishing has always been his great passion and the moment he set eyes on the estate, he knew he had found his idyll. Creatively, Kinnaird has also been his making as a cook but there is a certain fatalistic quality about his route to Perthshire – a tendency which appears to have been a common thread throughout his working life. Easy-going, undriven though dedicated, and utterly selfless in his outlook (surely unique in a chef), he has never actively pursued advancement. Glittering opportunities have just come his way, each one with a purpose which seems to have predetermined the next.

Kinnaird today is owned by Mrs Constance Ward, the widow of Reggie, Sir John and Lady Ward's second son. It was Connie Ward, a breezy but shrewd East Coast American, who had the wit to revive her neglected house by transforming it into a small hotel. Antiques, family portraits and heirlooms – including the famous salmon in the billiard room – were dusted off and rearranged, and Kinnaird now breathes again, grandly celebrating the nostalgia of the good old days. The odd eccentric folly contributes to the experience. The breakfast room is dominated by a sensuous portrait of Jean, Lady Ward, and a vast sideboard displays an extraordinary collection of ornate copper *bombe* and jelly moulds, each boldly engraved with her two initials. The amusing irony of the JW monogram is lost on most intrepid gastronomes for whom Kinnaird has now become a Highland address more closely associated with the home of John Webber and his illustrious kitchen.

" Easy-going, undriven though dedicated, and utterly selfless in his outlook . . . he has never actively pursued advancement "

While Connie Ward's restoration of the house was a *tour de force* in itself, she also knew that success as a country house hotel of this ilk would depend on the reputation of her dining room. The hand that played the ace came from another member of the family. Mrs Ward's son-in-law is Lord Thurso, formerly the Hon. John

Sinclair, the distinguished Savoy-trained hotelier who was John Webber's employer at Cliveden in Berkshire. It was Sinclair who artfully engineered Webber's transfer to Kinnaird, a move which finally established his place among the best in Britain's select league of country house chefs. 'John's craftsmanship is of the very highest order,' says John Sinclair. 'He is also the nicest chef I've ever met. Most of them have a streak of evil somewhere in their make-up. Not John. He is the most genuine chef I know.' This is an apt commentary on the life of a jovial, gentle and thoughtful human being who has risen quietly to the top in a singularly tough profession.

For a man who has spent most of his career working in some of the grandest mansions in the land, the first twenty years of John Webber's life were marked by far humbler surroundings. Born in Selly Oak, Birmingham, in 1951, he grew up the only child of a GPO engineer and his wife. Home was a council prefab erected on an unlit dirt-track by the edge of a municipal recreation ground.

When John was just eleven years old, his mother died, but the tragedy brought father and son closer together and they became best mates. If his father was called out on a night emergency, John would join him down manholes in the centre of Birmingham. 'We had a stove going,' he says. 'It was a bit like underground camping.' At weekends, they would often shoot down to Weston-super-Mare for the day – play a game of snooker in the halls above Burtons, eat a bag of chips on the pier and drive home again. In the house, John shared the domestic chores and, inevitably, lent a hand with the cooking, which he rather enjoyed. Early Webber specialities included a bread pudding which he cut into slabs. 'They would have made great British Rail sleepers,' he says, roaring with laughter. So, when the moment came for him to leave school, he decided that he would either follow his father into the GPO or try his luck as a chef. As Birmingham College of Food offered

him a place, he chose the second option, knowing that he could always fall back on the GPO if all else failed. Two years later, diploma in hand and now eighteen, John Webber suddenly found himself confronted by an uncomfortable dilemma. His tutors advised him to head for London but, at the same time, his father was on the point of retirement and he did not want to abandon him. In the end, his father persuaded him to go and he found his first job at the Park Lane Hotel. 'Not the best place to start your career,' he says, 'but in those days you had no idea.'

While Webber's first four years in London contributed little to his craft apart from a few bad habits, he did learn to survive the rawer edge of life in a big hotel kitchen. His roly-poly frame and amiable personality endeared him to his workmates but at heart he has always been something of a loner, perfectly content in his own company. In winter, to kill time between shifts, he would buy a newspaper and travel round the Circle Line just to keep warm. And in the summer, he took his rods to Hyde Park to fish for roach and tench in the Serpentine.

It was while he was at the Park Lane that John Webber faced his greatest personal crisis. In 1972, his father died. The shock affected him deeply and he was now forced to make another critical decision about his future. The options this time were either to pursue an embryonic career or return to Birmingham to claim his rights on the council house in Selly Oak. One offered uncertainty, the other represented security. After months of thought, he finally decided to sever his links with home. It was a terrible wrench from everything he had known and loved.

By 1973, John Webber was in a rut – going with the flow and getting nowhere. He was in a regular job and he felt safe. Meanwhile, his more ambitious pals were moving on, and one of them eventually persuaded him to join Eugene Kaufeler's more prestigious kitchen at the Dorchester. In 1976, Kaufeler retired as *Maître Chef des Cuisines* and the top job passed to a rising star, the twenty-nine-year-old Anton Mosimann.

In Britain, the Seventies ushered in the age of *nouvelle cuisine* and Mosimann became its leading protagonist. Much abused and more maligned, the principles of the new style remain good today. The only difference is that chefs are being more generous with their portions. Mosimann's gift to John Webber was to trans-

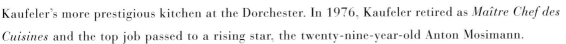

ʟʟ John Webber's four years at the Dorchester under Anton Mosimann were his seminal foundation ʟʟ

form him from an unthinking, mechanical jobbing cook into a chef who, for the first time, had to think about food and how it should taste. Learning the new techniques was the easy part and, besides, the lesser issue. Mosimann taught attitude. He awakened a proper respect and understanding of good raw ingredients and showed his pupils how they might assemble them harmoniously – always with the aim of enhancing the true, natural flavours of the original.

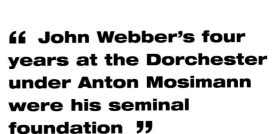

John Webber's four years under Mosimann were his seminal foundation and, by 1980, he had risen through the ranks to the position of *sous chef* in the Dorchester's Terrace Restaurant – a job he shared with Anton Edelmann, now the famous *Maître Chef* of the Savoy. Typically, Webber was in no rush to move on, although he had discussed his future with his mentor. Then, a chance meeting with a head-hunter put him in touch with Paul and Kay Henderson, the American owners of Gidleigh Park – at the time, a relatively new and unknown country house hotel in Devon.

The circumstances of Webber's removal from Park Lane to Dartmoor were worthy of an Ayckbourn farce. Paul Henderson – a mercurial and colourful man with a fondness for grand gestures and loud bow ties – organized a test dinner with friends in a house in south London. When Webber arrived, he found a box of provisions, no electricity and an oven that was dysfunctional. The menu, including a soufflé which refused to rise, took four hours to deliver, by which time Henderson and company were 'too pissed to notice'. And John Webber, notwithstanding this jolly charade, was offered the job anyway. Such was the power of a Mosimann pedigree.

After seven years at the Dorchester, Webber's departure for a remote West Country hotel was a courageous move. 'It was Paul Henderson's enthusiasm that persuaded me to give it a try,' he says. 'And if it wasn't to work, it would still have made a good holiday!' In the end, it was a happy and fruitful sojourn that lasted five years. Gidleigh Park was where he met and fell in love with his future wife Caroline and it was here that he discovered the peace and beauty of a setting which creatively would suit him best. Gidleigh Park was Kinnaird in waiting. But by 1985, Webber felt that the time had come to move on because,

" His menus display immense diversity. He is sensitive to both local and foreign palates, mixing themes which are ancient and modern, highbrow and populist "

effectively, the direction of the kitchen was still being controlled by the Hendersons. Professionally, John Webber was coming of age and he wanted to be his own man.

A reluctant Paul Henderson eventually resigned himself to the fact that he would be losing his chef and he spent several months with Webber exploring a variety of ideas. The search for a new opportunity coincided with the restoration of Cliveden. Billed as the grandest of them all, the Astors' stately home by the Thames became the most publicized hotel opening of the Eighties. The Hon. John Sinclair was appointed general manager and he needed a chef to match the stature of the house.

As career moves go, Webber's transfer to Cliveden was probably the most felicitous mistake a chef could make. While he was now in full command of a kitchen, his desire to develop his craft was overtaken by the technical demands of a large and complex catering operation. Webber is a cook, not an executive chef, and at Cliveden he became uncomfortably detached from his food. 'It was like the Ritz transposed to a country location,' he says. 'I could write my own menus, but I could not devote the time I wanted to work on my dishes.'

John Webber may have lost his way momentarily but he successfully secured Cliveden's gastronomic credibility and, crucially, he won the confidence and respect of John Sinclair. Moreover, the experience not only taught him the order of chef he wanted to become, he had learned how to open a kitchen from scratch: his first task at Kinnaird when he and Caroline finally moved North of the Border in November 1988.

The critics soon chased Webber to his Highland lair. The *Good Food Guide* described him as the 'golden boy of *nouvelle cuisine* in the provinces' and in September, 1989 – only four months after opening – that old sage Derek Cooper made his prediction in *Scotland on Sunday*. 'Like all creative people,' he wrote, 'good cooks don't stand still. It will be interesting to see how in the coming years Scotland and its fine raw materials influence Webber. Kinnaird . . . could well become one of the outstanding tables in Britain.' And so it came to pass.

The pleasure of John Webber's table today is a bit like feasting your eyes on a multi-coloured, intricate and carefully woven tapestry. His menus display immense diversity. And there is maturity and intelligence in his invention – dishes often taking months to perfect. He is sensitive to both local and foreign palates, mixing themes which are ancient and modern, highbrow and populist. Derek Cooper would be impressed to see the way he marshals all the best that Scotland offers in game and fungi, fish and seafood. He takes proper note of the seasons, and in winter he responds robustly with recipes that buttress the body against a vicious climate: oxtails and stews, for example, or a pease pudding flavoured with fresh mint and served with a good braised lamb shank.

This rusticity often comes in pretty sophisticated forms. Webber loves sausages and he uses a basic *boudin blanc* formulation to create a guinea fowl or pheasant sausage which he grills and sets on a mound of shredded parsnip spiced with ginger and moistened with a sweet truffled Madeira sauce. This convergence of the banal and the refined lends tremendous wit to a dish which is delicious, textural and deceptively light. It also demonstrates Webber's talent for applying his professional polish and unflashy creativity to the simplest ideas. Salmon from the Tay, queen scallops from Skye and small cuts of monkfish, halibut and snapper are plainly grilled and arranged in a medley on a plate dressed with a fruity olive oil infused by a *mirepoix* of vegetables. The dish sounds simple enough but in the eating it is a joy, the warm silkiness of the lubricant elevating the flavours of each individual fish.

The current mania for pasta also gets an outing at Kinnaird, although Webber's way with this medium exhibits the full range of his imagination and originality to good effect. Raw, finely cut slivers of turbot – a piscine *carpaccio* – lie luminescently on a marinade of citrus and olives. As a rich counterpoint to the tartness of the fish, the plate is crowned with a crab salad wrapped into a *raviolo*. A sprinkling of golden salmon roe, pink peppercorns and fresh thyme leaves provides colour and extra seasoning. It is an unusual and quite brilliant composition. Another – a wide bowl of marinated, chargrilled pigeon breasts, served with Puy lentils, chanterelles and smoked bacon in a red wine gravy – uses sheets of pasta arranged in loose folds as an extra textural dimension to the dish and as a sponge for the sauce. Again, it is a typical display of John Webber's painstaking care, finesse and virtuosity.

Puddings at Kinnaird tend to pay homage to the chef's sweet tooth (Mars Bars are his secret passion). On the official card, however, the best include a rich and moist hot marzipan soufflé cleansed by an equally voluptuous Amaretto ice cream – very much a John Webber invention – and a luxuriant gratin of summer fruits with a Grand Marnier glaze and a Sauternes sabayon which is exquisitely Mosimannesque in its presentation.

All this artistry is a far cry from the bread pudding he used to make in Selly Oak. But the tough decision he took to cut those home ties eventually won him the security which, for him, has always been a fundamental need in life. Kinnaird has also liberated the craftsman. Now in his mid-forties, it is only in the past five years that he has shown the extent of his creative potential and he is convinced that he has far more to give. 'I believe that you grow more quickly in the right surroundings,' he says. 'You need to have a feeling of well-being to work effectively.'

John Webber may not enjoy the celebrity profile of some of his peers – and neither does he seek it. But among the chefs of Britain's leading country house hotels, he is *primus inter pares*. He has worked in the best of them and as the first professional head chef in each one, he is largely responsible for establishing their starry reputations.

Guinea Fowl Sausage

with Gingered Parsnip and Madeira Sauce

—

40 g/1½ oz unsalted butter

75 g/3 oz shallots, finely chopped

2 slices of white bread, crusts removed

200 g/7 oz boneless breast of guinea fowl,
trimmed and roughly diced

125 g/4 oz finely sliced, rindless Parma ham

125 g/4 oz rindless pork back fat,
cut into 1 cm/½ inch dice

3 eggs, size 4

50 ml/2 fl oz double cream

salt, pepper, nutmeg

1 tablespoon Madeira

25 g/1 oz pistachio nuts, blanched, skinned
and roughly chopped

1 tablespoon chopped fresh flat leaf parsley

40 g/1½ oz gammon, cut in 5 mm/¼ inch dice

large natural sausage skin casings about 1.2
litres/2 pints boiling chicken stock

olive oil, for brushing

2.5 cm/½ inch fresh root ginger, finely grated

4 small parsnips, peeled, cored and grated

1 whole garlic clove

Truffled Madeira Sauce (see page 269)

Heat half the butter in a small pan and cook the shallots until softened but not coloured. Set aside to cool.

Soak the bread in milk for 10 minutes. Remove and squeeze out the excess moisture. Place in a food processor with the shallots, guinea fowl, Parma ham and pork fat and process briefly to a rough sausage texture.

Add the eggs, cream, salt, pepper, nutmeg and Madeira, and quickly process to combine and lighten the filling. Test-fry a little of the filling, taste and correct the seasoning and texture if necessary. Turn out into a clean bowl. Stir in the pistachio nuts, chopped parsley and gammon, then place in the refrigerator.

Select a string of sausage casing, about 90 cm/3 feet long, and soak in cold running water for 30 minutes. Wrap the remainder in foil, label and freeze for another use.

Fill the sausage casing with the guinea fowl mixture, and tie off with string into 7 sausages. If any air pockets form, prick the skin and press down the filling.

Place the sausages in a pan, add the boiling stock, and poach gently for 12–14 minutes (do not allow to boil, or the skins will split). Cool in the stock, then drain and refrigerate.

To assemble, remove the skins from the sausages, brush with a little olive oil and grill until crusty and golden.

Melt the remaining butter in a large pan. Add the ginger, cook very slowly for 2 minutes, then add the parsnips and garlic clove. Cook, stirring frequently, for 5 minutes or until just tender, then discard the garlic. Keep warm.

Place 1 heaped tablespoon of parsnips on 7 heated plates, then flatten slightly to make a nest for the sausage. Place the sausage on top and spoon around the truffled Madeira sauce. Serve as a first course or luncheon dish

Serves 7

Grilled Fillets of Saltwater Fish

with a Light Vegetable Dressing

——

frisée, oak leaf, lollo rosso and lamb's lettuce

sprigs of fresh dill

vinaigrette dressing

a selection of any 5 fish, filleted, from the list

below, plus one shellfish:

red mullet, red snapper, sea bass, salmon or

parrot fish (all grilled with the skin on)

turbot, brill, sole or monkfish (all grilled with

the skin off), and scallops, queen scallops,

prawns, lobster or blanched mussels

olive oil, for brushing

rock salt

Light Vegetable Dressing:

125 g/4 fl oz fruity, extra-virgin olive oil

a mirepoix of 15 g/½ oz each onion, carrot

and celery, all finely diced

1 bay leaf

1 sprig of thyme

1 small garlic clove, unpeeled

grated zest of 1 lemon

grated zest of 1 orange

25 ml/1 fl oz dry white wine

1 tablespoon lemon juice

Bacon and Vegetable Garnish:

15 g/½ oz smoked bacon, finely diced,

blanched and rinsed under cold water

15 g/½ oz carrots, finely diced

15 g/½ oz celery, finely diced

1 tablespoon chives, curt in 1 cm/½ inch batons

15 g/½ oz deseeded courgettes, finely diced

1 spring onion, finely sliced

15 g/½ oz cooked French beans, finely sliced

25 ml/1 fl oz vegetable stock

salt, pepper and lemon juice

Wash and dry the lettuces and dill and store in a covered container in the refrigerator. Toss in the vinaigrette just before serving. To prepare the vegetable dressing, place the ingredients in a stainless steel pan and bring to just below simmering point, for 15 minutes, then cover and allow to cool. Infuse overnight, then strain. Add the bacon, carrots and celery to the infused oil. Reheat and cook at just below boiling point for 10 minutes. Set aside.

Brush the fish with oil, season, and place under a very hot grill, skin-side up, until just cooked. Brush and season the scallops and sear in a very hot pan for 20 seconds each side.

Arrange the leaves in the centre of the plate or present in a filo pastry tartlet. Add the chives, courgettes, spring onion, beans and stock to the dressing and warm through. Add the salt, pepper and lemon juice to taste. Spoon the dressing around the plate and set the hot fish on top. Spoon a little more of the dressing over the fish and season with rock salt.

Serves 4

Open Ravioli of Pigeon Breast

with Red Wine, Lentils and Smoked Bacon

——

breasts of 4 wood pigeons, plus carcasses

1 teaspoon fresh thyme leaves

thinly sliced zest of ½ orange

about 1 tablespoon olive oil

40 g/1½ oz smoked bacon rashers, cut
crossways into 5 mm/¼ inch strips

75 g/3 oz cooked Puy lentils

125 g/4 oz fresh, small chanterelles

salt and freshly ground black pepper

crispy fried celeriac strips, to garnish

Red Wine Sauce:

1 tablespoon groundnut oil

25 g/1 oz carrot, chopped

25 g/1 oz celery, chopped

25 g/1 oz shallot, chopped

125 ml/4 fl oz red wine (Cabernet Sauvignon)

300 ml/½ pint beef stock

125 ml/4 fl oz chicken stock

2 juniper berries, crushed

1 large sprig of thyme

2 teaspoons redcurrant jelly

1 teaspoon arrowroot, slaked

Egg Pasta Dough:

8 pasta squares, 10 cm/4 inches, made from:

500 g/1 lb strong flour

9 egg yolks or 4 eggs and 1 teaspoon olive oil

1 teaspoon salt

a pinch of nutmeg

Mix all the egg pasta ingredients together in a bowl and knead the dough for about 5–10 minutes. Rest in the refrigerator for 1 hour before use (freeze any left over).

Sprinkle the pigeon breasts with the thyme, orange zest and olive oil. Set aside for 2 hours to 2 days in the refrigerator.

To make the red wine sauce, heat the groundnut oil in a heavy-based frying pan, add half the pigeon carcasses and legs and fry until evenly browned. Remove to a colander and repeat the process with the vegetables.

Add the red wine to the pan, scrape up all the juices, then pour into a stainless steel saucepan. Add the beef and chicken stock, the bones and vegetables, and bring slowly to the simmer, skimming as necessary. Continue to simmer for 35 minutes, then add the juniper berries and thyme. Simmer for 10 minutes, then strain through muslin into a clean pan. Add the redcurrant jelly, return to the heat and simmer until reduced by half and well flavoured.

Add the slaked arrowroot to the pan, cook until lightly thickened, cover and set aside.

Char-grill the pigeon breasts, if possible, to add extra flavour. Otherwise, heat a little of the marinade in a heavy-based frying pan and fry the breasts, skin-side down, for 2–3 minutes, then turn over and cook for a further 2 minutes (they should be a little underdone). Remove from the pan and set aside in a warm place to allow the meat to relax without cooling.

Heat the sauce to simmering point, add the bacon and cooked lentils and simmer for about 2 minutes, skimming as necessary.

Roll out the pasta dough and cut into eight 10 cm/4 inch squares. Cook in boiling, salted water (with a drop of oil) for a minute or so until done. Drain and return to the pan with another drop of olive oil and seasonings.

Heat a little more oil in a pan and sauté the chanterelles for 3 minutes. Add 2 teaspoons of water to the hot pan, then keep warm.

Place a pasta square in each plate, and spoon over the lentil mixture. Remove the skin from the pigeon, thinly slice the breasts, place on the bed of lentils and spoon the sauce around. Arrange a second square of pasta on top and spoon the mushrooms around. Garnish with the crispy celeriac strips.

Serves 4

Madeira Sauce

Serve this sauce with the Ravioli, left, or add truffles and serve with the Guinea Fowl Sausage on page 265.

450 ml/¾ pint Madeira (preferably Malmsey)

50 g/2 oz mushroom trimmings

3 shallots, finely sliced

450 ml/¾ pint beef stock

75 ml/3 fl oz port

¼ bay leaf

1 sprig of thyme

a dash of sherry wine vinegar

1 teaspoon arrowroot

Place one-third of the Madeira in a stainless steel pan, bring to the boil, then simmer until reduced to a thick syrup. Add the remaining Madeira and reduce by a quarter for the recipe left, or by half for other recipes.

Place the mushrooms, shallots, stock and port in another pan, and simmer until reduced by half. Skim, add to the Madeira and return to a slow simmer, skimming as required. Add the herbs and vinegar and cook for 5 minutes.

Strain into a clean pan through a double layer of damp muslin and bring slowly to the simmer, skimming as necessary.

Slake the arrowroot in a little cold water, then add to the sauce and cook until lightly thickened. Use as required, adding a little extra Madeira just before serving, if preferred.

For Truffle Sauce, add shaved fresh truffle, or chopped tinned truffle with its juice.

A Gratin of Summer Fruits

Flavoured with Grand Marnier

---

16 strawberries, washed, hulled and dried

24 raspberries

24 blueberries

½ mango, thinly sliced lengthways

½ papaya, thinly sliced lengthways

½ Charentais melon

4 red plums

2 small peaches

2 tablespoons Grand Marnier

4 scoops elderflower sorbet

4 sprigs of mint

Grand Marnier Glaze:

75 ml/3 fl oz chilled Sauternes

5 egg yolks, size 4

20 g/¾ oz caster sugar

25 ml/1 fl oz Grand Marnier

150 ml/¼ pint whipping cream, lightly
whipped with 25 g/1 oz caster sugar

Escoffier Paste Baskets:

150 g/5 oz unsalted butter, softened

250 g/8 oz icing sugar

125 ml/4 fl oz golden syrup

125 g/4 oz flour

Elderflower Sorbet:

475 ml/16 fl oz mineral water

150 g/5 oz caster sugar

6 strips of lemon zest and 1 tablespoon juice

6 strips of orange zest

125 ml/4 fl oz elderflower cordial

To make the sorbet, place the water, sugar, lemon juice and zests in a stainless steel pan. Bring to the boil, simmer for 5 minutes, pour into a bowl, cover with clingfilm, cool, and refrigerate overnight. Next day, strain the syrup, mix in the cordial and churn in a sorbetière until snowy. Store, covered, in the freezer.

To make the baskets, cream the butter and sugar, add syrup and fold in the flour. Chill 24 hours. Next day, mould into balls, place on non-stick baking paper and flatten with your hand. Bake in a preheated oven at 200°C (400°F) Gas Mark 6 until golden. Remove, cool, then press over moulds to form 5 cm/2 inch baskets.

Refrigerate the berries, mango and papaya. Scoop out balls of melon and sprinkle with some elderflower cordial. Slice the plums and peaches but do not peel, then store with the other fruits.

Pour the Sauternes into a stainless steel bowl with a curved base, add the egg yolks and sugar, and place over a pan of hot water. Using a whisk, beat the yolks until thickened, lifting as you whisk, to incorporate air. Remove from the heat and whisk for 2 minutes longer. Cover with clingfilm and set aside. Fold the egg mixture and Grand Marnier into the whipped cream.

Leave a space for the baskets in the middle of 4 large plates. Arrange the sliced fruit around the centre, then the large berries and melon, then fill in the spaces with the smaller berries. Drizzle with Grand Marnier, then the sauce.

Glaze the plate under a very hot grill. Place a ball of sorbet in the basket, place it in the centre of the fruits and garnish with mint.

Serves 4

Betty Allen

───

The Cross of St Andrew flutters lazily over Castle Stalker – claiming ownership, suggesting residency. But the place looks forlorn and deserted, a lonely forbidding stone tower rising absurdly on its islet in Loch Linnhe. It is a famous landmark in these parts and it is also a useful signpost alerting travellers that, if Port Appin is their destination and Airds their hotel, they have only two more miles to go. When they arrive, they will not be disappointed. Airds is, perhaps, the most romantic and agreeable small hotel in the Western Highlands.

Owned by the Allen family, this old ferry inn faces the northerly tip of Lismore – a long tongue of an island licking the eastern shores of Mull at the mouth of the loch. It was here that St Moluag established his church in the sixth century at the time that Columba came to Iona. As you gaze out of your gabled bedroom window, or from your table in the dining room, the view is awesome. Beyond Lismore, the mountains of Morvern rise out of the sea, creased and stubbled like an old man's face, clouds hanging round their folding brows like loose bandages. And as the evening light fades, the water turns slate-grey, a motionless stripe beneath a vast black wilderness cast against a western sky etched in pink and orange.

As a stranger visiting the region for the first time, I was struck by the mystery and beauty of this place – a curious intertwining sense of turbulence in times past and of exquisite peace today. This is Stuart country and memories of the Jacobite cause, genocide and treachery are still palpable. Drive through the majestic basin of Glencoe and the mountain slopes nudge the subconscious mind, murmuring a chilly reminder of the massacre in 1692. At Ballachulish, a cairn marks the spot where James Stuart of Acharn was shamefully hanged and left to rot for the Appin murder in 1752 – a strange, unresolved tale which Robert Louis Stevenson romanticized in his novel *Kidnapped*.

These days, life in Appin is altogether more beneficent and procreative, but if there is a death, a crisis or an emergency, it tends to be handled by the local garage, which also assumes the role of local fire station and local undertaker. Geographically, the area is a peninsula embraced by Loch Linnhe on one side and Loch Creran on the other. The raw materials which inspire much of Betty Allen's kitchen are abundant and visible everywhere. In late summer, the narrow lanes are fringed with rowans bursting scarlet bunches of fruit, waiting to be gathered for a rowanberry jelly to go with her venison. During the rutting season, you can hear the stags roaring in the hills above Glen Creran as eagles glide silently over the loch below. Meanwhile, on the rich salt meadows by the shores surrounding Appin, sheep and cattle graze peacefully. And in the early morning the only noise likely to disturb your sleep will be sound of hens clucking fitfully at the bottom of Mrs Allen's garden, laying their eggs obediently in time for your breakfast.

Predictably – and quite properly – visitors to Airds also enjoy the pick of Loch Linnhe's salmon. It is fished in Cuil Bay, a mile off the road to Ballachulish. Here Sandy MacLachan has kept his ancient limestone bothy for thirty years, as his father did before him. Inside, he stores his nets and tackle among the relics of a time when fishers lived in these Spartan huts. There's an old bedstead creaking under two hundredweight of rope, a rather fine Welsh dresser begging for repair and a fireplace that must have baked a few fish in its day. Outside, MacLachan shares his pebble beach with a flock of Canada geese who make the most appalling din. But the veteran trapper, ruddy-faced, eyebrows bleached by the Highland sun, is less vociferous as he talks quietly about the problems of over-fishing in the salmon's North Atlantic feeding grounds, of pollution and poaching, and of the impact of the burgeoning farmed trade. These

" Airds is, perhaps, the most romantic and agreeable small hotel in the Western Highlands "

> **❝ For Betty the laurels and symbols recognizing her skills arrived at a time when most chefs have either burned themselves out or are at least winding down ❞**

days the wild fish are smaller and scarcer, and I was left wondering what he would do without the keen support of people like the Allens in Port Appin.

Airds is a family affair in the continental tradition. Betty and Eric, their son Graeme and his wife Anne are all involved, and they care passionately about their hotel. The late Jane Grigson put it well in an article for the *New York Times* in 1989 where she wrote of their 'sweet willingness to make you feel at home ... a gift for conveying happiness that you are there'. That feeling is immediate from the moment you step inside this cosy, comfortable loch-side inn. And when you meet your host – pink-cheeked, bearded and magnificent in his Prince Charles jacket and kilt in the tartan of the MacDonalds of Clan Ranald – you will be forgiven if his face seems disconcertingly familiar. He looks the very picture of a Highland chieftain which may explain why he is to be found posing heroically on the front cover of the *Times Bartholomew Guide to Scotland*. In the tourist industry, Eric Allen is box office. To his friends in the trade, who like to keep a sense of proportion about these matters, he is known affectionately as 'sporran face'.

Those same friends also have a pet name for Betty Allen. She is known more flatteringly as 'Marlene' – a justifiable compliment to her fine features and womanhood but, as a human being, she hardly passes for the sultry femme fatale that immortalized Dietrich.

Betty's background is rooted in the Presbyterian ethic and strong community ties of Scottish village life. They taught her discretion, modesty and a stoicism without which she would never have scaled the hurdles which have led her to the top. Whereas, these days, talented and ambitious cooks often win their stripes early, for Betty the laurels and symbols recognizing her skills arrived at a time when most chefs have either burned themselves out or are at least winding down. Struggle and determination have been natural conditions of life since her early childhood. Behind her gentle, motherly disposition lies an indomitable will and an energy capable of being stretched to the limit.

Until her marriage to Eric in 1961, Betty lived in a small two-bedroomed cottage in the village of Blackridge near Bathgate, midway between Edinburgh and Glasgow. As the eldest of four children, and with a father away at war, household responsibilities and duty to family were disciplines learned young. She still recalls the air raid sirens and the terror as they listened, huddled beneath the kitchen table, to the bombs falling on Clydebank twenty miles away. Mother was fiercely house-proud and a good plain cook – there would always be a hot thick soup on the table made from the vegetables grown in their garden. But treats were few and far between, reserved for the village's annual gala day or the occasional Sunday school outing: rationed luxuries, like tinned peaches or salmon, were dutifully put away for the times when father returned home on leave.

And so Betty grew up to become a conscientious, practical and caring young woman. In her free time, she absorbed herself in her knitting, embroidery and crochet work. Cooking came later, although one entry in her diary when she was eight noted she 'made red and yellow jellies and chocolate crispy cakes for tea'. At school she worked hard and did well, leaving just before her sixteenth birthday with an armful of prizes.

For the next few years, Betty took a variety of office jobs and was even a nanny for a while until, one Saturday evening, she and her best friend Janette Sneddon took a bus from Blackridge to attend a concert by a chorus of Welsh male voice choirs in Glasgow. On the way, the bus stopped at Harthill, the next village, to take on more passengers bound for the concert. One was a dashing young soldier buttoned to the neck in an immaculate navy blue dress uniform. 'I thought he was in the Salvation Army,' Betty recalls. Indeed, this was Sergeant Drill Instructor Eric Allen of the Scots Guards. Cupid struck instantly. But, sensing Betty's coyness, Eric had to rely on the good will of Miss Sneddon to negotiate a proper introduction which took place three days later. Within the year Eric and Betty were married – but not before the admirable Miss Sneddon, a solicitor's assistant, had found the couple a suitable flat in Bathgate. At the wedding, Janette whispered crisply to her friend, 'I've got your man. I've got your house. Do you think you can manage the rest yourself?'

The evidence took five years to produce. In 1966, Betty gave birth to Graeme, and Janette was content. In the meantime, Eric left the army and took a job as a medical representative for a pharmaceutical company.

By the late Sixties, the young Allen family were living in Kirkintilloch, near Glasgow. It was here, more by accident than design, that Betty began to take her interest in cooking beyond the domestic circle. As a favour to a friend, she agreed to provide temporary lodgings for two French students. In the end, the girls stayed a year – charmed by the Allens' hospitality and, not least, by Betty's excellent home cooking. 'Because they were French,' she says, 'I felt I had to make a special effort. Their great favourite was my sherry trifle.' One of the students, Cecile Pottier, became a close friend and in 1970 she invited Eric and Betty to visit her family in St Etienne. Ever since, the Allens have returned to France almost every year and, by introducing them to the food and wine of her country, Cecile Pottier unwittingly laid the foundations for Betty's future.

The first big test came in 1974 when the Allens bought a twelve-bedroomed hotel in Largs on the Firth of Clyde. With Eric away on business for much of the time, the burden of running the Glen Eldon fell to Betty. With no help in the kitchen, she cooked a simple set menu for twenty or thirty people every night. She did the shopping herself, managed the books and all the hotel laundry too. And, of course, she had a rapidly growing son to care for. The strain became intolerable and she turned to her mother for support. 'If others can do it, you can do it,' she urged. From a woman who understood the meaning of hardship, it was a typically dour response but, with her encouragement, Betty persevered and the hotel prospered.

In 1976, to Betty's immense relief, Eric finally renounced his executive suits in favour of his tartan and the role of mine host. But their hearts had always been in the Western Highlands. They had honeymooned on Mull and they spent many of their holidays in the region. The search for the small hotel that now consumed their dreams took two years and eventually led them to Port Appin in 1978. The following year, a hesitant entry for Airds in *The Good Food Guide* recommended the Drambuie flummery, but observed that Mr Allen was taking bagpipe lessons.

Perhaps the bagpipes were a necessary diversion from the food, which was not to their taste. After the strain of the kitchen in Largs, Betty's intention was to step back and allow a professional team to take over. She was still, after all, a domestic cook and the menus at the Glen Eldon had been little more than her home repertoire delivered on a grander scale – with dishes like casseroles, roasts, some fresh fish and the famous trifle. Now, at Airds, she wanted a dash of style and sophistication, but the chefs she had inherited with the purchase of the business did not match up. In 1979, a brace of Cordon Bleu girls did no better and, by the middle of the season, Betty Allen was back in the kitchen. 'It took me a long time to get the confidence to do it myself,' she says, 'and even now, I feel anxious all the time.'

Through the 1980s, Betty's growing skills were slowly rewarded by the guide books, but the distinctions she won were never sought and, when they were conferred, they daunted rather than thrilled her. To the core, she is a perfectionist with a try-harder mentality – a Robert the Bruce of the stoves whose Bannockburn came in 1991 when she won her Michelin star.

In today's galaxy of British culinary talent, Betty Allen is something of an enigma. As a home-cook-turned-professional, she is not unique. But while Carole Evans and Rose Gray

" A perfectionist with a try-harder mentality — a Robert the Bruce of the stoves "

fall into this category, their food is informed by their early backgrounds. Betty Allen's cooking has passed through a gradual mutation – from simple Scottish domesticity to the high gloss of a smart French kitchen. At this level, she is self-taught, but her education bears none of the marks of academic rigour and studied rehearsal of, say, Stephen Bull or Rick Stein. Her development has been strangely organic and unstructured within a loose Gallic model: her success the outcome of a natural instinct for her subject, wide experience of eating out at home and in France (although she never takes notes on her travels) and some serious bedtime reading.

Betty's affinity with France – inspired originally by her friendship with Cecile Pottier – is not uncommon among the senior players of the Scottish gastronomic establishment. She shares it with people like David Wilson at the Peat Inn in Fife and Hilary Brown at La Potinière in Gullane. All of them, in their own individual ways, perpetuate that ancient love affair enshrined in the politics of the Auld Alliance. This inclination is not slavish in its content, but the stylistic influences are evident in much of the cooking.

Betty's menus owe little to fashion. She cooks what she likes to cook. A long-running classic is her Mousseline of Scallops with a Champagne and Chive Sauce. Fifteen years ago, munchless mousses were all the rage. In the hearty Nineties, we sneer and dismiss these little moulds as Gerber food. But, perfectly executed, to be reminded of a great dish is like listening to a golden oldie. It is actually quite thrilling. The flavour of the scallops – which come from Mallaig across the sound from Skye – is so intense it stings the palate, leaving a blissfully fresh after-taste that lingers around the gills.

Another starter – for the songs Betty plays do not get stuck in a groove – is more modern. She makes her own pasta – translucently thin sheets which she uses as a medium to present combinations of harmoniously matched components like sweetbreads, asparagus and wild mushrooms

"The fundamental classicism and poise of Betty Allen's kitchen today are especially manifest in her main courses, which demonstrate the professional polish and sophistication she has worked so hard to achieve "

from the Appin woodlands. A truffle sauce – precisely judged to avoid overwhelming the composition – imbues a simple plate of prime ingredients with a note of earthy luxuriance.

The fundamental classicism and poise of Betty Allen's kitchen today are especially manifest in her main courses which demonstrate the professional polish and sophistication she has worked so hard to achieve. Roast pigeon breasts – pink and succulent – squat on a croûte scraped with a film of chicken liver parfait, the richness nimbly foiled by the sweet tang of a date chutney. Morels, chanterelles and a shiny Madeira sauce complete the dish. It is a symphonic study of contrasting flavours and textures. The same finesse and thought are applied to a saddle of venison on a sauce infused with thyme and juniper. The slices of meat are arranged cheekily into a pyramid folded on to a rösti disc. This time, dramatic counterpoint is provided by a foundation of red cabbage bound in a subtle cocktail of spices, fruits and other aromatics and, in a final act of brio, the plate is ringed with a scatter of melting shallots and chestnuts.

Is this highly-tuned output such a far cry from the small cottage in Blackridge? Well, yes, but not quite. Betty Allen's four-course menus, for all their Epicurean felicity, also strike one endearingly dissonant bass note which echoes her childhood years. When you dine at Airds, your second course is likely to be a homely wholesome vegetable soup. Be it parsnip or a cream of swede and leek or any other, you will never taste soup as fragrant or so redolent of its origin.

To end your feast by Loch Linnhe, Betty's puddings are presented with typical *élan*, spiked here and there with a dram of Scottish wit. The star turn is a seductive raspberry ice cream made deceptively potent by a dash of Drambuie, Bonnie Prince Charlie's personal liqueur. It is a surprisingly successful match – damask pink, velvety, musky in tone and strangely exotic. Its effect is both refreshing and satisfying – a sense of final contentment before sinking into an armchair beside the fire in the drawing room, glass of malt to hand and the slow tick-tock of the grandfather clock for company.

While this has been Betty Allen's story, the credits in her kitchen today are shared by Graeme, who learned to cook at his mother's side. For Port Appin's happy pilgrims, there can be no better assurance of the succession at a hotel where good food conspires with the raw beauty of the Highlands. It is an alchemy which strikes deep into the human soul, made comfortable by a home that understands the immense pleasure of civilized hospitality.

Mousseline of Scallops

with a Champagne and Chive Sauce

━━━

250 g/8 oz fillets of sole, skinned

375 g/12 oz scallops, including corals

500 g/17 fl oz double cream

½ teaspoon salt

¼ teaspoon cayenne pepper

a little melted butter

Champagne and Chive Sauce:

300 ml/½ pint Champagne

300 ml/½ pint fish stock

3 shallots, finely chopped

300 ml/½ pint double cream

3 tablespoons chopped fresh chives

lemon juice, to taste

salt and freshly ground black pepper

To garnish:

8 sprigs of chervil

1 tablespoon chopped, pitted black olives

1 tablespoon chopped red pepper,

or salmon eggs

Cut the sole into 2.5 cm/1 inch pieces and place in a food processor. Dry the scallops thoroughly, add to the sole, and blend until smooth. Push the mixture through a sieve into a bowl set into a container of ice. Chill for 1 hour.

Using a hand-held electric whisk, gradually add the cream until the mixture falls easily from a spoon. Add the salt and cayenne pepper, then pour the mixture into 8 ramekins, brushed with melted butter.

Place the ramekins in a *bain-marie* filled with warm water to halfway up their sides. Place the *bain-marie* in a preheated oven at 180°C (350°F) Gas Mark 4 and cook for about 25 minutes, until the centres are just firm to the touch. Remove from the water and set aside to rest for about 5 minutes before turning out.

Meanwhile, make the sauce. Pour the Champagne and fish stock into a pan, add the finely chopped shallots, bring to the boil and reduce by half. Add the double cream, return to the boil and cook until the sauce thickens to a coating consistency. Add the finely chopped fresh chives, salt, freshly ground black pepper and lemon juice to taste.

To serve, place a scallop mousseline on each plate, top with a sprig of chervil, then spoon the sauce beside and garnish with the chopped olives and red pepper or salmon eggs.

Serves 8

Open Ravioli of Mushrooms

with Asparagus and a Truffle Sauce

———

25 g/1 oz butter

3 shallots, finely chopped

½ garlic clove, finely chopped

500 g/1 lb button mushrooms, thinly sliced

20 morels, fresh or dried and reconstituted in warm water for 30 minutes

20 asparagus tips

8 discs of fresh pasta, about 10 cm/4 inches in diameter

Truffle Sauce:

300 ml/½ pint cream

300 ml/½ pint chicken stock

300 ml/½ pint white wine

2 shallots, finely chopped

75 g/3 oz jar of truffle paste

6 fresh tarragon leaves, chopped

¼ teaspoon grated nutmeg

salt and freshly ground black pepper

Heat the butter in a pan and sauté the shallots and garlic until softened but not coloured. Stir in the mushrooms, cover and simmer slowly for 30 minutes. Remove the lid and continue cooking until most of the liquid has evaporated.

To make the truffle sauce, pour the cream into a heavy-based pan, bring to the boil and reduce until thickened to a coating consistency. Pour the stock and wine into a separate pan, add the shallots, and reduce to about 1 tablespoon. Add this to the cream, then add to the mushrooms and stir in the truffle paste and chopped tarragon, and season with salt, pepper and grated nutmeg.

Rinse the morels (if using dried ones, drain them first), then sauté in butter. Blanch the asparagus tips in boiling water for about 30 seconds and set aside to keep warm.

Quickly cook the discs of fresh pasta in boiling salted water for about 1 minute. To serve, place 1 pasta disc on each plate, add the morels and asparagus tips, then spoon over the sauce and top with another disc of pasta.

Serves 4

Saddle of Roe Deer

with Spiced Red Cabbage and Rowanberry Jelly

——

1 saddle of roe deer, about 1.5-2 kg/3-4 lb

65 g/2½ oz cold butter

salt and freshly ground black pepper

Venison Stock:

1 carrot, chopped

1 small onion, chopped

1 garlic clove

½ bottle of red wine

2 bay leaves

1 leek, chopped

1 sprig of fresh thyme

6 juniper berries

6 peppercorns

bones and trimmings from the saddle

Rowanberry Jelly:

rowanberries and Bramley apples

sugar (see recipe)

Spiced Red Cabbage:

500 g/1 lb dessert apples, peeled and cored

1 kg/2 lb red cabbage, shredded

250/8 oz onions, finely chopped

150 ml/¼ pint red wine

2 garlic cloves, finely chopped

2 tablespoons sherry vinegar

juice and grated zest of 1 orange

2 tablespoons light brown sugar

¼ teaspoon each of grated nutmeg, ground cinnamon, ground allspice and dried thyme

Make the stock the day before. Trim all fat and sinew from the saddle and remove the meat from the bone. Roast the bones in a preheated oven at 220°C (425°F) Gas Mark 7 until they start to colour. Add the carrot, onion and garlic and roast for a further 20 minutes.

Transfer to a saucepan, add three-quarters of the wine, the remaining stock ingredients and water to cover. Bring to the boil and simmer gently for 3 hours, skimming off any scum.

Strain through a fine sieve, return to a clean pan, add the remaining wine, bring to the boil and reduce to about 300 ml/½ pint. Set aside to cool, then refrigerate until needed.

To make the rowanberry jelly, measure equal quantities of rowanberries and Bramley apples. Remove all leaves and stalks from the berries, and quarter the apples. Place in a large saucepan and barely cover with water. Bring to the boil, uncovered, and simmer to a pulp. Transfer to a jelly bag and allow all the juice to drip into a bowl. Do not squeeze the bag.

Boil equal quantities of juice and sugar (e.g. 1.8 litres/3 pints of juice and 1.5 kg/3 lb sugar) for 6–8 minutes, then pour a spoonful on a saucer and leave in the refrigerator until cool. Push the cold jelly with your finger: if it begins to wrinkle, it is ready. Remove the scum and pour into clean jars.

To make the spiced cabbage, finely chop the apples, place in an ovenproof dish, and mix in the shredded cabbage and onions. Season with salt and pepper, stir all the remaining ingredients together and pour over the cabbage. Cover with foil and bake in a preheated oven at 200°C

(400°F) Gas Mark 6 for 45 minutes or until the cabbage is tender. Season to taste.

Melt 25 g/1 oz of the butter in a pan and seal the meat. Roast in a preheated oven at 220°C (425°F) Gas Mark 7 for 6–8 minutes, depending on thickness. (It should remain pink.) Cover and set aside to rest in a warm place for 15 minutes.

Reheat the stock, remove from the heat and whisk in the remaining cold butter, then taste and adjust the seasoning.

To serve, slice the venison and arrange on the cabbage, pour the sauce around, and serve with the rowanberry jelly. Roasted shallots and stir-fried cèpes are suitable accompaniments.

Serves 6

Breasts of Wood Pigeon

with Date Chutney and Madeira Sauce

———

4 tablespoons olive oil

4 wood pigeons

4 slices of white bread

50 g/2 oz butter, melted

Date Chutney:

500 g/1 lb pitted dates

250 g/8 oz onions

1 teaspoon allspice berries

15 g/½ oz salt

300 ml/½ pint soft brown sugar

salt and freshly ground black pepper

To serve:

Madeira sauce

sautéed morels and chanterelles

roasted shallots and chestnuts

To make the chutney, finely chop the dates and onions and tie the allspice berries in muslin. Place all the ingredients in the pan, stir until the sugar is dissolved, then simmer gently until thickened. When cool, pot and seal.

Heat the olive oil in a pan and brown the pigeons on all sides. Remove the breasts and use the carcasses to make stock.

Oil a roasting tin, sprinkle the breasts with salt and pepper and roast for about 5–6 minutes in a preheated oven at 200°C (400°F) Gas Mark 6, keeping them pink. Rest, covered, in a warm place for 10 minutes before serving.

Cut out rounds of bread, about 10 cm/4 inches in diameter, soak in melted butter and bake in the oven until golden brown and crisp.

To serve, warm the chutney slightly in a small pan and place a spoonful in the centre of 4 heated dinner plates, with a croûton on top, and the pigeon breast on top of that. Serve surrounded with the sautéed mushrooms, roasted shallots and chestnuts, with a classic Madeira sauce drizzled around.

Serves 4

Raspberry and Drambuie Ice Cream

———

4 tablespoons raspberry purée

juice of 1 large lemon

4 tablespoons Drambuie

475 ml/16 fl oz double cream

6 large eggs, separated

250 g/8 oz caster sugar

Mix together the raspberry purée, lemon juice and Drambuie. Whisk the cream lightly until it just hangs on the whisk, then fold in the juice mixture.

Place the egg whites in a large bowl and whisk until they hold stiff peaks. Gradually whisk in the sugar, then the yolks, until evenly blended. Fold in the cream, then transfer to a plastic container and freeze for 8 hours.

Remove from the freezer to the refrigerator about 2 hours before serving.

Serves 8

Index

Index of Recipes

General Index